KU-114-645

Collins Gem
Dictionary for Crossword Puzzles

Dictionary for Crossword Puzzles

J. A. MacAuslane

Collins
London and Glasgow

General Editor
W. T. McLeod

First Published 1971
Latest Reprint 1984

ISBN 0 00 458751 0

© **William Collins Sons & Co. Ltd. 1971**

Printed in Great Britain by
Collins Clear-Type Press

CONTENTS

v

INTRODUCTION

Interesting crosswords are based on the principle of hiding a simple word behind a complicated clue. Their entertainment value lies in the unravelling of the clue, not in searching the memory for a word one knows but cannot remember.

This book is designed to supply the word once the riddle of the clue has been solved. For this reason the words are arranged alphabetically according to their number of letters and in nine wide-ranging subject groups. These groups, with their sub-divisions, are listed in the Contents pages v and vi.

The word lists include foreign words, colloquialisms, slang, abbreviations and phrases, e.g. *fair play* will be found among the 8-letter words in the Sports and Pastimes section. An eight-page Supplement contains male and female first names and some of their commoner diminutives from 3 to 12 letters.

THE ARTS

This general heading covers the fields of Architecture and Building, Art, Education, Literature, Music, Theatre, which are dealt with in separate sections.

Architecture and Building

This section includes all types of building—houses, foreign houses, public buildings—apartments and rooms—parts of buildings—building materials—roofs and windows, arches and walls—fixtures—roadways and paths—bridges and towers—monuments and columns—burial places—architectural features and ornamentation.

w.c.	rib	bead	cove	eave
bay	tie	beam	cusp	exit
cob	adit	bell	cyma	face
cot	apse	bema	dado	farm
den	arch	berm	dais	flag
hut	area	boss	digs	flat
inn	aula	byre	dome	flue
kip	balk	cell	door	foil
nef	barn	coin	drip	fort
pub	base	cote	drum	foss

fret	rail	weir	croft	griff
gate	ramp	well	crown	groin
ha-ha	raze	wing	crypt	gutta
hall	reed	yard	décor	hatch
head	rima	zeta	ditch	helix
home	rind	abbey	*domus*	hinge
jamb	rise	abode	Doric	hoist
keep	road	adobe	dorse	hotel
lift	roof	adyta	dowel	house
list	room	agora	drain	hovel
loft	sash	aisle	drive	hutch
mews	seat	alley	eaves	igloo
mill	shed	ancon	entry	ingle
moat	shop	arena	facia	inlay
mole	sill	arris	fanal	Ionic
naos	silo	attic	fence	jetty
nave	site	berth	flats	joint
nook	slab	booth	floor	joist
ogee	slum	bothy	flush	jutty
pale	span	bower	flute	kiosk
pane	step	brick	folly	knosp
park	stoa	broch	forum	ledge
path	tent	brogh	fosse	level
pier	tige	cabin	foyer	lobby
pile	tile	cella	gable	lodge
plan	toft	cheek	glass	lotus
plot	tope	close	glebe	mains
post	vane	coign	glyph	manor
quad	wall	court	grate	manse

mitre	slums	villa	chalet
motel	socle	abacus	chapel
newel	sough	adytum	church
niche	speos	alcove	circus
ogive	spire	annexe	closet
order	splay	arbour	coffer
oriel	stage	arcade	column
ovolo	stair	aspect	concha
panel	stall	atrium	convex
patio	stele	avenue	coping
pitch	stile	awning	corbel
plaza	stoep	bagnio	corner
porch	stone	barrow	corona
pylon	stria	barton	course
quoin	strut	batten	cranny
ranch	study	belfry	crenel
range	stupa	billet	cupola
revet	suite	bistro	damper
ridge	talon	bridge	dentil
riser	tepee	brough	donjon
rooms	torus	by-room	dormer
salle	tower	camber	dorsal
salon	trave	canopy	dosser
scale	tread	canton	dry rot
sewer	trunk	castle	duplex
shack	tupek	caulis	durbar
shaft	tupik	cellar	estate
shore	*usine*	cement	exedra
slate	vault	centre	fabric

façade	header	pagoda	screen
facing	hearth	palace	scroll
fascia	hostel	*palais*	shanty
fillet	impost	paling	sluice
finial	insula	pandal	soffit
flèche	kennel	parget	spence
fluted	lancet	parvis	spiral
founds	lean-to	patera	spring
fresco	lintel	pharos	square
frieze	listel	*piazza*	stable
garage	loggia	picket	storey
garden	lounge	pillar	street
garret	louvre	plinth	stucco
gazebo	lyceum	podium	studio
ghetto	*maison*	portal	suburb
girder	mantel	*posada*	summer
godown	marble	prefab	tablet
gopura	metope	rafter	taenia
Gothic	milieu	recess	tavern
gradin	module	refuge	temple
grange	mortar	reglet	thatch
granny	mosaic	regula	tholos
gravel	mosque	relief	tholus
griffe	mud hut	rococo	timber
grille	muntin	rubble	toilet
ground	museum	saloon	torsel
gutter	mutule	school	trench
hangar	oculus	sconce	tunnel
hawhaw	office	scotia	turret

vallum	cabaret	crocket	granite
volute	canopy	cubicle	grating
wicket	canteen	culvert	grounds
wigwam	*cantina*	cushion	hallway
window	capital	derrick	hip roof
zoning	caracol	dinette	hospice
academy	carving	doorway	housing
address	cavetto	dungeon	hydrant
air duct	ceiling	echinus	keyhole
allette	chamber	edifice	kitchen
archlet	*chambre*	entasis	klinker
archway	chancel	estrade	lagging
areaway	chapter	eustyle	landing
armoury	charnel	factory	lantern
arsenal	*château*	fencing	larmier
asphalt	*chez moi*	festoon	lattice
astylar	chimney	fitment	library
balcony	choltry	fixture	lodging
barmkin	cipolin	fluting	mansard
baroque	cistern	Fossway	mansion
barrack	citadel	free end	marquee
beading	cloison	fusarol	masonry
bearing	cob-wall	galilee	megaron
bedroom	concave	gallery	minaret
boudoir	conduit	garland	mirador
box-room	console	gateway	moellon
bracing	contour	godroon	mudsill
bracket	cornice	gradine	mullion
bulwark	cottage	granary	munting

mutular	*Rathaus*	terrace
narthex	reredos	theatre
necking	roofage	tie-beam
new town	roofing	tracery
nursery	rooftop	transom
obelisk	roomlet	trefoil
offices	rosette	trellis
ossuary	rostrum	tribune
outlook	rotunda	tumulus
outwork	sanctum	upright
palazzo	*Schloss*	veranda
pannier	sea wall	viaduct
pantile	shelter	vitrail
parapet	shingle	abamurus
parlour	shore up	*abatjour*
parquet	shoring	abattoir
passage	shutter	*abatvoix*
pendant	sikhara	abutment
pension	sinkage	acanthus
pergola	skew-put	acrolith
plafond	skid row	air-drain
plaster	slating	anteroom
ponceau	station	aperture
portico	steeple	apophyge
postern	storied	aqueduct
purlieu	subbase	arcature
pyramid	sundial	archives
railing	surbase	artefact
rampart	Telamon	astragal

Atlantes	caracole	dwelling
aularian	caryatid	ebenezer
back door	casement	entrance
baguette	catacomb	*entresol*
baluster	chapiter	epistyle
bandelet	chaptrel	erection
banderol	*chez nous*	espalier
banister	cincture	*estancia*
bannerol	clithral	exterior
barbican	cloister	extrados
bartisan	colossus	fanlight
base line	concrete	farmyard
basement	corridor	fastness
basilica	cross-tie	*faubourg*
bathroom	cul-de-sac	fire plug
bed-mould	cupboard	fire stop
bell tent	curb roof	fireside
best room	cymatium	flat arch
blinding	dark-room	flat roof
brattice	dead wall	flooring
building	detached	fortress
bulkhead	diggings	fossette
bull's-eye	domicile	fountain
bungalow	doorhead	funk-hole
buttress	doorjamb	fusarole
caliduct	doorpost	gable-end
canephor	doorsill	game room
cantoned	downpipe	gargoyle
capstone	driveway	gatepost

hacienda   ogee arch   shutters
handrail   open plan   side door
headpost   ornament   skewback
headsill   outhouse   skylight
home roof   palisade   slum area
hospital   palmette   sod house
hothouse   Pantheon   solarium
housetop   parabema   spandril
interior   parclose   stairway
intrados   parterre   stockade
isodomon   pavilion   storeyed
keystone   peak arch   subtopia
kingpost   pedestal   suburbia
lavatory   pediment   sun porch
lich-gate   pilaster   tablinum
lodgings   pinnacle   tectonic
lodgment   platform   tenement
log cabin   playroom   teocalli
lotus-bud   pointing   terraced
love-nest   property   thalamus
magazine   propylon   tile roof
marquise   prospect   tolbooth
martello   quarters   top floor
mess hall   rocaille   tourelle
messuage   sacristy   town hall
mon repos   scaffold   transept
monolith   scullery   trap door
monument   semi-dome   traverse
moulding   shoulder   triglyph

triptych	blueprint	cross-beam
tympanum	bolection	crossette
underpin	bottoming	crown post
upstairs	bow window	cubby-hole
verandah	box girder	cubiculum
voussoir	breezeway	curtilage
wainscot	brickwork	curvature
wall tent	bunkhouse	cyma recta
windmill	butt joint	decastyle
woodworm	campanile	door frame
ziggurat	cartouche	door panel
acoustics	cartulary	doorstone
acropolis	cathedral	dormitory
alignment	cauliculi	doss house
almshouse	clapboard	drainpipe
angle-bead	classical	dripstone
angle-iron	cleithral	dry fresco
anthemion	cloakroom	earthwork
apartment	clout nail	eavesdrop
architect	clubhouse	edificial
architolt	coal-house	elevation
Attic base	coffer-dam	esplanade
banderole	coffering	estaminet
banquette	colonnade	extension
bas relief	Colosseum	fan window
bay window	columella	farmhouse
bead-house	composite	fastigium
bell-tower	converted	fireplace
belvederé	courtyard	fixed arch

flagstone
flat house
floor plan
flophouse
footstone
forecourt
framework
front door
front room
fundament
gable roof
garderobe
glory hole
green-belt
guildhall
guttering
gymnasium
headboard
headmould
headpiece
hexastyle
hip rafter
homecroft
homestall
homestead
hoodmould
house plan
houseboat
inglenook

ingleside
landscape
low relief
marquetry
masonwork
mausoleum
mezzanine
mock Tudor
modillion
neo-Gothic
Nissen hut
octastyle
open floor
outskirts
paintwork
panelling
Parthenon
partition
penthouse
peridrome
peristyle
pontlevis
proseuche
prothesis
reception
refectory
reservoir
residence
revetment

ridgepole
rigid arch
ring fence
roadhouse
rough arch
roughcast
round arch
rus in urbe
sally-port
scagliola
scantling
shopfront
skew-table
slate roof
staircase
stairhead
stanchion
stateroom
still-room
stone wall
storeroom
storm door
structure
stylobate
sun lounge
sunk fence
swing door
synagogue
Telamones

threshold	breakwater	family seat
tierceron	bressummer	fan-tracery
tollbooth	canephorus	fire escape
tollhouse	cantilever	first floor
town house	cauliculus	first story
tree-house	cellar door	foot bridge
triforium	chimney-pot	French roof
truss beam	cinquefoil	garden wall
Tudor arch	clearstory	glass house
vallation	clerestory	glebe house
vestibule	clock tower	Greek Ionic
wallboard	colonnette	greenhouse
warehouse	common room	ground plan
whitewash	compluvium	groundsill
window bay	conversion	groundwork
window box	Corinthian	habitation
acroterion	covered way	hammer beam
arched door	crosswalls	hipped roof
arched roof	damp course	Ionic order
architrave	denticular	ivory tower
art gallery	diaconicon	jerkin-head
auditorium	dining hall	jerry-built
balustrade	dining room	lancet arch
barge-board	doll's house	*Lebensraum*
base course	Doric order	lighthouse
batter pile	downstairs	living room
battlement	drawbridge	luxury flat
bedchamber	earthworks	maisonette
blind alley	excavation	manor house

manteltree	retrochoir	university
masonry pin	ribbed arch	ventilator
mitre-joint	ridge strut	watch-tower
monolithic	rising arch	wicket door
opera house	rising damp	wicket gate
orthograph	road bridge	angle closer
orthostyle	Roman Doric	angle rafter
passageway	Romanesque	antechamber
paving flag	rose window	barge-couple
pebble-dash	rumpus room	barge-stones
pendentive	Saxon tower	barrel vault
pentastyle	screenings	buttressing
pied à terre	scrollhead	campaniform
pigeonhole	sewing room	caravansary
pilastrade	skew-bridge	chimney tops
pile bridge	skew-corbel	common stair
portcullis	skyscraper	compartment
priest hole	split level	concert hall
projection	stillicide	coping stone
proportion	storehouse	cornerstone
propylaeum	stronghold	country seat
proscenium	structural	crazy paving
quadrangle	sun parlour	crenellated
quatrefoil	terra-cotta	cyma reversa
Quonset hut	true fresco	drawing room
ranch house	trust house	duplex house
real estate	tumbledown	eating house
repository	turret room	entablature
restaurant	undercroft	fan-vaulting

footing beam
foundations
gambrel roof
ground floor
ground table
hanging post
hearthstone
ichnography
inhabitancy
kitchenette
lancet style
latticework
laundry room
leaded glass
lecture hall
linen closet
little boxes
mansard roof
mantelpiece
mantelshelf
masonry arch
mews cottage
morning room
Norman tower
oeil-de-boeuf
outbuilding
pantile roof
paving stone
pendant post

peristylium
perpend wall
picket fence
pitched roof
plasterwork
plate girder
pointed arch
public house
rampant arch
restoration
roofing tile
room divider
rowlock arch
scaffolding
service lane
service lift
shingle roof
sitting room
smoking room
stately home
step terrace
street floor
summerhouse
sunken fence
trefoil arch
triple porch
Tuscan order
utility room
ventilation

wainscoting
waiting room
water closet
weathercock
willow cabin
window frame
window glass
wrought iron
zigzag fence
amphitheatre
ante-solarium
architecture
assembly hall
audience hall
Bailey bridge
balustrading
bead-moulding
billiard room
breastsummer
building line
buttress pier
caravanserai
chapter-house
charnel-house
chimney jambs
chimney shaft
chimney stack
city planning
common bricks

compass brick	hitching post	*porte-cochère*
conservatory	*hôtel de ville*	prefabricate
construction	hunting lodge	privy-chamber
country house	inner sanctum	rooming house
dividing wall	lake dwelling	*salle à manger*
double scroll	lancet window	semi-detached
double-glazed	lodging place	shutting post
entrance hall	machicolated	smallholding
espagnolette	maiden castle	snubbing post
false ceiling	main entrance	stained glass
fluted column	mansion house	string-course
French Gothic	meeting house	substructure
french window	Nelson column	swinging post
frontispiece	phrontistery	thatched roof
galilee porch	picture frame	town planning
garden suburb	pier buttress	underpinning
head moulding	plaster board	weatherboard

Art

This section includes all types of artist and crafts-man—lists of art forms and crafts, including sculpture and pottery—pottery ware—artists' mater-ials, paints and dyes—schools and styles of art—photography and photographic equipment.

R.A.	art	dye	hue	oil	pot
3-D	cut	gum	lac	pen	sit

urn	nude	craft	piece
arty	oils	crock	pin-up
bite	oven	curio	plate
boss	pose	delft	point
bust	roll	drawn	prime
calk	seal	dryer	print
cast	shot	easel	prism
clay	show	fired	rough
copy	snap	frame	scape
daub	soup	genre	scene
dope	stat	glass	sculp
draw	tile	glaze	shade
etch	tint	gloss	shape
film	tone	glyph	slide
fire	tool	graph	smear
flat	turn	grave	Spode
flux	vase	hatch	spool
form	view	image	stain
gild	wash	inlay	stamp
gilt	work	Japan	still
glue	batik	kodak	stone
head	block	lines	study
kiln	brush	model	style
lake	burin	motif	throw
lens	cameo	mould	tinct
limn	carve	mural	tinge
line	chalk	op art	trace
mark	chase	paint	turps
mask	china	photo	virtu

wheel	dyeing	pastel	carving
artist	eat out	pencil	ceramic
azo dye	effigy	plaque	chasing
bedaub	enamel	pop art	classic
bisque	engild	poster	close-up
bite in	etcher	potter	coating
blazon	figure	primer	collage
blowup	filter	relief	colours
bronze	firing	rococo	copyist
calque	fresco	school	Dadaism
camera	garret	screen	dash off
canvas	glazed	sculpt	develop
carved	graven	shadow	diorama
carver	graver	sketch	draught
chased	incise	statue	drawing
chaser	limner	studio	*ébauché*
chisel	madder	symbol	*écorché*
chroma	magilp	talent	enchase
colour	mallet	tripod	engrave
crayon	marble	viewer	enlarge
criblé	master	acid dye	etching
cubism	medium	aniline	faïence
cubist	megilp	art form	fast dye
dauber	mobile	art-work	Fauvism
déjà-vu	mock-up	atelier	furnace
depict	mosaic	baroque	gallery
design	museum	biscuit	garance
doodle	opaque	camaieu	gilding
drawer	parget	cartoon	glyphic

glyptic	scenist	art class	dry-plate
gouache	scratch	art paper	dyestuff
graphic	shading	artcraft	eclectic
graving	shutter	artefact	eggshell
gravure	spatula	artifact	emblazon
high art	stencil	artiness	emulsion
imagism	stipple	artistic	enchased
incised	tableau	artistry	engraved
lacquer	tachism	autotype	engraver
linocut	tempera	autotypy	enlarger
megilph	tessera	Barbizon	exposure
montage	the arts	basic dye	exterior
moulded	thinner	burinist	fair copy
moulder	tinting	calotype	figurine
off-tone	tintype	cassette	fine arts
outline	tooling	ceramics	fire clay
painter	touch up	charcoal	fixative
palette	tracery	chromism	freehand
pattern	tracing	ciselure	frescoes
picture	varnish	clayware	fretwork
pigment	vehicle	colorama	futurism
plaster	woodcut	cracklin	glyptics
portray	abstract	creation	graffiti
pottery	acid kiln	curlicue	graffito
preview	aesthete	dark room	graphics
primary	airscape	demitint	Greek urn
profile	anaglyph	depicter	grouping
realism	aquatint	designer	half-tint
relievo	art autre	dry-paint	half-tone

hatching	portrait	anastasis
hue cycle	positive	anastatic
in relief	potsherd	aquarelle
inscribe	printing	art critic
intaglio	repoussé	art lesson
interior	sculptor	art school
intimism	seapiece	art-minded
lapidary	seascape	bas-relief
likeness	sketcher	*beaux-arts*
limekiln	skiagram	blackware
majolica	skyscape	blueprint
mandorla	slapdash	box camera
modelled	snapshot	bric-à-brac
modeller	spectrum	brickkiln
monument	staining	*brouillon*
movement	statuary	brushwork
negative	stop bath	cameraman
original	symbolic	cameo ware
paintbox	tachisme	cartridge
painting	tapestry	cerograph
paint-pot	tessella	champlevé
panorama	the brush	china clay
pargeter	tinction	chinaware
pastiche	tincture	chiseller
pastille	turn a pot	chromatic
pastoral	vignette	cityscape
photomap	virtuoso	clean line
picturer	zoom lens	cloisonné
plein-air	aesthetic	collodion

collotype	inscriber	photostat
colorific	kalamkari	pictorial
colourful	landscape	porcelain
colouring	lay-figure	portrayal
colourist	lithotint	portrayer
crayonist	lithotype	prefigure
cyanotype	low relief	prismatic
cyclorama	manual art	projector
decorator	medallion	reflector
delftware	mezzotint	represent
designing	microcopy	rice paper
developer	microfilm	rotograph
distemper	miniature	rough copy
enameller	modelling	scrimshaw
encaustic	modern art	sculpture
enchasing	modernism	secondary
engraving	*objet d'art*	sgraffito
ferrotype	off-colour	sketch pad
figuriste	oil paints	sketching
flash bulb	old master	skiagraph
flash tube	oleograph	statuette
glassware	paintress	still-life
goldsmith	paper clip	stippling
Gothicism	pargeting	stoneware
grisaille	parge-work	symbolism
grotesque	*pasticcio*	symbology
headpiece	pen-and-ink	tablature
heliotype	photocopy	tailpiece
heliotypy	photogram	talbotype

9–10

technique	*avant garde*	decoration
telephoto	background	delineator
tenebrist	beaten work	draughting
throw a pot	Berlin ware	drawing pin
townscape	bibliofilm	emblazonry
treatment	block print	embossment
triquetra	cameo glass	enamel kiln
undercoat	caricature	enamelling
vitascope	cartoonist	enamellist
vorticism	cement kiln	enamelware
wax figure	ceramicist	exhibition
whiteware	cerography	figuration
whitewash	china stone	figurehead
wirephoto	chiselling	flashlight
wood block	chromatics	foreground
woodcraft	chromatism	full colour
woodprint	chromogram	functional
work of art	chromotype	futuristic
xylograph	cinecamera	glazed ware
zinc plate	classicism	grand style
acid colour	cloudscape	graphic art
aesthetics	coloration	Grecian urn
anaglyphic	colour film	half relief
anaglyptic	colourless	handicraft
aniline dye	comic strip	heliograph
art gallery	crosshatch	high colour
art nouveau	crouch ware	high relief
arty-crafty	Crown Derby	illuminate
automatism	dead-colour	illustrate

impression	photogenic	sketchbook
jasper ware	photograph	sling paint
kinetic art	photometer	statuesque
light-meter	photomural	steel plate
lignograph	photoprint	stereotype
linography	phylactery	*stiacciato*
linseed oil	picaresque	stonecraft
lithograph	pigmentary	stovehouse
luminarist	plasticine	surrealism
lustreware	polychrome	surrealist
masterwork	port-crayon	terra cotta
metalcraft	power wheel	tessellate
micrograph	proportion	turpentine
microprint	pure colour	view finder
monochrome	queen's ware	warm colour
monumental	Raphaelite	water glass
mordant dye	repoussage	waterscape
muffle kiln	rich colour	wax etching
natural dye	riverscape	wax process
naturalism	Rockingham	wood carver
neoclassic	scenograph	zylography
oil colours	sculptress	zincograph
oil painter	sculptural	abstract art
ornamental	sculptured	abstraction
paintbrush	sculpturer	achromatism
pastellist	Sèvres ware	*alto-relievo*
pedal wheel	shadowgram	anaglyptics
photoflash	show of work	brush stroke
photoflood	silhouette	*cavo-relievo*

ceramic ware
cerographer
ceroplastic
chaleograph
charcoalist
chef d'oeuvre
chiaroscuro
Chinese clay
cloisonnage
coat of paint
colorimeter
colour cycle
colour gamut
colour print
colouration
colour-blind
composition
connoisseur
copperplate
crackleware
delineation
dichromatic
discoloured
draughtsman
earthenware
eclecticism
electrotype
engravement
enlargement

etching ball
flash camera
French chalk
gild the lily
glass blower
glyphograph
glyptograph
graphic arts
heliochrome
ichnography
illuminator
illustrator
in low relief
insculpture
landscapist
life drawing
Limoges ware
linographer
lithography
living image
local colour
madder bloom
masterpiece
Meissen ware
miniaturist
museum piece
object of art
objet trouvé
oil painting

ornamentist
Palissy ware
papier-collé
papier-mâché
perspective
photography
photorelief
picturesque
pinacotheca
plein-airist
pointillism
pointillist
portraiture
potter's clay
press camera
primitivism
proportions
psychedelic
range finder
romanticism
rotogravure
rough sketch
Satsuma ware
scenewright
scenography
sculpturing
shadowgraph
silversmith
snap shooter

snapshotter
solid colour
still camera
tile painter
tissue paper
water colour
wood carving
xylographer
zincography
aestheticism
architecture
artist's model
artist's proof
arts of design
basso-relievo
brass-rubbing
bright colour
broken colour
camera lucida
candid camera
cave painting
caricaturist
ceramography
ceroplastics
chaleography
chiaro-oscuro
Chinese paper
chromaticity
colour circle

colour-filter
cottage china
design centre
drawing paper
drawing-board
Dresden china
Elgin marbles
etching point
fashion plate
genre painter
glyphography
heliogravure
hollow relief
illumination
illustration
in high relief
kaleidoscope
lantern slide
Leeds pottery
lignographer
line engraver
lithographer
lithographic
lithogravure
magic lantern
metallograph
mezzo-relievo
old Worcester
opaque colour

paint the lily
palette knife
panchromatic
photoengrave
photoetching
photographer
photographic
photogravure
photomontage
picture frame
pointillisme
pointilliste
portrait bust
poster colour
potter's earth
potter's wheel
reflex camera
reproduction
riot of colour
rough draught
rough outline
scene painter
sculptograph
self-portrait
shadow figure
sneak preview
spectrograph
stained glass
stereo camera

street artist	wall painting	well-composed
technicolour	water colours	white pottery
time exposure	wax engraving	zincographer
tracing paper	wax modelling	
tripod camera	Wedgwood ware	

Education

This section includes names for teachers and members of staff in schools and universities—scholars, students and pupils—types of teaching institution—writing materials and schoolbooks—examinations and qualifications.

B.A.	ambo	gown	quiz	atlas
Dr.	blot	grad	read	board
go	book	guru	roll	chair
I.Q.	co-ed	head	sage	chalk
M.A.	copy	lore	seat	class
O.B.	cram	mark	soph	coach
ABC	crib	mods	swat	dunce
con	dean	note	swot	école
den	demy	nous	talk	edify
dux	desk	oral	tech	élève
fag	exam	pass	term	essay
ink	fact	prep	test	final
jot	fail	prof	text	flunk
pen	form	quad	tyro	fresh

forum	tutor	infant	remove
gaudy	usher	infuse	report
gloss	alumna	inkpot	rubber
grade	biblos	jotter	savant
grind	biblus	junior	school
guide	brains	lector	*Schule*
hadji	brainy	lesson	scroll
house	browse	lyceum	senior
imbue	bursar	manual	sermon
khoja	campus	master	smalls
kudos	course	matron	syndic
learn	crèche	mentor	taught
lines	debate	mullah	teaser
lycée	degree	munshi	theory
major	docent	novice	tripos
merit	doctor	old boy	truant
minor	duenna	optime	vellum
paper	eraser	pandit	academy
poser	examen	pedant	alumnus
prime	fellow	pencil	amateur
prize	fescue	period	*bas bleu*
pupil	finals	peruse	boarder
quill	genius	preach	bookish
sizar	grader	primer	bookman
slate	grades	pundit	Braille
spell	gradus	reader	brush up
staff	greats	recite	bursary
study	ground	rector	coacher
teach	homily	regius	college

7-8

crammer	letters	teacher	dry nurse
culture	lexicon	the arts	educable
dabbler	lowbrow	theatre	educated
degrees	maestro	thinker	educatee
diploma	major in	three R's	educator
dominie	minor in	trainee	elective
Dunciad	monitor	tuition	emeritus
egghead	nursery	tutorer	examiner
entrant	old girl	varsity	exercise
erudite	oppidan	writing	foolscap
examine	pandect	written	freshman
explain	papyrus	academic	Gamaliel
expound	passman	aegrotat	glossary
faculty	pointer	agitprop	gownsman
failure	precept	aularian	graduand
fresher	prefect	bachelor	graduate
freshie	primary	beginner	guidance
grammar	problem	book lore	half-term
great go	proctor	bookworm	harangue
grinder	qualify	classman	highbrow
hearing	read for	coaching	homework
honours	reading	commoner	humanism
inkhorn	satchel	copybook	inceptor
inkwell	scholar	cramming	informed
instill	schools	cultural	inkstand
learned	seminar	cultured	instruct
learner	student	didactic	Latinist
lectern	studier	disciple	learning
lecture	studies	division	lecturer

26

lettered	roll-call	brainwave
liripipe	sciolist	brainwork
liripoop	semester	catechize
literacy	seminary	catechism
literate	servitor	chalk talk
little go	spelling	chalkdust
memorize	studious	classmate
mistress	studying	classroom
moralize	teaching	collegian
neophyte	textbook	day school
note book	training	dean of men
Oxbridge	treatise	desk-bound
pansophy	tutelage	didactics
pass-mark	tutorage	diligence
pedagogy	tutoress	direction
pedantic	tutorial	discourse
pedantry	tutoring	doctorate
playtime	vacation	dunce's cap
polemics	versed in	education
polyglot	well-read	enlighten
pore over	wordbook	erudition
postgrad	wrangler	extempore
preacher	absey book	fifth form
punditry	alma mater	final year
question	art school	first form
read up on	assistant	first year
red-brick	associate	formalist
research	Athenaeum	gaudeamus
revision	booklover	gazetteer

governess	proselyte	tutorhood
greenhorn	qualified	tutorship
Gymnasium	receptive	undergrad
homiletic	refresher	abiturient
honour man	rough note	academical
hortatory	scholarch	arithmetic
ignoramus	scholarly	bibliology
ingestion	school kid	bibliomane
inspector	school lad	biblionost
institute	schoolboy	bibliosoph
knowledge	schooling	blackboard
law school	schoolish	brain storm
lucubrate	schoolman	brain trust
masterate	sermonize	brain-child
note paper	sixth form	cap and gown
novitiate	smatterer	catechumen
palaestra	sophister	chautauqua
parchment	sophomore	classicism
pedagogic	staffroom	classicist
pedagogue	star pupil	college boy
pensioner	supplicat	collegiate
play group	syndicate	common room
portioner	take notes	coryphaeus
precentor	teachable	curricular
preceptor	thesaurus	curriculum
prelector	third form	dame school
pre-school	third year	dictionary
principal	timetable	dilettante
professor	tuitional	discipline

dual school
educatress
eleven-plus
escritoire
exposition
extramural
fellowship
form master
fourth form
fraternity
free period
free school
graduation
hard lesson
headmaster
high school
humanities
illiterate
illuminate
illuminati
imposition
inquisitor
instructed
instructor
intramural
junior high
lead pencil
learned man
lower fifth

lower sixth
lower third
memorandum
middle-brow
Nobel prize
past master
pedagogics
pedagogist
pensionnat
Philistine
playground
playschool
postmaster
preceptive
prelection
prep school
prize idiot
prolocutor
propaganda
quadrangle
quadrivium
quiz master
readership
real school
report card
Sabbatical
scholastic
school chum
school meal

school miss
schoolbook
schooldame
schoolgirl
schoolma'am
schoolmaid
schoolmarm
schoolmate
schoolroom
scrutinize
second form
second head
second year
self-taught
senior high
shibboleth
smattering
specialize
specialist
sub-culture
supervisor
tenderfoot
university
upper fifth
upper sixth
upper third
vocabulary
well-versed
widely read

abecedarian	enlightened	moral lesson
abecedarium	examination	mortarboard
academician	fellow pupil	music lesson
arts college	former pupil	music school
attainments	give a lesson	naval school
Bible school	grade school	night school
bibliolater	half scholar	omniscience
bibliolatry	head teacher	point a moral
bibliomania	house master	polytechnic
bibliophile	inculcation	preceptress
board school	information	preparation
bookishness	informative	prize-giving
brain-teaser	institution	prize-winner
bright pupil	instruction	probationer
certificate	instructive	questionist
chalk-talker	intelligent	read a lesson
charm school	invigilator	reading desk
class fellow	lecture hall	re-education
coeducation	lecture room	researchist
college girl	lectureship	responsions
college-bred	liberal arts	*salle d'asile*
collegianer	literary man	scholarship
crash course	*littérateur*	School Board
dame's school	lower fourth	school child
dean of women	matriculate	school lunch
directorate	meritocracy	school meals
distinction	midnight oil	school of art
edification	misteaching	schoolhouse
educational	moderations	scrutinizer

sharp lesson
spelling bee
student body
teacher's pet
teachership
teaching aid
trade school
upper fourth
wide reading
writing desk
amphitheatre
aptitude test
assimilation
baccalaureus
battle of wits
bibliomaniac
blue stocking
book learning
brain twister
church school
classicalist
College Board
conservatory
disciplinary
disquisition

encyclopedia
exercise book
exhibitioner
form mistress
French lesson
ground school
headmistress
indoctrinate
infant school
instructress
intellectual
intelligence
junior school
kindergarten
learn by heart
make the grade
man of letters
master of arts
matter of fact
memorization
mental labour
middle school
naval academy
normal school
object lesson

old school tie
painting book
parish school
perscrutator
phrontistery
postgraduate
professorate
professorial
public school
pupil teacher
riding school
roll of honour
school dinner
schoolfellow
schoolkeeper
schoolmaster
self-educated
senior school
spelling book
summer school
Sunday school
teach a lesson
training ship
underteacher
writing table

Literature

This section includes forms of literature, drama and poetry—books and booklovers—writers and poets (no personal names)—grammatical terminology—scansion—figures of speech—punctuation—writing materials—printing terms and typefaces—the Press and journalism.

Ed.	pad	code	mode	quad
em	pen	coin	mood	read
en	pie	copy	mora	root
MS	pun	dash	muse	ruby
op	rag	dele	myth	rune
pi	saw	demy	note	saga
P.S.	set	edit	noun	scan
ABC	tie	epic	opus	scop
act	anas	epos	page	slip
ana	anon	font	part	slug
bar	bard	foot	past	song
cap	beat	gest	pica	star
dot	bold	hack	plan	stem
gem	book	hero	play	stet
ink	bull	iamb	plot	tale
lay	cant	idea	poem	term
log	card	joke	poet	text
mot	case	leaf	puff	tome
ode	Clio	line	pull	type

verb	daily	idyll	proof	tense
word	ditto	index	prose	thema
work	devil	Ionic	prosy	theme
yarn	diary	irony	quill	tilde
acute	divan	issue	quote	title
adage	draft	lingo	rebus	topic
affix	drama	*livre*	recto	tract
album	dummy	lyric	reply	trope
Aldus	elegy	maxim	rhyme	twist
annal	envoi	metre	Roman	usage
argot	envoy	moral	runes	verse
arsis	epode	motto	runic	verso
atlas	essay	muses	scald	voice
axiom	extra	novel	scene	vowel
bible	fable	odist	scrip	words
blurb	farce	organ	serif	works
books	final	paean	set up	*abrégé*
brace	folio	paper	sheet	accent
Bragi	forel	parse	skald	action
breve	fount	pearl	slang	adverb
brief	genre	phone	slant	Alcaic
canon	geste	piece	slate	Aldine
canto	ghost	plume	space	annals
caret	gloss	poesy	spell	annual
codex	gnome	point	stamp	aorist
colon	grave	press	story	*aperçu*
comic	heads	prime	study	Apollo
comma	ictus	print	style	author
cover	idiom	proem	summa	ballad

bathos	em quad	italic	offset
biblos	ending	jacket	old saw
biblus	eponym	jargon	parens
binder	epopee	jingle	pathos
bon mot	errata	leader	patois
browse	etymon	legend	pencil
burden	eulogy	letter	penman
byword	exposé	loglog	penned
chorus	fabler	lyrist	pen-pal
clause	favour	mackle	period
cliché	figure	macron	person
climax	flimsy	macule	phrase
colour	folder	make-up	poetry
column	future	manual	postil
comedy	galley	margin	potted
copula	gender	matter	praxis
crambo	gerund	memoir	précis
critic	gnomic	metric	prefix
dactyl	Gothic	minion	primer
dagger	gradus	monody	prolix
dative	heroic	morgue	pundit
delete	hiatus	neuter	purist
depict	homily	notice	quarto
dictum	hybrid	number	quotes
diesis	hyphen	obelus	reader
digest	iambic	object	recant
dipody	iambus	octave	record
doodle	impose	octavo	relate
editor	inkpot	offcut	remark

report	stanza	article	creator
résumé	strain	autonym	dash off
Reuter	stress	ballade	daybook
review	stylus	binding	decline
revise	suffix	bookery	delenda
rhymer	syntax	book-fed	demotic
rhymic	tablet	bookish	descant
rondel	tercet	booklet	dialect
run off	theory	bookman	diamond
satire	thesis	Boswell	dimeter
saying	tongue	brevier	distich
scheme	truism	bucolic	eclogue
scrawl	umlaut	caconym	edition
screed	uncial	caesura	elegiac
scribe	vellum	calamus	English
script	verbal	capital	enstamp
scrive	volume	capsule	epigram
scroll	weekly	cedilla	episode
sequel	writer	chapter	epistle
serial	zeugma	classic	epitaph
series	abridge	codices	epithet
seriph	account	coinage	epitome
sermon	acronym	comment	eponymy
sestet	addenda	compend	erratum
sextet	adjunct	compose	excerpt
simile	anagram	context	extract
sketch	antique	copyman	fabliau
sonnet	antonym	coterie	factual
spread	apostil	couplet	fad word

fantasy	journal	nominal	prelims
feature	jussive	notepad	present
fiction	justify	*novella*	printed
flowers	laconic	obelisk	printer
fluency	lampoon	octapla	profile
flyleaf	leaders	old joke	pronoun
garland	leaflet	omnibus	proofer
gazette	Leonine	on paper	prosaic
georgic	letters	opuscle	prosody
grammar	lexicon	outline	proverb
graphic	library	overrun	publish
handout	literal	oxytone	quadrat
heading	litotes	pandect	recount
Helicon	log book	papyrus	refrain
heroine	lyrical	parable	reissue
history	*Märchen*	paradox	release
Homeric	meaning	paragon	reprint
homonym	measure	parsing	reverso
huitain	memoirs	passage	reviser
idyllic	message	pen-name	rewrite
imagery	metonym	perfect	rhyming
impress	missive	phoneme	romance
imprint	monthly	playlet	rondeau
in print	*morçeau*	Pléiade	roundel
initial	mystery	poetess	sagaman
inkhorn	narrate	poetics	Sapphic
inkwell	neology	poetise	sarcasm
insight	new word	portray	scaldic
italics	newsman	preface	scholia

section	virelay	appendix	chapbook
sestina	virgule	archaism	chestnut
shocker	vocable	archives	chiasmus
sorites	western	asterisk	China ink
special	wordage	Atticism	choliamb
spondee	write-up	autotype	circular
storied	writing	ballader	city desk
strophe	written	banality	city room
subject	ablative	biweekly	classics
summary	abstract	bold hand	clerihew
synesis	acrostic	boldface	co-author
synonym	allegory	book club	colophon
tabloid	allusion	book mark	compiler
telling	alphabet	bookcase	composer
textual	analecta	book-ends	construe
the Nine	analects	bookrack	contents
themata	analogue	book-read	copy desk
theorem	analysis	bookrest	copybook
tragedy	anapaest	bookroom	creative
treat of	anaphora	bookshop	critique
trilogy	anecdote	bookworm	cuttings
triolet	annalist	*bout-rimé*	dactylic
triplet	annotate	brackets	delectus
tripody	antihero	brochure	describe
triseme	aphorism	bulletin	despatch
trochee	apodosis	cacology	dispatch
typeset	apologia	calendar	document
verbose	apologue	Calliope	doggerel
versify	apothegm	causerie	dramatic

elegiast
ellipsis
emphasis
enallage
end rhyme
end-paper
epanodos
epic poet
epigraph
epilogue
epitasis
epopoeia
essayist
eulogium
euphuism
excerpta
excursus
exegesis
extracts
eye rhyme
fabulist
fabulous
fair copy
fascicle
feminine
folk tale
foolscap
footnote
fragment

full stop
fullface
genitive
glossary
Good Book
graffiti
graffito
handbook
headline
hexapody
hieratic
historic
hornbook
humorist
ideogram
idyllist
India ink
inkstand
inscribe
inscroll
Irishism
jongleur
kyrielle
laconics
language
laureate
libretto
ligature
limerick

link verb
linotype
lipogram
literacy
literate
logogram
logotype
longhand
love poem
madrigal
magazine
malaprop
measured
metaphor
metonymy
metrical
minstrel
misnomer
misprint
misusage
modifier
molossus
monotype
morpheme
mot juste
mythical
narrator
notation
notebook

nouvelle	poetling	satirist
novelist	poetship	scanning
novellae	polyglot	scansion
obituary	post-card	scholion
octapody	pressman	scholium
offprint	printers	scribble
old story	printery	sentence
open book	printing	skeleton
opuscule	prologue	slip case
original	prosaism	slipslop
oxymoron	protasis	solecism
palinode	put to bed	spelling
pamphlet	quatrain	spondaic
parabole	rare book	subtitle
paradigm	read copy	syllable
paragoge	ready pen	syllabus
paragram	relation	symploce
particle	reporter	synopsis
password	rescript	synoptic
pastoral	reviewer	textbook
pencraft	revision	the Press
pie a form	rewriter	thematic
Pierides	rhapsode	thriller
Pindaric	rhapsody	toponymy
playbook	rhetoric	tractate
pleonasm	romancer	treasury
poethood	romantic	treatise
poetizer	root word	tribrach
poet-king	ruby type	trigraph

trimeter	amphigory	bookshelf
tristich	anacrusis	bookstall
trochaic	anecdotal	bookstand
trouvère	annotator	bookstore
trouveur	anonymous	bourgeois
type face	anthology	brilliant
type page	anti-novel	bucoliast
type size	antispast	cap rhymes
verbatim	apostille	cap verses
verbiage	assonance	catalogue
verselet	Athenaeum	catch line
verseman	Attic salt	catchword
versicle	attribute	character
vignette	authoress	chronicle
vocative	autograph	clarendon
web press	ballpoint	classical
whodunit	battology	clippings
word form	bimonthly	coin a word
wordbook	biography	collector
yearbook	blackface	collotype
accidence	bold-faced	columnist
acrostics	book cloth	comic book
adjective	book cover	commenter
adventure	book token	composing
adverbial	book trade	condensed
albertype	bookboard	conjugate
allograph	bookcraft	consonant
amoebaean	booklover	conundrum
ampersand	bookmaker	copy chief

copy paper	fairy tale	in measure
copyright	fictional	Indian ink
criticism	folk story	intensive
crossword	fragments	Irish bull
cuneiform	free lance	late extra
Decameron	free verse	legendary
depiction	full-faced	lettering
depictive	gazetteer	librarian
descanter	gerundive	life story
diaeresis	ghost word	lightface
diphthong	gleanings	limp-cover
directory	go to press	lithotype
discourse	great work	livraison
dithyramb	guidebook	local room
dramatist	hair space	logogriph
editorial	half-title	logomachy
end-reader	hard cover	love story
ephemeris	headlines	lower case
epic verse	heptapody	macaronic
epithesis	heteronym	major poet
epizeuxis	hexameter	majuscule
eponymism	hexastich	masculine
epopoeist	historian	Meliboean
etymology	historify	melodrama
euphemism	holograph	Menippean
exegetics	hypallage	minor poet
expositor	hyperbole	minuscule
expounder	idiomatic	monograph
extrabold	idioticon	monostich

mythmaker
narration
narrative
necrology
neologism
neoterism
newspaper
newsprint
nonce word
nonpareil
note paper
novelette
octastich
onomastic
page proof
palillogy
paper-back
parabolic
paragraph
parchment
Parnassus
partitive
past tense
pen and ink
penscript
pentapody
personify
philology
phonemics

phonetics
phonology
phototypy
pictorial
platitude
poetaster
poetastry
poetcraft
poeticule
Poet's Poet
portrayal
potboiler
potential
predicate
pressroom
presswork
preterite
print shop
prolative
prolepsis
prolixity
proofread
proofroom
pseudonym
publicist
punch-line
punctuate
qualifier
quarterly

quodlibet
quotation
raconteur
rationale
recountal
recounter
reference
reflexive
represent
retelling
rhymester
rigmarole
romancist
rotograph
roundelay
round-hand
runesmith
sans serif
satirical
scholiast
scribbler
scription
scrivener
scrivenry
secret ink
secretary
selection
semanteme
semantics

semicolon	tetraseme	adversaria
semiotics	thesaurus	*Aldine book*
sgraffito	thin space	alliterate
sheetwork	title page	amanuensis
shorthand	treatment	amphibrach
signature	triticism	*amphigouri*
slip cover	trovatore	amphimacer
small pica	true story	anapaestic
soft-cover	type mould	anastrophe
songsmith	upper case	anecdotage
sonneteer	vade-mecum	anecdotist
spin a yarn	verbalism	annotation
statement	verbarian	antecedent
stenotype	verbosity	anticlimax
storiette	*vers libre*	antithesis
story book	verse form	apocalypse
story line	versifier	apostrophe
strike off	vocabular	atmosphere
subeditor	vogue word	authorship
substance	vulgarism	background
summarize	witticism	back number
sumpsimus	wordiness	bad grammar
syllabary	write upon	Bard of Avon
syllepsis	zincotype	battledore
symbolism	abridgment	best seller
symposium	accusative	bibliology
tail rhyme	active verb	bibliomane
tall story	adaptation	biblionost
tetrapody	adjectival	bibliopegy

bibliopole	colloquial	dissertate
bibliosoph	colportage	dust jacket
bibliothec	colporteur	embroidery
billet doux	comic strip	epanaphora
biographer	commentary	epic poetry
black-faced	common noun	exposition
blank verse	compendium	expression
Bloomsbury	compositor	fairy story
book jacket	conspectus	*feuilleton*
book review	continuity	fictionist
bookbinder	copulative	figurative
bookdealer	copyholder	filing room
bookholder	copying ink	finite verb
book-loving	copyreader	funeral ode
bookmaking	corruption	ghost story
bookmonger	cradle book	glossarist
bookseller	cryptogram	glossology
bookwright	curate's egg	glottogony
brain child	cyclopedia	glottology
broadsheet	dead letter	grammarian
cacography	dead matter	hack writer
catalectic	declension	Heptameron
chapel text	dedication	heptameter
Chinese ink	definition	heptastich
chromotypy	denotation	historical
chronicler	derivation	house organ
circumflex	diaskeuast	hybrid word
classicism	dictionary	hyperbaton
collection	discourser	imperative

imposition	make-up room	participle
impression	manuscript	pen pushing
incunabula	metalepsis	pentameter
indicative	metaphrase	pentastich
infinitive	metathesis	periodical
inflection	metrically	permissive
inkslinger	miscellany	plate proof
job printer	mock-heroic	playwright
journalese	morphology	pleonastic
journalism	neuter verb	pluperfect
journalist	news editor	poccilonym
lame verses	news writer	poet-artist
lead pencil	newsletter	poetastery
letter card	*nom-de-plume*	poet-farmer
lexicology	nominative	poet-priest
lexiconist	non-fiction	possessive
librettist	noun clause	press proof
light-faced	obligative	production
light verse	obsoletism	pronominal
literature	open letter	proof sheet
live matter	orismology	proper noun
long accent	*ottava rima*	prosaicism
long primer	palaeotype	prospectus
love letter	palimpsest	publishers
logorrhoea	palindrome	publishing
macaronics	palinodist	put to press
magazinist	paper tiger	recounting
magnum opus	paraphrase	rhapsodist
make a proof	Parnassian	rhyme royal

round robin
runic verse
schoolbook
scratch pad
scribbling
scriptural
scrivening
sealed book
set in print
shibboleth
short story
slim volume
socio-drama
soubriquet
spoonerism
stereotype
storiology
storymaker
subheading
Swan of Avon
synecdoche
syntactics
taleteller
tell a story
tetrameter
tetrastich
thick space
transitive
troubadour

true to life
type matter
typescript
typesetter
typewriter
typography
verbal note
verbal noun
vernacular
versecraft
versemaker
versesmith
villanelle
vocabulary
word-coiner
word-seller
writership
abecedarian
active voice
acute accent
adversative
alexandrine
alphabetics
anacoluthia
Anacreontic
anachronism
Anglo-Saxon
antiphrasis
antispastic

antistrophe
antonomasia
attributive
authorcraft
author's copy
ballad maker
bastard type
bibliognost
bibliolater
bibliophage
bibliophile
bibliotheca
biographist
black letter
black comedy
Book of books
book of verse
book printer
book support
bookbinding
bookishness
book-learned
bookselling
bring to book
catachresis
catch phrase
circulation
cliff hanger
collectanea

commentator	engrossment	local colour
compendious	exclamation	logographer
compilation	festschrift	lucubration
composition	first person	lyric poetry
concordance	Fleet Street	malapropism
conditional	flow of words	memorabilia
confessions	fortnightly	memorialist
conjugation	fountain pen	miracle play
conjunction	future tense	miscellanea
conjunctive	galley proof	monographer
connotation	ghostwriter	Mrs Malaprop
contributor	glottal stop	Mrs Slipslop
correlative	grammatical	*nom de guerre*
corrigendum	grave accent	novelettist
counterterm	great primer	nursery tale
crabbed hand	gutter press	onomasticon
crambo-clink	handwriting	onomatology
cub reporter	happy ending	orthography
description	heroic verse	pamphleteer
descriptive	incunabulum	paragrapher
disjunctive	inscription	parenthesis
dissertator	inspiration	participial
dissyllable	interviewer	Passion play
dithyrambic	letter paper	passive verb
dithyrambus	letterpress	past perfect
dittography	library book	patent space
electrotype	linguistics	penny-a-liner
Elzevir book	literary man	perissology
enchiridion	littérateur	phrasemaker

phraseology	semasiology	word painter
picture book	short accent	word picture
Pindaric ode	solid matter	written word
play on words	stenography	yarn spinner
poetic prose	story writer	Yellow press
poetic works	storyteller	abbreviation
poet-patriot	subjunctive	abbreviature
poet-pilgrim	substantive	abstract noun
poet-thinker	superscribe	adherent noun
poet-warrior	tachygraphy	advance proof
point tenses	taletelling	alliteration
preposition	terminology	author's proof
press revise	the Good Book	balladmonger
printed word	third person	ballpoint pen
printer's ink	tragi-comedy	bastard title
proofreader	transcriber	bedtime story
psychodrama	translation	bibliography
public press	true meaning	bibliologist
publication	tuneful Nine	bibliomaniac
punctuation	type foundry	bibliopegist
reading room	typesetting	bibliopolist
real meaning	typographer	bibliothèque
retold story	typographic	binder's title
rhyme scheme	unfold a tale	block capital
rotary press	verbigerate	book learning
rotogravure	vers librist	book reviewer
sad to relate	versemaking	bookstitcher
scriptorial	war reporter	brachygraphy
semantology	word history	calligrapher

chrestomathy
chronography
classicalism
collaborator
collectarium
commentation
complete work
complication
condensation
construction
dead language
deponent verb
direct object
direct speech
disquisition
dissertation
double dagger
early edition
elegiac verse
encyclopedia
epigrammatic
fat-faced type
first edition
foundry proof
fourth estate
frontispiece
gnomic aorist
gossip column
halting rhyme

hermeneutics
hieroglyphic
Hudibrastics
indelible ink
initial rhyme
instrumental
interjection
intransitive
introduction
invisible ink
king's English
leader writer
letter writer
lexicography
literary hack
literary lion
logodaedalus
man of letters
metaphorical
metrical foot
metrical unit
monkish Latin
monosyllable
morality play
mother tongue
newspaperman
nomenclature
nursery rhyme
onomatopoeia

palaeography
paragraphist
part of speech
passive voice
pastoral poet
perfect rhyme
perfect tense
plain English
poet laureate
poetastering
poetic genius
poet-novelist
poet-satirist
polysyllable
present tense
press release
question mark
quill driving
rhyming slang
Rosetta stone
second person
slanting hand
slip of the pen
society verse
space fiction
speed writing
spelling book
stock of words
story telling

strip cartoon	versemongery	writing paper
turn of phrase	western story	yarn spinning
type printing	word painting	writer's cramp
uncial letter	writer's cramp	

Music

This section includes all musical forms, classical and popular—musical instruments—musicians (but no personal names)—common foreign words for terms and symbols in musical notation—dances.

f	te	hum	sax	bell	flue
p	ut	jig	soh	bind	form
D.C.	act	key	sol	blow	fret
do	air	kit	tie	*brio*	glee
D.S.	bar	lah	uke	clef	gong
E.P.	bop	lay	wax	coda	harp
fa	bow	lip	alto	dash	horn
ff	cat	lur	*arco*	disc	hymn
fp	cue	nut	*aria*	disk	jack
la	doh	ode	*arpa*	diva	jazz
L.P.	dot	peg	ayre	drum	jive
me	duo	pes	band	duet	jota
op	fah	pop	bard	dump	juba
pp	hay	rag	base	fife	keen
re	hey	ray	bass	*fine*	lead
sf	hit	run	beat	flat	*Lied*

lilt	root	album	chime	gigue
lira	rota	anima	choir	grace
loco	rote	A-side	chord	*grave*
lure	scat	ad lib	close	gymel
lute	sing	*assai*	comma	ictus
lyra	slur	atone	*corno*	idyll
lyre	solo	aulos	crook	jazzy
mass	song	banjo	croon	jodel
mode	stop	basso	dance	kyrie
mood	time	baton	*desto*	large
mute	tone	bebop	dirge	*largo*
neck	toot	bells	ditty	*lento*
node	trio	belly	*dolce*	luter
noël	tuba	blues	drone	lyric
note	tuck	bones	drums	major
oboe	tune	brace	elegy	march
open	turn	brass	Erato	melic
opus	vamp	brawl	*étude*	metre
part	vina	breve	fancy	minim
peal	viol	B-side	farce	minor
pick	*vivo*	*buffo*	fifer	modal
port	*voce*	bugle	fifth	motet
prom	wait	*burla*	final	motif
rank	wind	canon	flute	musak
reed	wood	*canto*	forte	music
reel	work	carol	fugue	naker
rest	*a poco*	catch	galop	nebel
ribs	*ad lib*	'cello	gamba	neume
roll	adapt	chant	gamut	ninth

nonet	rondo	swell	volte
notes	rosin	swing	waits
octet	rotte	table	waltz
odeon	round	tabor	winds
opera	rumba	*tacet*	woods
organ	runic	tambo	yodel
paean	scale	tango	accent
pause	scena	*tempo*	accord
pavan	score	tenor	*adagio*
pedal	*segno*	theme	almain
piano	*segue*	third	almand
piece	shake	throb	answer
piper	shalm	thrum	anthem
pitch	sharp	tonic	Apollo
pleno	shawm	touch	*arioso*
pluck	siren	triad	atonal
point	sixth	trill	*aubade*
polka	slide	troll	ballad
presa	snare	trope	ballet
primo	sol-fa	tuned	bolero
proms	*sordo*	*tutti*	bowing
psalm	sound	up bow	*branle*
pulse	space	*valse*	bridge
quint	staff	valve	bugler
range	stave	verse	burden
rebec	Strad	vibes	cadent
reeds	strum	viola	*caisse*
regal	study	voice	can-can
resin	suite	volta	cantor

6

cantus	fading	*Lieder*	potted
caoine	fiasco	line-up	*presto*
catchy	fiddle	litany	quaver
catgut	figure	lituus	racket
chanty	finale	lutist	rattle
chimes	firing	lyrist	rebeck
choral	fourth	maggot	record
chorus	fugato	manual	repeat
cither	gallop	medley	rhythm
citole	*geigen*	melody	*rigore*
copula	*giusto*	minuet	rounds
cornet	graces	monody	*rubato*
corona	*grazia*	motion	rubebe
cue-ing	great C	motive	scorer
cymbal	guitar	musico	second
da capo	hammer	needle	*sempre*
damper	harper	neumes	septet
decani	hepcat	*nobile*	serena
diesis	hocket	nowell	sestet
direct	horner	oboist	sextet
do-re-mi	hymnal	octave	shanty
double	hymner	off-key	shofar
drones	in tune	*ottava*	*simile*
dulcet	jingle	pavane	singer
ecbole	keener	period	snatch
eighth	kettle	phrase	sonata
encore	lament	pipe up	spinet
entrée	leader	piston	stanza
euphon	*legato*	player	strain

53

string	vielle	bandore	celesta
subito	violin	banjuke	cellist
syrinx	*vivace*	bar beat	cembalo
tabret	voices	bar line	*chanson*
tampon	volume	baryton	chanter
tam-tam	waxing	bass bar	chantry
tattoo	zambra	bassist	chekker
temper	zither	bassoon	chikara
tenor C	zufolo	battery	chiming
tenuto	a tempo	*battuta*	chorale
tercet	*agitato*	bazooka	chorine
terzet	*allegro*	bellows	chorist
timbal	althorn	bombard	cithara
timbre	*amabile*	bourdon	cithern
tom-tom	*amoroso*	*bourrée*	cittern
tooter	*andante*	boutade	clapper
top ten	*animato*	brasses	clarion
treble	*arietta*	*bravura*	classic
tromba	*ariette*	buccina	*clavier*
troppo	arrange	cadence	*codetta*
tucket	*ars nova*	cadency	compass
tune up	art song	*cadenza*	compose
tuning	*attacca*	*calando*	*con brio*
tymbal	*attacco*	calypso	*con moto*
tympan	attuned	*canarie*	concent
unison	bagpipe	*cantata*	concert
up-beat	ballade	*canzona*	concord
vagans	bandman	*canzone*	conduct
veloce	bandora	caprice	consort

cornett	*giocoso*	mazurka	pianist
cornist	gittern	measure	pianola
coupler	gradual	mediant	pibgorn
Cremona	G-string	melisma	pibroch
crooner	halling	melodia	piccolo
curtall	harmony	melodic	*pietoso*
cymbals	harpist	middle C	piffero
descant	hautboy	mixture	*pomposo*
discord	hit song	*morceau*	pop song
double C	hit tune	mordent	potlids
doubles	hornist	*morendo*	prelude
down bow	hot jazz	musette	Psalter
drummer	humming	musical	quartet
episode	hymnist	natural	quintet
euphony	hymnody	ocarina	ragtime
Euterpe	intrada	octette	recital
fagotto	introit	offbeat	refrain
fanfare	ivories	one-step	reprise
fermata	juke box	organum	requiem
fiddle G	*Kapelle*	Orpheus	respond
fiddler	keening	pandora	ribible
flutina	key note	pandore	*ripieno*
fluting	*Ländler*	pandura	romance
flutist	Lorelei	Panpipe	*rondeau*
forlana	lullaby	partial	*rondino*
fox trot	*maestro*	passage	*rosalia*
furioso	mandola	*pesante*	*roulade*
furlana	mandora	*piacere*	sackbut
gavotte	marimba	*pianino*	salicet

sambuca	tambura	ziganka	boat song
samisen	tangent	*a capella*	bouffons
Sanctus	the Nine	*a piacere*	*burlesca*
saxhorn	theorbo	*Agnus Dei*	*burletta*
saxtuba	timbrel	*agrément*	Calliope
scherzo	timpani	*air varié*	canticle
sciolto	tirasse	alto clef	canticum
scoring	*toccata*	alto horn	cantoris
secondo	top note	alto viol	*canzonet*
septuor	tracker	*anglaise*	carillon
serpent	treble C	antiphon	*castrato*
service	*tremolo*	archlute	*cavatina*
seventh	trillet	*arpeggio*	chaconne
sfogato	triplet	arranger	chanting
singing	tritone	Ave Maria	choirboy
sithara	trumpet	bagpipes	choirman
skiffle	tuneful	bandsman	choragus
soloist	two-step	banjoist	choregus
song hit	ukelele	baritone	clappers
soprano	upright	barytone	clarinet
sordino	vespers	bass clef	*clavecin*
spinnet	*vibrato*	bass drum	composer
stopped	vihuela	bass horn	*con amore*
stretto	violist	bass note	*con anima*
strings	violone	bass oboe	concerto
subject	war song	bass viol	*continuo*
syncope	warbler	beat time	coronach
taborer	wassail	bell harp	courante
taboret	whistle	*berceuse*	cromorna

cromorne	fantasie	keyboard
crooning	flautist	key-bugle
crotchet	flourish	last post
cylinder	flue-pipe	lay clerk
dal segno	flue-work	lay vicar
deep bass	folderol	left hand
diapason	folk song	*leggiero*
diapente	*fughetta*	*libretto*
diatonic	galliard	*lieblich*
doh-ray-me	gemshorn	ligature
doloroso	glee club	love song
dominant	habanera	low pitch
down beat	half rest	lutanist
doxology	hand bell	madrigal
drumbeat	harmonic	*maestoso*
drumhead	harp lute	*maggiore*
drumskin	hornpipe	major key
duettino	humstrum	mazourka
duettist	hymeneal	meantone
dulciana	hymn tune	measured
dulcimer	in accord	melodeon
emphasis	in chorus	melodica
ensemble	in unison	melodics
entr'acte	interval	melodist
faburden	jazz band	minor key
falderal	jazzed up	minstrel
falsetto	jew's harp	*moderato*
fandango	jongleur	monotone
fantasia	Jubilate	movement

music box	plangent	septette
musicale	plectron	sequence
musician	plectrum	serenade
nocturne	pop group	*serenata*
notation	pop music	sextette
oliphant	post horn	sextolet
open note	postlude	side drum
operatic	psalmody	sing-song
operetta	psaltery	sliphorn
oratorio	pure tone	*soggetto*
organist	purfling	sol-faist
ornament	quintole	solo stop
ostinato	ragtimer	sonatina
overtone	recorder	song book
overture	reed pipe	songbird
Panpipes	reed stop	songplay
parallel	register	songster
parlando	response	sour note
parlante	reveille	*spianato*
part song	rhapsody	*spiccato*
partials	*ricochet*	spinette
pastoral	rigadoon	squiffer
phagotus	*ritenuto*	*staccato*
phantasy	saraband	strike up
phrasing	*sautillé*	strummer
pianette	Schalmey	subtonic
pianiste	*scordato*	swan song
Pierides	semitone	swell-box
pipe tune	*semplice*	symphony

tamboura	vocalion	band major
tenor cor	vocalism	bandstand
tenoroon	vocalist	bandurria
terzetto	*Vorspiel*	banjolele
the Muses	warbling	banjorine
threnody	wind band	barcarole
tonalist	woodwind	blow a horn
tonality	yodeller	blues song
tone deaf	zambomba	bombardon
tone down	zarzuela	bow fiddle
tone poem	*a cappella*	brass band
tone poet	accompany	*Brautlied*
tonguing	accordion	*brillante*
tonic key	acoustics	bugle call
tourdion	*ad libitum*	bugle horn
triangle	*adagietto*	cacophony
trihoris	*agilmente*	*cantabile*
trombone	*alla breve*	*cantilena*
trouvère	*alla zoppa*	*capriccio*
tunester	*allemande*	carolling
tympanon	*andamento*	castanets
tympanum	*andantino*	celestina
una corda	antiphony	chalumeau
vamp horn	arabesque	chantress
Victrola	archilute	charivari
virginal	*aria buffa*	choralist
virtuosa	baby grand	chorister
virtuosi	*bagatelle*	chromatic
virtuoso	*balalaika*	citharist

clarionet	epinicion	harmonist
classical	euphonium	harmonium
claviharp	execution	head voice
colla voce	extempore	hexachord
concentus	farandole	high pitch
conductor	figurante	hit-parade
conductus	fine-toned	*Hohlflöte*
consonate	fingering	homophony
contralto	*fioritura*	hydraulus
cornopean	flageolet	hymnology
crescendo	*flûte-à-bec*	*imbroglio*
croon song	folk dance	imitation
cymbalist	folk music	*impromptu*
dance band	fugue form	improvise
dance form	full close	inflexion
dead march	full organ	interlude
death song	full score	invention
diaphonia	*gallopade*	inversion
dithyramb	*glissando*	jazz stick
double bar	grace note	jitterbug
drone bass	*grandioso*	kent-bugle
drum corps	Gregorian	krummhorn
drum major	guitarist	*Kunstlied*
drumstick	half-close	langspiel
dulcitone	hand bells	*larghetto*
duple time	hand organ	leger line
echo organ	harmonica	*Leitmotiv*
écossaise	harmonics	lost chord
epicedium	harmonize	lyric bass

lyrichord
major mode
malaguena
mando-bass
mandoline
mandolute
manichord
matassins
matelotte
mediation
melodious
melodrama
melomania
metronome
mezza voce
minor mode
modulator
monochord
monophony
mouth harp
music demy
music hall
music roll
music room
music wire
mute pedal
obbligato
octachord
octo basse

offertory
open notes
open score
orchestra
organ stop
orpharion
out of tune
overtones
part music
Parthenia
passepied
pasticcio
pastorale
pedal note
performer
piacevole
piangendo
piano keys
piano wire
pianolist
pipe organ
pitch pipe
pizzicato
plainsong
play by ear
polonaise
polychord
polyphony
pop record

port a beul
potpourri
precentor
pricksong
principal
programme
prolation
promenade
quadrille
quartette
quintaton
quintette
quodlibet
recording
reed organ
remote key
rendering
rendition
resonance
rhythmics
ricercare
right hand
rondo form
roundelay
saxcornet
saxophone
scherzoso
schneller
scrape-gut

semibreve	tablature	variation
semitonic	tabor pipe	viola alto
serenader	tail piece	violin-bow
seraphina	tambourin	violinist
seraphine	tempo mark	virginals
sforzando	tenor clef	virtuosic
shantyman	tenor drum	*vivamente*
siciliana	tenor horn	vocalizer
signature	tenor tuba	voice part
singspiel	tenor viol	*Volkslied*
sink-a-pace	tessitura	voluntary
slow march	theme song	*vox humana*
smerzando	theorbist	waltz time
soap opera	time-value	whole note
soft pedal	timpanist	whole rest
solfeggio	top twenty	whole step
solo organ	torch song	whole-tone
song sheet	transpose	wind chest
sonometer	*tremolant*	wind music
sostenuto	*tremoloso*	wind trunk
sotto voce	tremulant	woodwinds
sound hole	triangles	wrest-pins
sound post	*trillando*	wrong note
spiritoso	trumpeter	xylophone
spiritual	tubuphone	zitherist
stockhorn	tuning bar	*a capriccio*
succentor	tymp stick	*Abendmusik*
swing band	tympanist	accidental
symphonic	undertone	adaptation

added sixth
affettuoso
allargando
allegretto
alteration
Antiphoner
aria da capo
aria fugata
ars antiqua
attunement
background
ballad horn
band leader
band master
band-waggon
barcarolle
basse danse
basset horn
basset oboe
basso buffo
bassoonist
bell-ringer
Benedictus
binary form
bottom note
brass winds
bridal hymn
bull fiddle
cancionero

cancrizans
cantatrice
canto fermo
canzonetta
chest voice
chime-bells
chitarrone
choir organ
chorus girl
cinquepace
clavichord
colla parte
coloratura
comic opera
common time
con affetto
con sordini
concertina
concertino
concertist
concordant
conducting
consonance
contrabass
cor anglais
cornermuse
cornettist
Coryphaeus
cradlesong

dance music
diminuendo
diminution
disc jockey
dissonance
doodlesack
dotted note
double bass
double flat
double time
drummer boy
dulcetness
Eisteddfod
enharmonic
euphonious
exposition
expression
fipple pipe
five-finger
Flügelhorn
folk singer
fortepiano
fortissimo
French harp
French horn
golden disc
grace notes
gramophone
grand opera

grand piano	major chord	music stand
great organ	major scale	musical bow
great stave	major sixth	musical box
Greek modes	major third	musical ear
grind organ	major triad	musical use
ground bass	mando-cello	musicology
hand bassel	manuscript	*Nachtmusik*
harmonicon	marimbaist	nail violin
harmonizer	mellophone	oboe d'amore
homophonic	melody part	*opera buffa*
hornplayer	*mezzo forte*	opera score
horse opera	*mezzo piano*	ophicleide
humoresque	minor canon	orchestral
hurdy-gurdy	minor chord	organ point
incidental	minor scale	*partimenti*
instrument	minor sixth	*passamezzo*
intermezzo	minor third	patent note
intonation	minor triad	patter song
Irish tenor	minstrelsy	pedal board
jam session	mixed times	pedal organ
kettledrum	modal scale	pedal point
leger lines	modern jazz	pentachord
light music	modulation	pentatonic
light opera	mouth music	percussion
long-player	mouth organ	*perdendosi*
lyre-guitar	mouthpiece	phonograph
lyric drama	music lover	*pianissimo*
lyric tenor	music maker	piano score
mainstream	music paper	piano stool

pianoforte	sacred Nine	suabe flute
pianologue	salicional	submediant
piccoloist	saltarello	supertonic
plagal mode	saxotromba	suspension
Polyhymnia	*scherzando*	swell organ
polyphonic	*scordatura*	swell pedal
ponticello	Scotch snap	symphonion
pop concert	*seguidilla*	symphonist
popular air	semichorus	syncopated
portamento	semiquaver	syncopator
prima donna	set to music	tambourine
prima volta	shaped note	tarantella
proportion	sheet music	tetrachord
proprietas	short score	tin whistle
quick march	silver disc	tone poetry
recitalist	simple time	tonic chord
recitative	sonata form	tonic major
recitativo	song leader	tonic minor
related key	song writer	tonic sol-fa
repertoire	songstress	*tranquillo*
repetition	*sordamente*	transcribe
resolution	sound board	transcript
responsory	sousaphone	transition
rhapsodist	speaker note	treble clef
ritardando	squeeze box	treble viol
ritornelle	Stradivari	*tremolando*
ritornello	strathspey	trenchmore
rondoletto	street band	triple time
round dance	*stringendo*	trombonist

troubadour	beat a tattoo	damper pedal
tuning fork	beat the drum	*decrescendo*
tuning pipe	binary scale	descant viol
tuning wire	blues singer	discography
tweedledee	bell-ringing	divided stop
tweedledum	broken chord	dominant key
twelve note	calliophone	Dorian modes
Tyrolienne	campanology	dotted minim
Union pipes	canned music	double chant
variations	*capriccetto*	double fugue
vibraphone	*capriccioso*	double sharp
villanella	cat's concert	double touch
vocal music	chansonette	dulcet tones
vocal score	chanterelle	ear for music
wrest-plank	choirmaster	English horn
accelerando	clarinetist	equal voices
accompanist	clarion call	eunuch flute
accrescendo	clavicymbal	eurhythmics
Aeolian harp	common chord	extemporize
affrettando	composition	faux bourdon
alla tedesca	concert band	fiddlestick
alternativo	concert hall	fife and drum
arrangement	*concertante*	figured bass
ballad maker	consecutive	finger board
ballad opera	*contrapunto*	fipple flute
banjo-zither	*contredanse*	first fiddle
barrel organ	couched harp	first violin
bass passage	counterbase	French pitch
basson russe	curtain tune	French sixth

fundamental
funeral song
gedackt-work
German flute
German sixth
golden-toned
graphophone
great octave
half cadence
harmonizing
harpsichord
hunting horn
in the groove
inscription
keyed guitar
lamentabile
leading note
long-playing
Lydian modes
madrigalist
major second
mandolinist
manichordon
mellifluent
mellifluous
mellisonant
Minnesinger
minor second
mixed voices

morris dance
music lesson
music school
musica ficta
musical copy
musical joke
musical note
music-loving
nickelodeon
normal pitch
nyastaranga
opera ballet
opéra bouffe
orchestrate
orchestrina
orchestrion
organ player
organophone
ottava bassa
over-blowing
Pandean pipe
part playing
part singing
part writing
partial tone
passacaglia
passing note
passing-bell
percussions

percussives
performance
piano player
piano-violin
pitch accent
plagal modes
player piano
polyphonism
popular tune
preparation
prestissimo
primary form
progression
psalm singer
quarter note
quarter rest
ragtime band
rallentando
rattlebones
relative key
Requiem mass
retardation
rock and roll
sacred music
saxophonist
scat singing
Schottische
Scotch catch
short octave

11–12

silver-toned
singing sand
small octave
solmization
sonorophone
soprano clef
sound in tune
square piano
Stabat Mater
street organ
street piano
string music
stopped pipe
string plate
subdominant
sweet potato
sweet-voiced
synchronism
syncopation
temperament
tempo giusto
teneramente
ternary form
Terpsichore
time pattern
Tin Pan alley
tonic accent
torch singer
transposing

tuneful Nine
tunefulness
tuning slide
veiled voice
vicar choral
viol da gamba
viola d'amore
violin piano
violoncello
vivacissimo
voce di petto
voce di testa
voix céleste
wedding song
willow pipes
acciaccatura
accompanyist
accordionist
acoustic bass
agogic accent
andante tempo
anticipation
appassionata
appoggiatura
aria da chiesa
aria parlante
augmentation
ballad singer
balladmonger

banjo-ukelele
bass baritone
bass clarinet
bass trombone
bathtub tenor
beat a retreat
boogie-woogie
brass section
carillonneur
cembal d'ambre
chamber music
chamber organ
changing note
chest of viols
chorus singer
clavicembalo
clavicithern
comedy ballet
compound time
concert grand
concert music
concert pitch
concertinist
Concertstück
conservatory
contraoctave
contrapuntal
corno Inglese
counterpoint

68

country dance
cushion dance
divertimento
dominant note
dotted quaver
drinking song
Dutch concert
extended play
extravaganza
false cadence
fiddlesticks
fiddlestring
florid phrase
funeral march
Glockenspiel
gravicembalo
harmonic tone
harmonichord
heavy harmony
hidden fifths
hurdy-gurdist
hymnographer
improvisator
instrumental
introduction
inverted turn
Italian sixth
ivory thumper
ivory tickler

jazz musician
key signature
less semitone
light harmony
lyric cantata
major seventh
marching song
martial music
mean semitone
medieval mode
mellifluence
melodic minor
metallophone
mezzo-soprano
military band
minor seventh
minstrel song
mixed cadence
monochordist
musical scale
musical score
musicianship
musicologist
mutation stop
nota cambiata
opening notes
opéra comique
orchestra pit
orchestrater

organ grinder
parlour grand
passion music
pastoral oboe
penny whistle
perfect fifth
philharmonic
Phrygian mode
pianofortist
piobaireachd
pipe and tabor
polytonality
popular music
pralltriller
reciting note
record player
Regent's bugle
registration
repercussion
rhythmic mode
sarrusophone
seconda volta
sesquialtera
skiffle group
sing in chorus
siren strains
slow movement
speaking stop
steam whistle

Stradivarius tintinnabula **upright piano**
street singer tone measurer viola da gamba
stress accent tone painting vocalization
symphonic ode top of the pops wedding march
tape recorder tromba marina wind musician
theatre-organ trumpet major *Zigeunerlied*
theatrophone tutti passage
thorough-bass upper partial

Theatre

This section includes list of entertainers and all
forms of entertainment—the theatre as a building—
theatre staff—stagecraft—stage directions—cinema
and television.

TV	mug	dock	hoke	play
act	*pas*	dots	idol	plot
bit	run	drop	joke	prop
bow	set	epic	lead	rant
box	tab	film	line	rave
cue	bill	flat	loft	ring
fan	bowl	flop	loge	rôle
gag	busk	foil	mask	rush
ham	cast	fool	mike	shot
pit	clap	gods	mime	show
rag	crew	grid	mute	side
rep	dais	hall	oleo	skit
hit	diva	hero	part	sock

solo	dry up	queue	chorus
spot	éclat	radio	cinema
star	enact	revue	circle
tail	épode	rodeo	circus
text	extra	scena	claque
turn	farce	scene	comedy
tutu	flick	score	critic
unit	flies	spout	dancer
wing	floor	stage	depict
zany	focus	stagy	direct
actor	foots	stall	effect
ad lib	foyer	stand	encore
agent	front	still	Equity
angel	heavy	stunt	exodus
arena	hokum	usher	farcer
aside	house	wings	feeder
barre	lines	act out	filler
break	mimer	acting	finale
buffo	mimic	action	floats
chips	movie	appear	flyman
cloth	odeon	backer	gagman
clown	odeum	ballet	guiser
comic	on cue	barker	jester
corps	opera	Big Top	juicer
début	oscar	boards	Kabuki
décor	piece	border	lights
drama	props	buskin	limber
drame	Punch	camera	lyceum
drill	put on	chaser	make-up

masque	singer	bit part	drive-in
method	sketch	booking	*estrade*
motley	speech	box seat	fan club
movies	stager	buffoon	*farceur*
mummer	stalls	cabaret	farcist
number	stanza	callboy	feature
on tour	stooge	cartoon	film set
one act	studio	casting	flicker
patron	talent	cat-call	flipper
patter	talkie	cat-walk	gallery
person	teaser	charade	gate man
pit man	Thalia	chorine	grimace
player	ticket	circuit	guisard
podium	tights	clapper	ham it up
prompt	timing	close-up	heroine
puppet	tragic	*comedia*	histrio
relief	troupe	*comédie*	hoke act
repeat	TV show	commère	ingénue
re-take	up left	company	last act
review	walk-on	compère	leg show
ring up	warm-up	costume	leotard
rushes	writer	cothurn	long run
satire	acrobat	coxcomb	manager
scenic	act-drop	creepie	marquee
screen	actress	curtain	matinée
script	all-star	dancing	mimicry
season	artiste	*danseur*	miracle
serial	balcony	dead-pan	mummery
series	benefit	dress up	musical

mystery	spieler	Broadway	*farceuse*
New Wave	sponsor	burletta	farcical
No drama	stadium	business	fauteuil
on stage	stagery	carnival	festival
overact	staging	Cinerama	figurant
pageant	stand-by	clapping	film club
parquet	stand-in	claqueur	film crew
perform	stardom	clowning	film star
Pierrot	starlet	coliseum	film unit
play-act	support	comedian	film-goer
playing	tableau	*comédien*	first act
playlet	the gods	conjuror	front row
pop idol	theatre	*coryphée*	funny man
pop star	Thespis	costumer	gridiron
portray	tragedy	coulisse	grimacer
present	trailer	*danseuse*	ham actor
preview	trouper	dialogue	headline
produce	tumbler	Dionysus	hokum act
protean	up right	director	interval
proverb	upstage	disguise	juvenile
re-enact	vehicle	down left	libretto
rep show	antimask	dramatic	live show
rostrum	applause	dumb show	location
scenery	asbestos	duologue	magician
scenist	audience	entr'acte	morality
show off	audition	entrance	newsreel
showman	backdrop	epilogue	off stage
Roscius	balletic	epitasis	operatic
soap-box	big scene	exit line	operetta

overture	stagedom	backcloth
paradise	stageman	backstage
parterre	stage-set	*baignoire*
pastoral	star turn	ballerina
peep show	stasimon	bandstand
pictures	straight	barnstorm
pit stall	stroller	bit player
platform	sub-title	box-office
playbook	take a bow	breakaway
play-goer	telecast	broadcast
playland	telefilm	burlesque
playwork	the dance	cameraman
practice	the stage	carpenter
première	theatron	character
producer	Thespian	chorus boy
prologue	third act	chorus man
prompter	tragical	cinematic
property	travesty	clip-joint
protasis	typecast	Colosseum
quiz show	usheress	Columbine
rehearse	wardrobe	costumier
ring down	wigmaker	cothurnus
scenario	wireless	coulisses
sceneman	act as foil	criticism
set-piece	animation	cyclorama
showboat	announcer	dead stage
side show	arabesque	direction
smash-hit	astrodome	discovery
stage-box	back scene	double act

down right
downstage
dramatics
dramatize
dramatist
drop scene
entertain
entrechat
epirrhema
exhibitor
featuring
figurante
film actor
film extra
film-strip
flash-back
floor-show
greenroom
grimacier
guest star
ham acting
ham chewer
ham fatter
Hanswurst
harlequin
headliner
heavy lead
hoardings
hoke comic

horseshoe
incognito
interlude
interview
left stage
limelight
live stage
love scene
low comedy
major rôle
make-up man
melodrama
Melpomene
menagerie
minor rôle
monodrama
monologue
movie show
movie star
movie-goer
music hall
night club
old stager
open a show
orchestra
panel game
pantaloon
pantomime
parabasis

pas de deux
patronage
patroness
performer
personage
photoplay
Pierrette
pirouette
play-actor
playhouse
portrayal
practical
programme
prompt-box
publicity
punch-line
raw comedy
recording
rehearsal
repertory
represent
scenarist
scene plot
second act
side scene
slapstick
soap opera
soliloquy
soubrette

spectacle	bandwaggon	high comedy
spectator	buffoonery	hippodrome
spotlight	chorus girl	histrionic
stage door	chorus show	hokum comic
stage name	clog dancer	home-movies
stage play	clown white	horror film
stagehand	comedienne	horse opera
stageland	*comedietta*	impresario
staginess	comic opera	impression
take a part	commercial	in the round
tap dancer	continuity	in the wings
the big top	coryphaeus	intermezzo
the boards	costumière	leading man
theatrics	crowd scene	legitimate
title rôle	*dénouement*	librettist
tormentor	disc jockey	management
tragedian	drama group	marionette
tragédien	dramalogue	masquerade
triologue	dramatizer	microphone
usherette	dramaturge	milk a scene
wisecrack	dramaturgy	mimologist
act curtain	engagement	motley fool
act the goat	exhibition	mountebank
act the part	expository	movie actor
afterpiece	fantoccini	music drama
appearance	first house	newscaster
apron stage	first night	on location
arena stage	footlights	on the stage
auditorium	get the bird	*opera buffa*

opera house	socio-drama	bag of tricks
pantomimic	stage boxes	balletomane
pass holder	stage fever	ballyhoo man
performing	stagecraft	barnstormer
play acting	step dancer	black comedy
playbroker	stet finale	broad comedy
playreader	strip-tease	broadcaster
playwright	substitute	cap and bells
playwriter	tap-dancing	catastrophe
presenting	tear-jerker	charity show
prima buffa	television	Cinemascope
prima donna	the critics	cliff hanger
production	the unities	comedy drama
promptbook	theatre box	comic relief
properties	theatreman	commentator
proscenium	theatrical	concert hall
Pulcinella	tragicomic	credit title
puppet show	trial scene	curtain call
put on a show	understudy	documentary
rave notice	utility man	drama school
repertoire	variety act	dramatic art
right stage	vaudeville	dramaticism
sand-dancer	walk-on part	dramaturgic
Scaramouch	act as feeder	dress circle
scenariost	actor's agent	drop curtain
screenplay	actor's lines	echo chamber
shadow show	all-star bill	electrician
silent film	all-star cast	entertainer
slapsticky	a star is born	exeunt omnes

feature film
fire curtain
galanty show
grease paint
Greek chorus
hammy acting
histrionics
histrionism
illusionist
impersonate
jackpudding
kitchen-sink
leading lady
light comedy
limbering up
low comedian
make-believe
matinée idol
merry-andrew
method actor
mimographer
miracle play
mise en scène
off Broadway
on the boards
pantomimist
pas de quatre
Passion play
performance

personality
personation
picture show
play-actress
play the fool
play the part
practicable
protagonist
psychodrama
Punchinello
radiocaster
scene change
scenewright
set designer
set the scene
set the stage
showmanship
show-stopper
Simon Legree
skirt dancer
sound effect
spectacular
stage design
stage player
stage school
stage-effect
stage-fright
stage-struck
stageworthy

stagewright
star billing
star quality
star vehicle
star-studded
straight man
strip teaser
talent scout
talking film
terpsichore
theatregoer
theatreland
theatricals
theatrician
Thespian art
tragedienne
tragedietta
tragic drama
tragicomedy
upper circle
ventriloquy
waiting line
walking part
walk-through
word perfect
academy award
acting device
actor-manager
advance agent

amphitheatre
ballet dancer
booking agent
borderlights
character man
characterize
choreography
clapperboard
comédie rosse
comedy ballet
dramatic play
dramaturgist
dressing room
entrepreneur
extravaganza
film festival
first-nighter
Greek theatre
harlequinade
hold the stage
impersonator
introduction
juvenile lead

make-up artist
masked comedy
melodramatic
method acting
minstrel show
modern ballet
morality play
nom de théâtre
old stage hand
opera glasses
orchestra pit
Pepper's ghost
picture house
presentation
publicity man
Punch and Judy
scene painter
sceneshifter
scene-stealer
scenic effect
screenwriter
scriptwriter
season ticket

show business
show must go on
silver screen
song and dance
sound effects
stage manager
stage setting
stage whisper
standing room
starring rôle
steal the show
stock company
stole the show
straight part
take the floor
technicolour
ten-percenter
theatrecraft
theatromania
top of the bill
vaudevillian
vaudevillist

INSTITUTIONS

This general heading is divided into two sections, Church, covering all aspects of religion, and Law and Government.

Church

This section includes people, places, tribes and books of the bible—religions—participants of various religions—the church as a building—furnishings, vessels and vestments—church government—parts of the service—church music—holy days and festivals—funerals and burial.

Ai	ark	Ham	pie	Abel
A.V.	Asa	Hur	pye	Abib
No	Bar	Jah	pyx	Acts
N.T.	Bul	Jew	R.I.P.	Adam
Og	Dan	Job	see	Adar
O.T.	Dom	Lot	sin	Agag
R.C.	Eli	Nob	Toi	Agur
R.V.	Eve	Nod	vow	Ahab
So	Gad	Noe	Zin	Ahaz
St.	Gog	Nun	Zur	alba
Ur	goy	Ono	Abba	alms
alb	Hai	pew	Abda	ambo

amen	Elam	Juda	Obed	Sion
Amok	Elon	Jude	Oded	soul
Amon	Emim	Kain	Omri	Tema
Amos	Esau	keen	Oreb	text
Anna	Ezra	kirk	Ozni	Tola
apse	fast	Kish	pall	tomb
Aram	font	lama	Paul	tope
Aven	Gath	Lamb	Peor	Tyre
Baal	Gaza	Leah	Pope	Ulai
Baca	Geba	Levi	pray	Urim
bell	guru	Lois	pyre	veil
bema	halo	Luke	Rama	vows
Beth	harp	Magi	Reba	wake
bier	Heli	Maon	rite	zeal
Boaz	Hell	Mara	robe	Zela
bull	Hiel	Mark	rood	Ziba
Cain	holy	Mary	Rota	Zion
Cana	hymn	mass	Ruth	Zoan
cant	icon	Meah	Sara	Zoar
cell	idol	Mica	Saul	Aaron
cope	Ishi	Moab	Seba	Abana
cowl	Jael	monk	sect	abbey
cure	Jehu	Moph	seer	abbot
Cush	Joab	Myra	Sela	Abdon
dean	Joda	naos	Seth	Abner
Doeg	Joel	nave	sext	Abyss
dome	John	Nebo	Shem	Accad
Eden	Jona	Noah	Shen	Achan
Edom	joss	oath	Shur	Achor

Adria	Caleb	dulia	Gomer	Jesse
agape	canon	Eglon	goyim	Jesus
aisle	carol	Egypt	grace	Jewry
Akkad	cella	Ekron	grail	Joash
Aleph	chant	Eldad	grave	Jobab
Allah	chela	elder	Hadad	Jonah
almug	Chios	Eliab	Hades	Jonas
Alpha	Chiun	Elias	Hagar	Joppa
altar	Chloe	Elihu	Haman	Joram
ambry	choir	Endor	Hamor	Jubal
amice	*ci-gît*	Enoch	Hanum	Judah
Amnon	cotta	ephod	Haran	Judas
Amram	credo	Erech	Harod	Judea
angel	creed	exile	Hazor	judge
Annas	cross	extol	Herod	Kenan
apron	crypt	faith	Hiram	Kings
apsis	Curia	fanon	Hobab	knell
Arpad	curse	Felix	Hoham	Koran
Asher	Cyrus	feral	Horam	Laban
Baali	Dagon	Flood	Horeb	Lahmi
Babel	David	friar	Hosea	lauds
Balak	Dedan	frock	Islam	laver
banns	Demas	Gaius	Jabal	leper
Barak	demon	Gebal	Jacob	Linus
beads	Derbe	Gezar	James	Logos
Bible	Devil	Gihon	Jason	Lycia
bigot	Dinah	glebe	Javan	Lydda
bless	dogma	glory	Jaziz	Lydia
cairn	druid	Golan	Jebus	Magog

magus	nones	Rezon	Tamar
Mahol	Omega	Rhoda	Tekoa
Maker	Ophel	Rufus	Teman
Mamre	Ophir	saint	Terah
manna	Ophni	Salem	tiara
manse	Padan	Sarah	Timna
Marah	padre	Sarai	Timon
Mazda	paean	Sarum	Titus
Mecca	pagan	Satan	Torah
Medes	Paran	scarf	tract
Media	paten	Sheba	Troas
Merab	Pekah	Sidon	tunic
Meroz	Perga	Sihon	Uriah
Mesha	Peter	Silas	Uzzah
Micah	Petra	Simar	vault
Millo	piety	Simon	vicar
mitre	pious	Sinai	Zabad
Moreh	prior	Sodom	Zadok
Moses	psalm	Solon	Zebah
motet	Purim	spire	Zebul
mound	Raama	staff	Zenas
myrrh	rabbi	stall	Zerah
Nabal	Rahab	stole	Zidon
Nadab	Rahel	stoup	Zimra
Nahum	Ramah	stupa	Zohar
Naomi	Rapha	Sumer	Zorah
Negeb	Rekem	synod	Abarim
Niger	relic	Syria	abbess
Nogah	Rezin	taber	Abdiel

Achaia	Bethel	Cyrene	Gehazi
Achsah	Beulah	Daniel	Geshur
Adonai	bishop	Darius	Gibeah
Agabus	Bozrah	deacon	Gibeon
Ahijah	Brahma	Deluge	Gideon
Ahikam	Buddha	devout	Gilboa
Aholah	burial	diadem	Gilead
Amalek	Byblos	divine	Gilgal
amulet	Caesar	dolmen	Goshen
Anakim	Canaan	Dorcas	gospel
Andrew	cantor	Easter	gradin
anoint	Carmel	Elijah	Haggai
anthem	Carpus	Elisha	Hallel
Aquila	casket	Elymas	hallow
Arabah	censer	embalm	Hamath
Ararat	chapel	Engedi	Hannah
armlet	Chebar	Esaias	Hattin
Ashdod	cherub	Esther	Hazael
Azazel	Chidon	Eunice	hearse
Baalim	chimer	eunuch	Heaven
Baanah	chrism	Euodia	Hebrew
Baasha	church	Exodus	Hebron
Balaam	clergy	famine	heresy
barrow	cleric	fannel	Hermas
Baruch	coffin	Father	Hermes
Bashan	Coptic	Festus	hermit
beadle	corban	flamen	Hermon
Belial	curacy	Gadara	homage
Benoni	curate	Gallio	homily

Hophni	keener	Midian	office
Hormah	Kenite	Migdol	Oholah
Hoshea	Kidron	Milcah	Olivet
Idumea	Kishon	Miriam	Ophrah
Isaiah	Kittim	Mishna	orator
Israel	Lamech	missal	ordain
Jabbok	latria	Mizpah	orison
Jabesh	lavabo	Mizpeh	Ormuzd
Jachin	lector	Mnason	pagoda
Jahweh	lemuel	Molech	palace
Jairus	Levite	Moloch	papacy
Jannes	litany	Moriah	parish
Jashar	Lystra	Mormon	parson
Jemima	Maacah	Moslem	pastor
Jesuit	Madmen	mosque	Patmos
Jethro	magian	mystic	Philip
Jewish	Mahlon	Naamah	Phoebe
Joanna	manger	Naaman	Pilate
Jordan	Manoah	Naboth	Pisgah
Joseph	mantle	Nahash	plague
Joshua	mantra	Nathan	Pontus
Josiah	manual	Nereus	prayer
josser	Martha	Nergal	preach
Jotham	martyr	nimbus	priest
jubbah	matins	Nimrod	primus
Judaea	maundy	nipter	priory
Judges	Melita	Noamon	Psalms
Justus	Merari	novena	pulpit
Kadesh	Michal	novice	Quaker

Raamah	sermon	Talmud	Zillah
Rabbah	sexton	Tammuz	Zilpah
Rachel	shaman	Tarsus	Zophar
Raddai	Sharon	Tartan	Abaddon
Rechab	Shebah	temple	Abigail
rector	Shelah	Thomas	Abilene
Red Sea	Shibah	tierce	Abishag
Reuben	Shihor	tippet	Abishai
Riblah	Shiloh	Tirzah	Abraham
Rimmon	Shinar	Tophet	Absalom
ritual	shrine	unholy	acolyte
Rizpah	shroud	Urijah	Adullam
rochet	Shunem	Uzziah	Agrippa
Romans	Siloah	vakass	Ahaziah
rosary	Siloam	Vashni	Ahinoam
rubric	Simeon	Vashti	Alcoran
Sabean	sinner	verger	almoner
sacred	Sirion	vestry	Amaziah
Salmon	Sisera	vigils	Amittai
Salome	sister	Virgin	Ananias
Samson	Smyrna	vision	angelic
Samuel	stalls	Xerxes	angelus
Sargon	Sunday	Yahweh	Antioch
satrap	suttee	Zeboim	Antipas
schism	Symeon	zealot	Antonia
Scribe	Tabeal	Zeresh	Apollos
sedile	tablet	Zeruia	apostle
Semite	talent	Zethar	Araunah
Senate	Talmai	Ziklag	Artemas

ascents	chapman	diptych	Genesis
Asherah	chapter	diviner	gentile
Assyria	charity	doubter	Gerizim
atheist	charnel	Dry Mass	Gershom
Babylon	chimere	Eleazar	gittith
baptism	chorale	Eliphaz	glorify
Baptist	Cilicia	Elishah	godhead
Benaiah	collect	Elkanah	Goliath
Bernice	complin	Enrogel	good man
Bethany	convent	Ephraim	gradino
Bezalel	convert	Epistle	Haggada
biretta	Corinth	epitaph	Harsith
blessed	cortège	Erastus	Havilah
bondage	Creator	Eshtaol	heathen
bondman	Crispus	Essenes	Hebrews
brother	crosier	Ethanim	heretic
burying	crozier	Eubulus	Hilkiah
buskins	crusade	Eupator	Hittite
cabbala	cuculla	Ezekias	holy day
calotte	daysman	Ezekiel	holy see
Calvary	Daystar	fanatic	holy war
Candace	Dead Sea	fasting	Hosanna
Cantuar	deanery	frontal	hymnary
capuche	Deborah	*funèbre*	Ichabod
cassock	deodate	funeral	impiety
Chaldea	devotee	Gabriel	impious
chancel	Didymus	gaiters	incense
chantry	diocese	Galatia	infidel
chaplet		Galilee	introit

Ishmael	Megiddo	Othniel	Rebecca
Jainist	memoria	pallium	Rebekah
Jambres	Menahem	papyrus	rectory
Japheth	Meshach	parable	religio
Jehoram	Messiah	Pathros	Rephaim
Jehovah	Messias	Pauline	requiem
Jericho	Micaiah	periapt	reredos
Jezebel	Michael	Pharaoh	retable
Jezreel	Midrash	Phrygia	Rituale
jubilee	minaret	pietism	Sabbath
Judaism	minster	pilgrim	Salt Sea
keening	miracle	piscina	Samaria
Keturah	mission	pontiff	sanctum
Lachish	Moabite	prayers	sandals
Lambeth	mourner	prebend	Sarepta
Lazarus	muezzin	prelate	Saviour
Lebanon	mummify	primate	sceptic
lectern	narthex	profane	scourge
lection	Nicanor	prophet	secular
liturgy	Nineveh	psalter	sedilia
Low Mass	Nisroch	Ptolemy	Semitic
Magadan	Numbers	Publius	Seraiah
Magdala	nunnery	Puritan	serpent
Malachi	Nymphas	pyramid	service
Malchus	Obadiah	pyx veil	session
maniple	obelisk	rabboni	Shallum
Maonite	Olympas	raiment	Shamgar
mastaba	oratory	Ramadan	Shammah
Matthew	ossuary	Rameses	Shammua

Shaphan	vespers	Barjonah	cemetery
Shaphat	Vulgate	Barnabas	cenotaph
Shebuel	Wise Men	basilica	ceremony
Shechem	worship	beadroll	Chaldees
Shittim	Zabulon	beadsman	chaplain
Shubael	Zebedee	bedesman	chasuble
Shushan	Zebulun	Behemoth	cherubim
sistrum	Abednego	believer	choirboy
Solomon	Abinadab	Ben Hadad	Chorazin
Sopater	Adonijah	*bénitier*	chrismal
soutane	aetheist	Benjamin	cincture
steeple	agnostic	berretta	cingulum
Stephen	Akeldama	Bethpeor	cloister
stipend	Almighty	Bithynia	compline
Succoth	Amorites	bless you	conclave
Susanna	Amraphel	blessing	corporal
Taanach	anathema	bondmaid	covenant
Tabitha	Anathoth	Borsippa	Creation
Taphath	Anglican	brethren	credence
Tertius	antipope	breviary	credenda
Theudas	Apollyon	Buddhist	cromlech
Thummin	Apostles	Caesarea	crucifix
Timothy	Ashkelon	Caiaphas	Crusader
tonsure	Asnappar	canonics	Cyrenius
Trinity	Athaliah	canonize	Dalmatia
tumulus	Ave Maria	canticle	dalmatic
tunicle	Baalpeor	capuchin	Damascus
unction	Barabbas	cardinal	delubrum
Vatican	Barjesus	catholic	disciple

divinity	Gomorrah	Iscariot
doctrine	Good Book	Issachar
doxology	governor	Jehoahaz
druidess	Great Sea	Jephthah
Drusilla	Habakkuk	Jeremiah
Ebenezer	Hadassah	Jeroboam
Ecbatana	Hail Mary	Job's Well
embolism	hallowed	Jochebed
Emmanuel	hecatomb	Jonathan
Epaphras	here lies	Laodicea
Epheseus	Herodias	lay-vicar
Epiphany	Herodion	Lebbaeus
Epistles	Hezekiah	lich gate
Ethiopia	*hic jacet*	Lord's day
Eutychus	Hiddekel	Lost Coin
evensong	High Mass	Lot's wife
exegesis	holiness	Lutheran
exequial	holy city	Lycaonia
exequies	holy coat	Mahalath
exorcism	Holy Land	Makkedah
faithful	Holy Week	Manasseh
funerary	Holy Writ	marabout
funereal	holyrood	Mareshah
Gabbatha	Huguenot	Mark John
Gamaliel	hymn book	Mass book
Gehennah	idolater	Matrites
Gentiles	idolatry	Matthias
God's acre	Immanuel	mediator
Golgotha	inner man	megalith

memorial	obituary	publican
menology	oblation	pyx cloth
Merodach	offering	quindene
Michmash	Onesimus	Rabsaris
minister	orthodox	Rehoboam
ministry	Osnappar	religion
Mitylene	Paradise	Rephidim
monachal	Parmenas	Rich Fool
monastic	Parousia	Romanism
monolith	Parthian	rood-loft
monument	Passover	sacellum
Mordecai	Pekahiah	sacristy
mourning	penitent	Sadducee
mozzetta	Pergamos	sanctity
Naphtali	Pergamum	Sapphira
Nazarene	Pharisee	scapular
Nazareth	Philemon	Scythian
Nazirite	Philetus	Secundus
Neapolis	Philippi	Seleucus
Nehemiah	Phinehas	seraphic
Nehiloth	pontifex	seraphim
neophyte	Potiphar	Shadrach
Nephilim	praise be	Shepherd
Nephtoah	preacher	Silvanus
Nethanel	predella	skullcap
Nethinim	prie-dieu	Sodomite
Nicolaus	Proverbs	Son of Man
Noah's Ark	province	surplice
Obed-Edom	psaltery	Syntiche

Syracuse	adoration	Beelzebub
Tahpenes	Agapemone	Beer-sheba
Tarshish	Ahasuerus	Bethhoron
Tartuffe	Alexander	Bethlehem
Tattenai	Allelujah	Bethphage
Temanite	altar desk	Bethsaida
tenebrae	altar rail	black mass
Teraphim	Ammonites	blasphemy
theology	Antiochus	Boanerges
thurible	Antipater	Brazen Sea
thurifer	Apocrypha	Calvinist
Thyatira	archangel	Canaanite
Tiberias	arch-druid	canonical
Tirhakah	Archelaus	cantharus
Tishbite	arch-enemy	canticles
transept	arch-fiend	Capernaum
Tychicus	Areopagus	Carmelite
Tyrannus	Arimathea	carpenter
versicle	Ascension	cartulary
vestment	Ashtaroth	catacombs
viaticum	Ashtoreth	catechism
vicarage	atonement	cathedral
Virginal	Baalzebub	celebrant
Wesleyan	Babylonia	cerecloth
Zedekiah	baldachin	cerements
ziggurat	barbarian	Chaldeans
Zipporah	Barsabbas	Christian
Aaron's rod	Bathsheba	churchman
Abimelech	Beatitude	claustral

clergyman	episcopal	Hexateuch
cloisters	episcopus	hierarchy
coadjutor	Eucharist	hierology
Communion	Euphrates	high altar
concubine	exchanger	holocaust
confessor	family pew	holy cross
converted	firmament	Holy Ghost
Cornelius	firstborn	Holy Grail
cremation	firstling	holy table
cupbearer	fishermen	holy water
Cyrenaica	footstone	Hymenaeus
deaconess	Galatians	incumbent
decalogue	god-father	interment
Decapolis	godliness	Israelite
dei gratia	god-mother	Jansenist
Demetrius	god-parent	Jashobeam
desecrate	good works	Jehoiadah
devotions	gospeller	Jehoiakim
dignitary	graveside	Jehosheba
Dionysius	graveyard	Jerusalem
dog-collar	Hadadezer	joss-house
dogmatics	hagiarchy	joss-stick
Dominican	hagiology	Judas kiss
Elect Lady	Hammurabi	Lamb of God
Elimelech	headstone	land of Nod
Elisabeth	Hereafter	Lappidoth
embalming	Herodians	last rites
Epaenetus	Hesychast	laudation
Ephesians	heterodox	lay-reader

lay-sister
Leviathan
Leviticus
loin-cloth
Lost Sheep
Maccabees
Macedonia
Machpelah
mactation
Magdalene
martyrdom
mausoleum
Mazzarath
mercy seat
Methodist
Midianite
monastery
Monsignor
mort-cloth
Mosaic law
Mount Seir
Mount Sion
mummy case
Mussulman
mysticism
Narcissus
Nathanael
Nicodemus
obsequial

obsequies
Octateuch
offertory
officiant
orthodoxy
ossuarium
Palestine
Pamphylia
papal bull
Paraclete
parchment
parsonage
patriarch
pay homage
Pentecost
Phoenicia
piousness
plainsong
postulant
prayer mat
prayer rug
precentor
presbyter
priestess
prime song
Priscilla
Prochorus
profanity
proselyte

proseuche
prothesis
psalmbook
quindecim
Quirinius
Rechabite
reliquary
reverence
righteous
river Nile
rood stair
rood tower
rural dean
sackcloth
sacrament
sacrarium
sacrifice
sacrilege
sacristan
sainthood
saintship
salvation
Samaritan
Sanballat
sanctuary
Sanhedrin
scapegoat
scapulary
schoolman

9–10

Scripture	Zalmunnah	archdeacon
sepulchre	Zarephath	arch-flamen
sepulture	Zechariah	arch-priest
shewbread	Zephaniah	Armageddon
Shintoist	Zoroaster	Artaxerxes
shovel hat	zucchetta	Band of Hope
spiritual	zucchetto	baptistery
Stephanas	absolution	Bartimaeus
suffragan	Ahithophel	battle hymn
synagogue	Alexandria	Beatitudes
Synoptics	allocution	Belshazzar
Tertullus	allotheist	benedicite
testament	almsgiving	benefactor
Thaddaeus	altar cloth	Bethhaggan
Timotheus	altar front	Bible class
Tirshatha	altar mound	birthright
tombstone	altar stead	blind faith
triforium	altarpiece	blindstory
Trophimus	Amalekites	Book of Life
Tubal Cain	amen corner	canonicals
Tyrian dye	Amphipolis	Carchemish
undersong	Anabaptist	Carthusian
unfrocked	Anammelech	catafalque
Unitarian	Andronicus	catechumen
unworldly	anklechain	chartulary
venerable	antichrist	choirstall
Zacchaeus	Antipatris	Chronicles
Zachariah	Apocalypse	Church Army
Zacharias	archbishop	church bell

95

churchgoer
churchyard
Cistercian
City of Salt
clear-story
clerestory
cloistered
collection
Colossians
confession
consecrate
conversion
dedication
diaconicon
Diotrephes
divination
doctrinism
Douay Bible
encyclical
entombment
Epicureans
episcopacy
episcopant
Esarhaddon
Evangelist
Evil Spirit
exaltation
false piety
fellowship

Fortunatus
Franciscan
funeral ode
funeral urn
Geneva gown
Gennesaret
Gethsemane
god-fearing
golden calf
goody-goody
Gospel side
gravestone
hagiolatry
hagioscope
Hallelujah
hierolatry
hieromancy
hierophant
Heptateuch
Hermogenes
high church
high places
high priest
Holy Family
Holy Father
Holy Orders
Holy Spirit
Holy Willie
House of God

hyperdulia
iconoclast
idolatrous
immolation
in memoriam
incumbency
inhumation
irreligion
Ishbosheth
Ishmaelite
Jacob's Well
Jehoiachin
Kohathites
Lady-chapel
Last Supper
lay-brother
lectionary
Libertines
lie in state
lip service
Lord's house
Lord's table
magnificat
mantellone
Mark of Cain
Methuselah
missionary
Mithredath
Mohammedan

Mount Sinai	Revelation	Theophilus
Mount Tabor	Roman Curia	unbeliever
Mt. of Olives	rood screen	undertaker
necropolis	Sabbath day	veneration
Needle's eye	sacerdotal	watch night
Oholibamah	sacredness	widow's mite
pallbearer	sacrosanct	wilderness
papal brief	sanctimony	worshipper
Papal Court	Scepticism	Wycliffite
paraphrase	Schismatic	Zelophehad
Pelethites	scholastic	Zerubbabel
Pentateuch	Scriptures	agnosticism
Pharisaism	secularism	altar carpet
Philistine	Septuagint	altar facing
phylactery	sepulchral	apologetics
pilgrimage	shibboleth	arch-heretic
pontifical	Shulammite	arch-prelate
poor sinner	Shunammite	Aristarchus
praetorium	Simon Peter	Aristobulus
prayer-bead	solifidian	aspergillum
prayer-book	soothsayer	Augustinian
prebendary	superaltar	Bartholomew
Presbytery	synthronus	Benedictine
priesthood	tabernacle	benediction
procurator	tartuffery	bishop's ring
prophetess	temperance	bitter herbs
Protestant	temptation	blasphemous
Providence	theologian	body and soul
regenerate	theologist	Book of Books

Book of Death
burning bush
Catholicism
chapel royal
choir-stalls
Christendom
Christening
church court
church mouse
City of David
commandment
communicant
conventicle
Convocation
Corinthians
crematorium
Crucifixion
Curia Romana
decanal side
Deuteronomy
Divine right
Epistle side
eschatology
family bible
first-fruits
funeral pile
funeral pyre
Geneva bands
Geneva cloak

Good Tidings
graven image
Greek Church
Hagiographa
hagiologist
hierography
incarnation
irreligious
Jehoshaphat
Jubilee Year
Kingdom Come
kirk session
last offices
lawn sleeves
Lion of Judah
Lord of Hosts
Lord's prayer
Lord's supper
mantelletta
missal stand
Mithridates
monasterial
Mount Ararat
Mount Pisgah
Nebuzaradan
Nicene Creed
Nicolaitans
nullifidian
original sin

parish clerk
paternoster
patron saint
Philippians
pillar saint
pontificals
pontificate
prayer wheel
Prodigal Son
protomartyr
pure in heart
reading desk
Reformation
religiosity
remembrance
requiem mass
rest in peace
river Jordan
Sacred Heart
saintliness
Sanctus bell
sarcophagus
secular hymn
Sennacherib
Shalmaneser
Shesh Bazzar
Sons of Javan
soteriology
subcingulum

take the veil
theological
triple crown
Vatican City
vine of Sodom
Virgin's Well
Wise Virgins
Annunciation
anxious bench
burial ground
canonization
cardinal's hat
chancel table
chapel of ease
chapter house
charnel house
Charterhouse
Chosen People
Christianity
church living
church parade
churchmaster
church-nation
churchwarden
City of Refuge
collectarium
Commandments
Common Prayer
confessional

confirmation
congregation
consecration
Coptic church
Damascus road
Day of the Lord
denomination
Ecclesiastes
ecclesiastic
enshrinement
Epaphroditus
Evil Merodach
Field of Blood
fiery serpent
frankincense
Garden of Eden
Good Shepherd
hagiographer
herald angels
Holy Alliance
Holy of Holies
Holy Thursday
hot-gospeller
Jacob's ladder
jot and tittle
Judgment Hall
Judgment Seat
Lamentations
Last Judgment

major prophet
marriage vows
Mephibosheth
minimifidian
minor prophet
money-changer
New Testament
Old Testament
penitent form
Philadelphia
Pillar of Salt
Potter's Field
prayer carpet
Priestly Code
Promised Land
Queen of Sheba
Ramoth Gilead
resting place
Resurrection
river of Egypt
Rose of Sharon
sacred ground
sacrilegious
Saul of Tarsus
Sea of Galilee
Second Coming
Sunday school
thanksgiving
theologian

Thessalonian   ultramontane   wear the cloth
Three Wise Men   Vale of Siddim   winding sheet
Tower of Babel   Valley of Salt

Law and Government

This section includes crimes and criminals—prisons
and forms of punishment—officers of the law—
courts of law—legal terms—forms of government
and government officials—political parties—foreign
parliaments and legislatures—political terminology
and office holders—rank and rulers, past, present
and foreign.

C.D.	C.I.D.	nob	alod	clan
J.P.	con	rap	axis	code
K.C.	cop	red	bail	czar
M.P.	dip	rex	beak	dame
P.C.	don	rob	beat	deed
P.M.	dot	rod	bill	deny
Q.C.	F.B.I.	soc	bloc	diet
U.N.	feu	S.O.S.	bond	dock
act	H.M.S.	sue	brig	*doge*
aga	jug	tax	bull	*dona*
bar	*jus*	try	cadi	*Duce*
beg	lag	U.N.O.	camp	duke
bey	law	wig	case	duty
bug	*lex*	ally	cell	earl

emir	memo	stir	bench	crime
exon	mute	suit	birch	crimp
eyre	nick	swag	blimp	crook
feme	oath	sway	board	crown
feod	O.H.M.S.	tail	bobby	curia
feud	oyer	tana	bonds	deeds
fiat	oyes	thug	booty	divan
fief	oyez	toft	boule	dower
file	pact	tort	bribe	dowry
fine	peer	Tory	brief	doyen
gaol	pink	tsar	bulla	draft
G-man	plea	veto	burgh	duchy
gyve	poll	visa	by-law	edict
hang	pomp	vote	cabal	elder
heir	rack	ward	canon	elect
imam	raja	Whig	caste	elite
Inca	rani	whip	cause	ephor
jack	rank	will	chair	felon
jail	rape	writ	chief	fence
jury	rent	aegis	choky	feoff
just	rota	agent	civic	filch
kadi	rule	agora	claim	forum
king	sack	alias	class	frame
lady	seal	alibi	clink	fraud
left	seat	amban	comyn	front
levy	serf	annat	co-opt	gavel
lien	shah	arson	corps	graft
lord	silk	baron	count	grass
mace	soke	begum	court	guard

guild	noose	screw	aristo
guilt	panel	sheik	arrest
hakim	party	slate	asylum
in-law	pasha	snout	bagnio
judge	pinch	Solon	bailie
junta	plead	staff	ballot
junto	plebs	swear	bandit
jurat	poach	thane	barony
juror	polls	theft	bigamy
laird	Porte	thief	breach
lease	posse	trial	brevet
legal	power	tribe	bureau
libel	proof	truce	bye-law
licit	proxy	trust	Caesar
liege	quash	ulema	caliph
lobby	queen	usher	caucus
Mafia	rajah	usurp	caveat
major	rally	vakil	censor
manor	realm	visne	census
mayor	rebel	voter	charge
minor	reeve	Whigs	clause
Mogul	regal	abjure	clique
mores	*Reich*	action	coheir
mufti	reign	accede	colony
mulct	reset	acquit	con-man
nabob	rider	adjure	consul
nawab	right	agenda	cooler
negus	royal	appeal	copper
noble	ruler	archon	cordon

Cortes	Fabian	kidnap	mutiny
county	faggot	knight	Nazism
curfew	*fasces*	laches	nonage
debate	*fascio*	lagger	notice
debtor	felony	Lammas	nuncio
decree	fetter	lawful	octroi
delate	fiscal	lawman	office
delict	forger	lawyer	old lag
denial	Führer	leader	on oath
depute	gag law	leaser	orator
deputy	gaoler	legacy	ordeal
despot	gentry	legate	outlaw
détenu	guilty	legist	papacy
dharma	gunman	lessee	parage
dictum	harman	lessor	pardon
digest	heriot	lethal	parole
dogate	holder	lictor	patrol
domain	holdup	*Majlis*	patron
dry law	homage	master	payola
durbar	honour	mayhem	peeler
dynast	indict	mikado	piracy
empire	induna	milady	pirate
emptio	jailer	milord	pledge
emptor	junior	moiety	pogrom
entail	junker	mollah	police
eparch	jurant	morgue	policy
equity	jurist	motion	polity
estate	Kaiser	motive	pow-wow
exarch	keeper	murder	prince

103

prison	socage	abscond	blue law
puisne	soviet	abstain	borstal
puppet	speech	accused	borough
quorum	squire	accuser	bribery
ransom	status	acquest	bullary
rapine	stocks	adjourn	burglar
rating	suitor	admiral	cabinet
recess	sultan	adviser	cacique
record	summit	Aga Khan	canvass
reform	*sûreté*	*alcalde*	capital
regent	syndic	alimony	Capitol
régime	tenant	alodium	captain
remand	tenure	amnesty	captive
report	throne	anarchy	case-law
return	ticket	annuity	cashier
reward	tie-wig	arbiter	caution
robber	tocsin	armiger	Chamber
rozzer	Tories	arraign	charter
rubric	treaty	assault	chattel
ruling	truant	assizes	circuit
sachem	Tyburn	autarky	closure
satrap	tyrant	autopsy	club law
sconce	umpire	bailiff	codicil
search	vassal	baronet	cojuror
senate	vizier	Beltane	colonel
shogun	voting	bencher	command
simony	warden	bequest	Commons
sircar	warder	binding	compact
sirdar	yeoman	biparty	con-game

consort	dyarchy	garotte	Knesset
convict	dynasty	general	Kremlin
coroner	earldom	Gestapo	ladrone
corsair	elector	grandee	*Lagting*
council	embargo	grassum	land tax
counsel	embassy	hanging	larceny
crimper	emperor	hangman	latitat
custode	empress	harbour	law-list
custody	enclave	harmans	law-lord
Customs	enfeoff	harmost	lawsuit
czarina	escheat	hearing	leftist
damages	esquire	hearsay	legatee
deed-box	estover	heiress	legator
defence	estreat	heritor	libelee
delator	faction	hidalgo	Liberal
demesne	fair cop	his nibs	looting
deodand	Fascism	hot seat	majesty
deposit	Fascist	illicit	manacle
devisor	federal	impeach	mandate
diarchy	fee tail	infanta	marquis
dictate	felonry	inquest	marshal
divorce	feoffee	inquiry	Marxism
dossier	feu duty	jeofail	Marxist
dowager	footpad	John Doe	measure
dragnet	foreman	jury box	mediate
duarchy	forfeit	juryman	militia
duchess	forgery	just men	minutes
dukedom	frame-up	justice	mob rule
dungeon	gallows	khedive	mobsman

mobster	Premier	samurai	tenancy
monarch	primary	sceptre	testate
mormaor	probate	senator	testify
neutral	process	settler	toisech
New Deal	proctor	shackle	torture
nonsuit	protest	sheriff	Toryism
offence	proviso	shrieve	traitor
officer	provost	shyster	treason
on trial	prowler	slander	tribune
pageant	purloin	soapbox	trustee
parolee	purview	soccage	tsarina
patriot	questor	Speaker	turnkey
peerage	quietus	spy ring	Tynwald
peeress	radical	station	uniform
penalty	reality	statist	Vatican
pension	recount	statute	verdict
perjury	red tape	steward	viceroy
Pharaoh	referee	stick-up	villain
pillage	refugee	stretch	villein
pillory	regency	sultana	warrant
pinched	regimen	summons	witness
pleader	returns	Sun King	abaction
plunder	*Rigsdag*	support	abdicate
poacher	*Riksdag*	suspect	abductor
podesta	Riot Act	swear in	abrogate
politic	robbery	swindle	accolade
praetor	royalet	sworn in	accusant
precept	royalty	tallage	activism
prefect	sacking	Templar	adultery

advocate	brass hat	deedpoll
alienate	buncombe	defender
alliance	burglary	delegate
amortise	calendar	delictum
archduke	campaign	demagogy
argument	canon law	Democrat
arrogate	caudillo	demurrer
articled	ceremony	deponent
articles	chairman	detainee
aspirant	chambers	diadochi
assassin	champion	dictator
Assembly	chancery	diplomat
assessor	chantage	distrain
atheling	chartism	distress
attorney	citation	division
autarchy	civil law	doctrine
autonomy	civilian	domicile
averment	claimant	dominion
balloter	Conclave	don't-know
bankrupt	congress	election
baronage	contempt	embezzle
baroness	contract	embracer
bastardy	copyhold	eviction
Bastille	countess	evidence
bicamera	criminal	executor
black cap	crown law	Fair Deal
Black Rod	cursitor	feme sole
blood-tax	danegeld	findings
bluecoat	dead hand	*Fine Gael*

flatfoot	hung jury	litigate
forensic	hustings	lobbying
foul play	imperial	lobbyist
free vote	in camera	local law
freehold	incivism	loophole
fugitive	informer	lordling
game laws	innocent	lordship
gangster	Interpol	loyalist
garrotte	item veto	lynch law
Gaullist	jailbird	lynching
gendarme	Jingoism	maharani
genocide	John Bull	majority
governor	jointure	*mandamus*
gravamen	judgment	mandarin
Gray's Inn	judicial	marauder
green bag	kingship	margrave
grilling	ladyship	martinet
guardian	law agent	mayoress
gynarchy	law court	mem-sahib
hanger-on	lawgiver	messuage
heckling	lawmaker	Minister
hegemony	lay judge	ministry
heirloom	left wing	minority
henchman	legal aid	mistrial
heritage	legalism	mittimus
High Gate	legality	monarchy
highness	legation	monition
home rule	libelant	mortgage
homicide	litigant	mortmain

mortuary	picaroon	reprieve
Mounties	platform	republic
movement	pleading	Roman law
narratio	politico	royalist
navicert	politics	sabotage
nihilism	polygamy	saboteur
nobility	porridge	sanction
nobleman	preamble	scaffold
nomology	precinct	scot-free
nonvoter	princess	security
offender	prisoner	seigneur
official	promisor	sentence
oligarch	protocol	sergeant
on the run	puissant	sessions
outlawry	put-up job	shanghai
overlord	quaestor	silk gown
overrule	question	Sing-Sing
pacifism	quisling	smuggler
palatine	quit-rent	*Sobranje*
pandects	rack-rent	solatium
partisan	rebuttal	speed-cop
party man	receiver	splinter
passport	recorder	squad car
patentee	reformer	stealage
peculate	regicide	stealing
penal law	regnancy	stir bird
penology	reigning	Stormont
Pentagon	rent-free	subpoena
petition	rent-roll	suffrage

summitry	upper ten	authority
suzerain	usufruct	autocracy
swindler	vendetta	avizandum
tail male	verbatim	back bench
take silk	vice-king	bailiwick
talesman	vice-ring	ballot box
tanaiste	viscount	barmaster
taxation	wardmote	barrister
tenement	Whiggism	black book
tenendum	Wool Sack	blackmail
testamur	abduction	blood-feud
testator	absconder	blue blood
testatum	accession	bridewell
test-case	accessory	body of law
the Bench	acquittal	bodyguard
the chair	actionist	bolshevik
thearchy	ademption	bound over
thievery	Admiralty	bourgeois
thirlage	affidavit	brain-wash
tipstaff	alarm bell	brief-case
top brass	amendment	bring suit
town hall	anarchist	buccaneer
treasury	annulment	Bumbledom
trespass	appellant	*Bundesrat*
triarchy	appellate	*Bundestag*
tribunal	Areopagus	caliphate
true bill	attainder	candidate
ultraist	attestant	capitular
Uncle Sam	Aula Regis	captaincy

case lists
cassation
catchpole
cell-block
centumvir
chain-gang
champerty
Chief Whip
chieftain
civil case
civil list
civil suit
class rule
coalition
collegian
colonelcy
Cominform
Comintern
commander
committee
common law
communism
communist
complaint
concordat
constable
consulate
coparceny
copyright

cosmocrat
coup d'état
court list
court roll
courtroom
cracksman
custodian
Dalai Lama
death duty
deathblow
defendant
demagogue
democracy
desertion
desperado
detective
detention
diplomacy
direct tax
dir: eption
discharge
disseisin
disseizin
distraint
dogmatist
doing time
drug squad
Eduskunta
embezzler

embracery
enactment
equity bar
espionage
ex officio
exchequer
exciseman
ex-convict
execution
executive
exonerate
extortion
extremist
fair trial
fee simple
felonious
feudal law
feudal tax
feudalism
feudatory
fire alarm
first lady
first lord
Folketing
forest law
formality
franchise
frithborh
frithgild

gavelkind	judicator	major-domo
generalcy	judiciary	majorship
grand duke	jungle law	manifesto
grand jury	jurywoman	matricide
Grand Turk	justiciar	mayoralty
Great Seal	kidnapper	means test
guardroom	kingcraft	menshevik
handcuffs	kingmaker	mercy seat
heir-at-law	Labourite	miscreant
high birth	landgrave	mobocracy
High Court	landslide	mock court
hit-and-run	*Landsting*	moderator
Identi-kit	law reform	monocracy
impartial	law report	moot court
imperator	law school	moot point
incognito	leasehold	moral code
income tax	legal heir	mortgagee
incumbent	legal term	mortgager
indemnity	legal year	Mosaic Law
influence	lend-lease	Mr. Justice
injustice	licitness	next of kin
inspector	liege lord	*nisi prius*
intestate	life owner	not guilty
inventory	litigator	not proven
Iron Guard	litigious	novodamus
Jack Ketch	logroller	objection
jailbreak	Lord Mayor	*Odelsting*
judge-made	maharajah	Old Bailey
judgement	maharanee	oligarchy

ombudsman
open court
ordinance
oubliette
pageantry
palsgrave
paramount
parricide
party line
party whip
patriarch
patrician
patrimony
patrol car
patrolman
patronage
peculator
penal code
pendragon
petit jury
petty jury
pilfering
plaintiff
pleadings
plutocrat
police car
police dog
police van
policeman

Politburo
political
polyandry
portfolio
portreeve
potentate
power game
precedent
prescript
president
presidium
pretender
princedom
princelet
privateer
probation
procedure
programme
prolicide
pronounce
prosecute
protector
public law
publicist
put in suit
queenship
quittance
racketeer
recaption

receiving
red-handed
red-tapism
registrar
remainder
remission
represent
reprimand
resetting
right wing
riot squad
Royal seal
rule of law
sanctions
sanhedrin
secretary
selectman
seneschal
sheriffry
smuggling
socialism
socialist
solicitor
sovereign
stamp duty
statement
statesman
straw poll
straw vote

stuff gown	waldgrave	blood royal
Stünderat	wanted man	blue murder
sub judice	witch hunt	Brain Trust
suit at law	abalienate	breath-test
suit in law	abdication	brevet rank
summing-up	aborticide	bureaucrat
supporter	absolutism	by-election
synedrion	abstention	Caesarship
talkathon	accomplice	campaigner
taoiseach	accusation	canvassing
tenements	aggression	capitalist
terrorism	aid and abet	capitulary
testament	allegation	cashiering
testatrix	allegiance	casual ward
testifier	ambassador	censorship
testimony	amercement	centralism
tetrarchy	androlepsy	*certiorari*
theocracy	annexation	chancellor
tidal wave	arbitrator	Chauvinism
title deed	aristarchy	chrematist
top secret	aristocrat	circuiteer
treasurer	autonomous	city father
trial jury	bank robber	civil death
truncheon	bankruptcy	classified
uxoricide	Big Brother	code of laws
vice squad	bill of sale	commandant
vigilante	birthright	commissary
violation	Black Maria	commission
viscounty	Black Shirt	common weal

communiqué	dispatches	government
confession	dotted line	grand juror
confiscate	doubletalk	Grand Mufti
conspiracy	duumvirate	grass roots
constraint	ear-witness	Green Cloth
contraband	electorate	guardhouse
contravene	encyclical	guillotine
conversion	entailment	gunrunning
conveyance	estate tail	hamesucken
conviction	eye witness	handshaker
coparcener	Falangists	hard labour
coronation	federation	harman-beck
corregidor	feme covert	hatchet-man
corruption	*Fianna Fail*	heteronomy
councillor	figurehead	highwayman
councilman	filibuster	hold a brief
counsellor	find guilty	hold office
court of law	fiscal year	Home Office
court order	forfeiture	illegality
court usher	fratricide	impediment
courthouse	fraud squad	imposition
crime sheet	free pardon	in articles
crime squad	freebooter	in chancery
death chair	frizzed wig	in jeopardy
decree nisi	front bench	indictment
delinquent	full pardon	inducement
department	Gallup poll	injunction
deposition	gas chamber	Inner House
disherison	glasshouse	invocation

judicature	magistrate	*Oireachtas*
jus commune	Magna Carta	on the fence
justiciary	maiden name	out of court
King's bench	mail robber	Outer House
king's peace	major party	palatinate
knighthood	man of straw	palliation
land-pirate	margravine	papal brief
land-tenure	marquisate	Papal Court
land-values	martial law	parliament
law officer	mass murder	party-liner
Law Society	matriarchy	patriarchy
law-abiding	memorandum	peccadillo
lawbreaker	metrocracy	peppercorn
law-burrows	metropolis	petitioner
lawfulness	militarism	petty juror
leadership	minor party	petty theft
left-winger	mitigation	pickpocket
legacy duty	morganatic	plebiscite
legal right	mouthpiece	plundering
legislator	muckraking	plural vote
legitimacy	mugwumpery	pocket veto
Liberalism	neutralism	point of law
lieutenant	neutrality	politician
litigation	no man's land	post mortem
logrolling	noble birth	Post Office
lower house	noblewoman	postliminy
mace-bearer	nomination	power-happy
machinator	nomography	praesidium
magistracy	ochlocracy	pray a tales

prefecture
presidency
princeling
private law
prize court
procession
procurator
prosecutor
protection
proveditor
punishment
purloining
pursuivant
put on trial
quarantine
quarter-day
queencraft
ransacking
ration book
real estate
recidivist
recognitor
referendum
reform bill
refutation
regulation
remand home
reparation
Republican

resolution
respondent
revolution
Richard Roe
right of way
ringleader
Rolls Court
sanctioned
search form
separation
sergeantcy
serve a writ
settlement
shoplifter
single vote
sneak-thief
speed limit
Square Deal
stadholder
state trial
statecraft
Statehouse
statistics
statute cap
statute law
stillicide
strategist
straw voter
succession

suffragist
suspension
suzerainty
the Commons
the Royal we
third party
third Reich
throne room
title deeds
trade union
trafficker
underworld
undress wig
upper class
upper crust
upper house
usurpation
vigilantes
voters' roll
White House
White Paper
witness box
written law
your honour
adjournment
agrarianism
androlepsia
appeal court
appointment

arbitration
archduchess
aristocracy
arm of the law
arraignment
assumed name
attestation
authorities
backbencher
bag-snatcher
bank robbery
bear witness
bill of costs
bill-chamber
black-and-tan
black market
blackmailer
body politic
buffer state
bureaucracy
burglarious
burgomaster
candidature
capital city
casting vote
cattle thief
chamberlain
civil arrest
civil rights

civvy street
co-existence
colonelship
colonialism
Common Pleas
complainant
compurgator
condominium
confederate
confinement
congressman
constituent
contract law
contractual
conveyancer
coparcenary
corporation
corpus juris
corroborate
county court
criminal law
criminology
crown prince
crowned head
Dail Eireann
declaration
delinquency
diet of proof
digest of law

diplomatics
disarmament
dissolution
divine right
doctrinaire
double-cross
duty officer
electioneer
embracement
empanelment
enfeoffment
engrossment
equity court
ergatocracy
escheatment
estate in fee
examination
exculpation
executioner
exoneration
extenuation
extradition
factory acts
fair hearing
false arrest
fieri facias
fifth column
fingerprint
firing squad

flying squad
foreclosure
found guilty
functionary
gallows bird
garnishment
generalship
gentlewoman
geopolitics
gerrymander
good offices
Grand Sachem
grand vizier
grave robber
guilty party
gynecocracy
head of state
heir general
high sheriff
high society
high steward
high treason
higher court
house arrest
House of Keys
hunger-march
impeachment
imperialist
impoundment

in duplicate
incarcerate
incriminate
inculpation
independent
indirect tax
infanticide
inheritance
Inner Temple
Inns of Court
inquisition
institution
insufflator
intercessor
investiture
Iron Curtain
jury-process
Kellogg Pact
king's speech
Labour party
last request
law and order
law merchant
lawbreaking
lawlessness
legal action
legal battle
legal estate
legal record

legal reform
legal remedy
legal tender
legislation
legislative
legislature
lèse majesté
libel action
lie detector
lieutenancy
limited veto
Lincoln's Inn
long stretch
Lord Justice
Machiavelli
magisterial
maintenance
malpractice
man on the run
marchioness
meritocracy
military law
ministerial
mosstrooper
mudslinging
murder squad
nationalism
Nationalrat
negotiation

nonpartisan
null and void
officialdom
officialism
omnibus bill
open verdict
Papal Nuncio
partisanism
partnership
party member
patent rolls
patent-right
pathologist
peace treaty
penal reform
pettifogger
police court
police force
police judge
police squad
police state
policewoman
policy maker
Politbureau
power of veto
powermonger
prerogative
proceedings
procuration

progressive
Prohibition
proletariat
prosecution
protest vote
public enemy
public works
puisne judge
Quarter Seal
queen mother
Queen's bench
Queen's peace
Queer Street
questioning
ransom money
reactionary
rear-admiral
reformatory
right to vote
right-winger
Royal Assent
royal family
royal palace
royal pardon
royal person
rubber stamp
rule of thumb
ruling class
safe-conduct

safecracker
sansculotte
secretariat
senatorship
shanghaiing
sheriffwick
ship of state
shoplifting
shore patrol
show of hands
sovereignty
speech maker
squirearchy
Star Chamber
stateswoman
statute book
stolen goods
stool pigeon
stratocracy
suffragette
summit talks
sympathizer
syndicalism
take to court
Tammany Hall
technocracy
tenant-right
testamental
third degree

traffic duty
train robber
trial by jury
triumvirate
under arrest
undersigned
vice-admiral
vindication
viscountess
voting paper
ward of court
Westminster
wirepulling
writ of error
your worship
absolute veto
adjudication
administrate
after the fact
amicus curiae
amortisement
ancien régime
appeal motion
apprehension
Aulic Council
bar of justice
bench warrant
bill of health
Bill of Rights

Board of Trade
breathalyser
bring charges
burglar alarm
capitularies
carpet-bagger
cause célèbre
cause in court
charterparty
chattels real
Chief Justice
circuit court
circuit judge
civil defence
civil service
codification
collectivism
Colonel Blimp
commissariat
commissioner
common lawyer
commonwealth
compensation
compurgation
condemnation
condemned man
confiscation
conscription
conservatism

Conservative
constabulary
constituency
constitution
conveyancing
coroner's jury
corporalship
court martial
court of wards
criminal code
criminal suit
cross-examine
cucking stool
customs union
death penalty
death warrant
debtor's court
den of thieves
dictatorship
dispensation
divorce court
dominion rule
dressing down
ducking stool
embezzlement
estate at will
estate in tail
false witness
Federal Union

feudal estate	Jack-in-office	legally bound
feudal system	jail sentence	lese-majestie
First Chamber	judge and jury	Liberal party
first offence	judge-made law	life sentence
floating vote	judgment debt	Lord Advocate
frankalmoign	judgment hall	lord temporal
gerontocracy	judgment seat	lower chamber
gobbledegook	judicial oath	lying-in-state
gold standard	jurisconsult	magistrature
grand duchess	jurisdiction	maiden assize
grand juryman	jurisprudent	maiden speech
grand larceny	Justice-clerk	majority rule
guardianship	King's counsel	majority vote
Habeas corpus	King's Proctor	manslaughter
hanging judge	knight-errant	marriage vows
heir apparent	*laissez-faire*	mercy killing
hereditament	Land Registry	mess sergeant
House of Lords	landed gentry	misdemeanour
House of Peers	law of nations	metropolitan
housebreaker	law of the land	mixed larceny
Imperial Diet	leading light	*modus vivendi*
imprisonment	left of centre	municipality
in litigation	legacy-hunter	office-bearer
in triplicate	legal adviser	officeholder
incriminator	legal aid fund	pantisocracy
independence	legal fiction	party machine
intromission	legal history	party to a suit
investigator	legal redress	pass sentence
isolationism	legal science	Patent Office

peace officer
penitentiary
people's front
petit larceny
petty juryman
petty larceny
plain clothes
plea for mercy
plural voting
point of order
police cordon
police office
police patrol
politicaster
polling booth
popular front
powers that be
prescription
Prince Regent
prison warder
Privy council
probate court
probate judge
procès-verbal
proletariate
protectorate
protest march

puppet régime
queen dowager
queen's speech
question time
reform school
registration
rent tribunal
resist arrest
rest one's case
return ticket
right of entry
rough justice
royal charter
royal command
Royal Majesty
run for office
safebreaking
safecracking
scene of crime
Scotland Yard
secret police
security risk
seignioralty
self-governed
sergeantship
sheriff court
silk-gownsman

smash-and-grab
snap judgment
split the vote
standing army
status symbol
strait jacket
stuffed shirt
subcommittee
Sublime Porte
summary trial
supreme court
tenant at will
thirdborough
totalitarian
Traitor's Gate
Union Council
unwritten law
upper chamber
violent death
viscountship
welfare state
whipping post
widow's-bench
witness stand
word of honour
worldly goods

LIVING CREATURES

This heading contains all living creatures of every type, excluding human beings, who are dealt with in the section People at Home, Work and Play.

It includes lists of beasts, birds, fish, insects and reptiles—young animals—male and female—groups of animals—animal homes—characteristics of animal anatomy—common genera—mythical and prehistoric creatures—some common breeds of domesticated animal.

ai	bog	daw	fur	kob	pie
id	bug	den	gam	Leo	pig
ox	cat	doe	gar	low	pod
ant	caw	dog	gnu	mew	pom
ape	cob	dor	gyp	moa	pug
asp	cod	eel	hag	moo	pup
ass	coo	eft	hen	nag	ram
auk	cow	elk	hob	nit	rat
bat	cry	emu	hog	owl	ray
bay	cub	ewe	jay	pad	roc
bee	cur	fin	kea	paw	roe
bib	dab	fly	kid	pen	run
bit	dam	fox	kit	pet	set

3–4

sow	bull	dove	hake	lamb
sty	byre	down	hare	lark
tat	cage	dray	hart	lice
teg	calf	drey	hawk	ling
tit	call	duck	herd	lion
tod	carp	erne	hern	loon
tom	cavy	eyas	hide	lory
tup	char	eyra	hind	luce
web	chat	eyry	hock	luth
yak	chow	fang	hole	lynx
zoo	chub	fawn	honk	mane
apar	chum	Fido	hoof	mare
Arab	clam	fish	hoot	maud
axis	claw	flea	horn	meow
barb	cleg	foal	howl	mews
bark	coho	form	hump	mice
barn	colt	fowl	huso	mina
bass	comb	game	ibex	mink
beak	cony	gang	ibis	mite
bear	coon	gaur	jill	moke
bevy	coop	gill	kaka	mole
bike	coot	gnat	kelt	mona
bill	crab	goat	keta	moth
bird	croc	goby	kine	mule
blay	crow	grig	kite	musk
bley	dace	grub	kiwi	mute
boar	deer	guan	kora	mutt
bray	dodo	gull	kudu	myna
buck	dory	hack	lair	neat

125

nest	rhea	titi	aphid	brush
newt	roan	toad	aphis	brute
nide	roar	tope	argus	bunny
oont	rook	tuna	aspic	burro
opah	rout	tusk	avian	camel
oryx	rudd	tyke	aweto	caple
oxen	ruff	unau	babok	capon
paca	runt	ursa	basse	capul
pack	saki	urus	beast	catch
pard	scad	urva	billy	cavie
parr	scup	vole	biped	charm
pavo	seal	wasp	bison	cheep
peba	sett	weka	bitch	chick
pelt	shad	wing	blain	chirp
pern	skua	wisp	blaze	civet
pest	slug	wolf	bleak	cloud
pika	smew	worm	bleat	cluck
pike	sole	wren	bongo	coati
poll	sord	yelp	booby	cobia
pony	stag	yoke	borer	cobra
pout	stud	yowl	boxer	cohoe
prad	swan	zebu	brace	cohog
prey	tail	addax	brant	coney
puma	teal	adder	bream	couch
pupa	team	aerie	brill	covey
puss	tern	agama	brize	coypu
quad	tick	agami	brock	crake
rail	tike	alula	brood	crane
rein	tine	apery	Bruin	crawl

crest	fitch	horse	llama	nymph
croak	flock	hound	loach	okapi
cuddy	fluke	husky	lodge	orang
culex	gaper	hutch	loris	ormer
daman	gayal	hutia	louse	ornis
dhole	gecko	hydra	macaw	otary
dingo	geese	hyena	madge	otter
diver	genet	hyrax	mamba	ounce
dogie	genus	imago	manis	ousel
dorse	girth	izard	manul	ouzel
drake	glede	jenny	mavis	oxeye
drill	goose	Jumbo	merle	owlet
drone	grebe	junco	miaow	panda
drove	grice	kaama	midge	peggy
dryft	griff	kalan	moose	pekan
eagle	growl	kiang	moray	perch
earth	grunt	kitty	morse	pewit
egret	guana	koala	moult	pibea
eider	guppy	krait	mount	picus
eland	haras	kulan	mouse	pi-dog
emmet	harpy	lance	murex	piggy
eyrie	hatch	lapin	murre	pinna
fauna	hathi	larus	murry	pinto
fauve	helot	larva	nandu	pipit
Felix	heron	leash	nanny	pitta
feral	hinny	leech	Neddy	pogge
field	hippo	lemur	neigh	poker
filly	hobby	liger	nidus	Polly
finch	homer	limax	noddy	polyp

pongo	satyr	snout	tribe
pooch	saury	solan	trill
porgy	scale	spawn	troop
pouch	sedge	spitz	trout
poult	serin	spoon	trunk
pound	shark	sprat	tunny
poyou	sheep	sprig	tweet
prawn	shell	squab	udder
pride	shire	squid	ululu
puppy	shoal	stall	urial
pussy	shoat	steed	veery
quack	shrew	steer	vespa
quail	siege	stilt	viper
rache	siren	sting	vireo
rasse	skart	stoat	vixen
ratel	skate	stork	wader
raven	skein	stray	waler
reeve	skink	swarm	watch
reins	skunk	swift	whale
rhino	slink	swine	whelk
roach	sloth	tabby	whelp
robin	smelt	takin	zebra
roker	smolt	talon	zibet
roost	snail	tapir	zoril
rotch	snake	tatou	zorro
sable	snarl	tench	acarus
saiga	snipe	tiger	agouta
saker	snook	tigon	agouti
sasin	snort	torsk	alauda

albino	bayard	caplin	cottus
alevin	beagle	caribe	coucal
alpaca	beaver	castor	cougar
angler	bedbug	cat-nap	covert
angora	bee fly	cattle	coyote
anguis	beetle	cayman	coypou
ant cow	bellow	chacma	cruive
antler	beluga	chafer	cuckoo
aoudad	bharal	cheven	culver
apiary	bident	chevin	curlew
aquila	blenny	chigoe	curtal
aranea	bobcat	chinch	cus-cus
argala	bonito	chough	cushat
argali	borzoi	cicada	cuttle
aswail	botfly	cicala	cygnet
auklet	bovine	circus	darter
aviary	bowfin	clotho	dassie
avocet	bow-wow	clutch	dayfly
aye-aye	breeze	coaita	desman
baboon	bridle	cocker	dipper
badger	bronco	cockle	dipsas
baleen	bulbul	cocoon	dobbin
bandog	burbot	collie	donkey
bantam	burnet	colony	dorado
barbel	burrow	colugo	dorfly
barbet	cackle	condor	dragon
barren	canary	conger	drongo
barton	Cancer	corbie	dugong
basset	canine	corral	dunlin

durgan	gavial	hog-rat	kakapo
eaglet	gee-gee	honker	keltie
earwig	genera	hooper	kennel
ellops	gennet	hoopoe	killer
embryo	gerbil	hooves	kindle
entire	gibbon	hop-fly	kipper
equine	gnawer	hornet	kit fox
ermine	gobble	houdah	kitten
falcon	godwit	howdah	koodoo
farrow	gopher	howlet	kraken
feline	gorgon	humble	langur
fennec	griffe	hummel	lanner
ferine	grilse	hunter	lap dog
ferret	grison	hyaena	launce
fisher	grivet	hybrid	limpet
flight	groper	iguana	linnet
fogash	grouse	impala	lionet
fossil	guenon	insect	litter
fox-bat	gun dog	instar	lizard
fulmar	gurnet	jabiru	locust
gadfly	hackee	jacana	lowing
gaggle	hackle	jackal	lowrie
gambet	hallux	jaeger	lupine
gander	heckle	jaguar	mad dog
gannet	he-goat	jennet	maggot
garron	heifer	jerboa	magpie
garrot	hen-run	jigger	maigre
garuda	herald	jumart	mammal
garvie	hogget	jungle	manati

manège	mulish	partan	puffer
manger	mullet	passer	puffin
mantid	murena	pastor	pug dog
mantis	murine	pavone	pullet
margay	murray	peahen	pye-dog
marlin	murrey	pecten	python
marmot	musk ox	peewee	quagga
marten	mussel	peewit	quahog
martin	muster	peludo	rabbit
maybug	muzzle	petrel	racoon
mayfly	mysore	phoebe	rallus
mazama	nandoo	pholas	ranger
meagre	nekton	phylum	red ant
medusa	nereid	pigeon	red fox
megrim	nilgai	piglet	redcap
merino	nilgau	pig-rat	redeye
merlin	ocelot	pig-sty	redfin
merman	onager	pincer	remora
miller	oriole	piraña	rhesus
milter	oscine	pisces	robalo
minnow	osprey	plaice	rodent
monkey	ostrea	plover	roller
mopoke	ox-bird	podura	saddle
motmot	oyster	pollan	salmon
motuca	palama	pollen	saluki
mouser	pallah	poodle	sambar
mud-eel	palolo	porker	sawfly
mud-hen	pariah	possum	scarab
mugger	parrot	pouter	school
		psocid	

scoter	sow bug	trogon	wombat
sea-ape	sphinx	tsetse	wrasse
sea-bat	spider	tunnel	wyvern
sea-cat	sponge	turbot	ynambu
sea-cob	spring	turdus	abalone
sea-cow	squama	turkey	acaleph
sea-dog	squawk	turtle	alewife
sea-ear	stable	tusker	anchovy
sea-eel	string	urgula	anguine
sea-fan	sucker	urchin	annelid
sea-fox	summer	ursine	ant-bear
sea-hog	tarpan	vermin	antbird
sea-mew	tarpon	vervel	antenna
sea-owl	taurus	vervet	ant heap
sea-pen	tautog	vicuna	ant hill
sea-pig	teetee	volary	ant lion
serran	teledu	walrus	aquatic
serval	tenree	wapiti	army ant
setter	teredo	warble	asinine
shelty	thrips	warren	aurochs
shiner	thrush	weasel	axolotl
shrike	tipula	weaver	barking
shrimp	tomcat	weever	barn owl
simian	toucan	weevil	basenji
simurg	towaco	wether	bat tick
siskin	towhee	whinny	bean-fly
sleuth	toy dog	wigeon	bear-cat
slough	tracer	wild ox	beavery
sorrel	triton	willet	bee-hive

beeline	bush-cat	chincha	dor-hawk
bee-moth	bush-tit	chirrup	dovecot
benthos	bustard	cichlid	dunnock
bergylt	buzzard	coal tit	earworm
bestial	capelin	codfish	echidna
bettong	carabus	codling	echinus
big game	caracal	colibri	eel-pout
bighorn	carcase	colobus	egg-bird
billbug	carcass	company	emperor
bird-dog	cariama	coon cat	emu-wren
bittern	caribou	cotinga	epizoon
bivalve	cat flea	courser	ewe lamb
blesbok	catbird	cowbird	extinct
blowfly	catfish	cowshed	fantail
blue fox	catling	creeper	feather
blue jay	cattalo	cricket	fern-owl
blue tit	centaur	croaker	fesnyng
bluecap	cervine	cutworm	fetlock
blue-eye	cestoid	cyclops	finback
boat fly	cetacea	dasyure	finnock
bobtail	chamois	deerdog	fin-toed
brocket	charger	deer-fly	firefly
brooder	cheetah	deer-hog	fischer
buffalo	Cheviot	deerlet	fish fly
bull-bat	chewink	denizen	fitchet
bulldog	chicken	dew claw	fitchew
bullock	chigger	dogfish	flapper
bummalo	chikara	dolphin	flicker
bunting	chimera	dopping	flipper

133

floccus	grampus	hencote	June fly
flyblow	grey fox	hennery	karakul
foreleg	grey hen	herring	katydid
forepaw	grey owl	hilding	keitloa
foumart	greylag	hindleg	kestrel
frog-fly	greyleg	hindpaw	killdee
fur-seal	griffin	hircine	kinglet
gadwall	griffon	hive-bee	knobber
gallfly	grouper	hoatzin	lacerta
gambrel	gryphon	hog-deer	ladybug
garfish	grysbok	hogfish	lady-cow
gar-pike	guanaco	hogwash	ladyfly
gazelle	gudgeon	homelyn	lambkin
gelding	guereza	hoot owl	lampfly
gemsbok	gurnard	hop flea	lamprey
giraffe	gymnura	hornbug	land-rat
gizzard	habitat	hornfly	lapwing
glowfly	hackney	hornowl	latrate
glutton	haddock	howling	lemming
gnu goat	haggard	ice bear	leonine
gobbler	halcyon	ice bird	leopard
goldbug	half-ape	ice worm	leveret
goldeye	halibut	jacamar	lich-owl
gorcock	hamster	jacchus	linsang
gor-crow	hanuman	jackass	lioness
gorilla	harness	jackdaw	lobster
goshawk	harrier	jawfish	lobworm
gosling	hawk owl	jewfish	longear
grackle	hen-coop	June bug	lugworm

lurcher	mouflon	papilio	pole cat
macaque	mudfish	Partlet	pollack
madoqua	mud-lark	pastern	pollard
mahseer	muraena	peacock	polypod
mallard	muridae	peafowl	pompero
mammoth	musimon	peccary	porcine
manakin	musk-hog	Pegasus	poulard
manatee	musk-rat	pelican	poultry
Manx cat	mustang	pellock	prepupa
marabou	mytilus	penguin	pricket
markhor	nandine	phasmid	primate
marmose	narwhal	phoenix	puttock
marsoon	nose-bag	piculet	pyralis
martlet	oarfish	piddock	quetzal
mastiff	octopod	piebald	raccoon
mawworm	octopus	pig-deer	rat-flea
meerkat	oilbird	pill bug	rathole
merling	ophidia	pinguin	rattler
mermaid	opossum	pinnock	red deer
metazoa	oquassa	pintado	red drum
migrant	ortolan	pintail	redbird
milk cow	osseter	pinworm	redfish
mole rat	ostrich	piranha	redhead
mollusc	pack rat	piscine	redpoll
mollusk	paddock	pismire	redwing
mongrel	painter	pit pony	reptant
monitor	palfrey	plumage	reptile
monster	palm-cat	pochard	Reynard
moor-hen	panther	pointer	ringlet

roatelo	sea-dove	spouter	toheroa
rock-cod	sea-duck	spreagh	torpedo
roebuck	seagull	staniel	tree-fox
roe-deer	sea-hare	striges	trepang
rookery	sea-hawk	strigil	trotter
rooster	sea-lark	sturnus	tuatara
rorqual	sea-lion	sumpter	tumbler
rose bug	sea-pike	sun-bear	turndun
rosella	sea-slug	sun-bird	twinter
rotifer	sea-star	sun-fish	twitter
ruddock	sea-wife	suthora	unicorn
sage hen	sea-wolf	swallow	urodele
saimiri	sea-worm	syrphus	vaccine
Samoyed	seriema	tadpole	vampire
sand-eel	serpent	tamarin	varmint
sand-fly	shad fly	tanager	vespoid
sapajou	she-goat	tarsier	viceroy
sardine	shippon	tatouay	voengra
saurian	siamang	tattler	vulpine
sawfish	simurgh	termite	vulture
scallop	sirenia	terpang	wagtail
scomber	sirgang	terrier	wallaby
sculpin	skimmer	tiddler	warbler
sea-bass	skylark	tiercel	wart-hog
sea-bear	sockeye	tigress	water ox
sea-bird	sounder	tinamou	wax-moth
sea-calf	spaniel	titlark	waxwing
sea-cock	sparrow	titling	web-foot
sea-dace	spawner	toad bug	web-toed

webworm	anguilla	bird's egg
whippet	animalia	black ant
whisker	anserine	black cat
whiting	anserous	black fly
widgeon	ant-pipit	black fox
wild ass	anteater	black rat
wild cat	antelope	blackcap
wistiti	antennae	blauwbok
withers	antilope	blinkers
wolf-dog	apterous	blow-hole
wood-ant	aquiline	blue-back
wood-owl	arachnid	bluebill
wood-rat	arapunga	bluebird
wren-tit	argonaut	blue-buck
wryneck	army worm	bluefish
yard-ant	avicular	bluegill
aardvark	avifauna	blue-hare
aardwolf	bactrian	bluewing
aasvogel	baldpate	boatbill
abattoir	band fish	boattail
accentor	barnacle	bobolink
acridian	basilisk	bobwhite
adjutant	bee-eater	bollworm
aigrette	bell-bird	bonefish
Airedale	berghaan	book-lice
albacore	bettonga	bookworm
alcatras	bird-bath	brancard
amadavat	bird-cage	brisling
anaconda	birdcall	brontops

brown owl
brown rat
bull-calf
bull-frog
bullhead
bush-baby
bush-buck
bush-wren
cachalot
cachelot
calamary
cannibal
capuchin
capybara
caracara
carapace
carcajou
cardinal
cargoose
cariacou
caseworm
castrate
cave-bear
cavicorn
ceratops
Cerberus
cetacean
chestnut
chigetai

chimaera
chipmunk
chipmuck
chowchow
civet cat
coach dog
coalfish
cockatoo
cockerel
congo eel
cowhouse
crane-fly
crawfish
crayfish
creature
curassow
curculio
dabchick
daggmask
dairy cow
dead duck
deal fish
deer park
demi-wolf
Derby dog
didapper
dinosaur
dobchick
Doberman

dog house
dog pound
dog's life
dormouse
dotterel
dovecote
dragonet
duck bill
duck hawk
duckling
duck-mole
duck-pond
eagle-owl
eagle-ray
earshell
earth hog
edentate
elephant
elkhound
entellus
entrails
ephemera
fauvette
feathers
filefish
fin-whale
firebird
firebrat
fireworm

fish hawk	grayling	horse-box
fish tank	great auk	horse-fly
fishpond	greenfly	hound-dog
flamingo	greenlet	house ant
flatfish	grey mare	house dog
flatworm	grey wolf	housebug
flesh-fly	grosbeak	house-fly
flounder	guacharo	humpback
fool-duck	gymnotus	hydrozoa
forewing	hair-seal	inchworm
foxhound	hair-tail	Irish elk
fox-shark	hair-worm	itch-mite
frog-fish	hangbird	javeline
frogling	hawfinch	jenny ass
froth-fly	hawk moth	John Dory
fruit-bat	hedgehog	kangaroo
fruit-fly	hedgepig	keeshond
gall-gnat	helminth	killdeer
Galloway	hemipode	kingbird
gall-wasp	henhouse	king-crab
game fish	hernshaw	king-crow
gamecock	hind-wing	kingfish
garefowl	hoggerel	kinkajou
garganey	honey-bee	kitty-cat
glow-worm	hookworm	kiwi-kiwi
goatfish	hornbeak	kolinsky
goat-moth	hornbill	labrador
goldfish	horntail	lacewing
gold-wasp	hornworm	ladybird

8

lame duck	mealy-bug	octopede
lancelot	megapode	oliphant
land-crab	menhaden	omnivore
landrail	Minotaur	ophidian
lannaret	moccasin	ouistiti
lava-crab	mongoose	ovenbird
laverock	monkfish	ox-pecker
lemon dab	monk-seal	pack-mule
leporine	moor-cock	paddling
linkworm	moor-fowl	palm-chat
lion fish	mosquito	palomino
lion's den	mud-puppy	pangolin
long horn	mule-deer	parakeet
loosebox	musk-deer	parasite
lovebird	musk-duck	pavonian
lump-fish	musquash	Pekinese
lungfish	mute swan	penny dog
mackerel	myriapod	pheasant
macropod	nauplius	philomel
mandrill	nautilus	physalia
man-eater	neat-herd	pickerel
mangabey	night-ape	pilchard
man-of-war	night-fly	pinniped
marmoset	nightjar	pinscher
martinet	night-owl	pipefish
mastodon	nose-band	pit-viper
matamata	nurse ant	plankton
maverick	nuthatch	plant bug
meal-worm	oak eggar	platanna

platypus	rhyncota	screamer
podargus	rice-bird	sea-acorn
polar fox	richesse	sea-adder
polliwog	ringdove	sea-beast
polo pony	ringtail	sea-bream
poorwill	river hog	sea-devil
popinjay	rock-bird	sea-eagle
porkling	rock-cook	sea-horse
porpoise	rock-dove	sea-hound
predator	rock-fish	sea-lemon
protozoa	rock-lark	sea-louse
puff bird	rockling	sea-lungs
puss moth	rose-fish	sealyham
pussy cat	ruminant	sea-otter
queen ant	sage-cock	sea-perch
queen bee	sailfish	sea-robin
quill pig	salmonid	sea-snail
rabbitry	sand mole	sea-snake
rara avis	sand-dart	sea-snipe
rare bird	sand-flea	sea-swine
rasorial	sand-lark	sea-trout
rat-shrew	sandling	serotine
red-belly	sand-peep	sheep dog
redbreast	sand-sole	shelduck
redshank	sand-wasp	shepherd
redstart	sapi-utan	Shetland
reedbird	sauropod	shipworm
reindeer	scarabee	shoebill
rhizopod	scorpion	silkworm

skewbald	swift fox	viscacha
skua-gull	swiftlet	vivarium
slave ant	tabby cat	wallfish
sleipner	tapaculo	wall-newt
slow-worm	tapeworm	wanderoo
small-fry	tawny owl	war-horse
smilodon	teal duck	warragal
snowbird	tentacle	watchdog
songbird	terrapin	water-boa
sparling	theropod	water-bug
spawning	thrasher	water-cow
spitz dog	throstle	water-dog
squirrel	tiger-cat	water-fly
stallion	titmouse	waterhen
starfish	toad-fish	water-rat
starling	tortoise	weakfish
stegodon	tragopan	wharf-rat
steinbok	tree-frog	wheatear
sting-ray	troupial	wheat-eel
stink bug	troutlet	wheatfly
stone-fly	tubeworm	whimbrel
stray cat	turn tail	whinchat
stray dog	turnspit	whirlwig
sturgeon	ungulate	whistler
subimago	univalve	white ant
suborder	urodella	white fly
sun grebe	vespiary	white fox
surfbird	viperish	whitecap
suricate	viperous	wild boar

wild duck	amazon ant	binturang
wild goat	amber-jack	birdhouse
wild life	amphibian	bird-louse
wildfowl	angel fish	bird's-nest
wingspan	angleworm	bird-table
wireworm	Angora cat	black bass
wolf-fish	ant patrol	black bear
wolf pack	anthropod	Black Bess
woodchat	ant-thrush	black kite
woodcock	aphid pest	black ruff
wood-duck	arachnoid	black swan
wood ibis	Arctic fox	black tern
woodlark	armadillo	blackbird
wood-lice	arthropod	blackbuck
wood-mite	babirussa	blackcock
wood-tick	babyrussa	blackfish
wood-wasp	badger dog	blackgame
woodworm	bald eagle	blackhead
wood-wren	bandicoot	blindfish
woof-woof	bangsring	blindworm
yeanling	barracuda	blood-bird
yearling	bassarisk	bloodworm
yoke-toed	bean-goose	blue heron
yoldring	beaver-rat	blue shark
zoiatria	beccafico	blue sheep
zoophyte	bee-beetle	blue whale
aepyornis	beef-eater	boarhound
albatross	berg-adder	book-louse
alligator	billy goat	bottle tit

bowerbird
brambling
brandling
breeze fly
brimstone
brood mare
broomtail
brown bear
brush deer
brush wolf
buck hound
bull snake
bullfinch
bull-trout
bumble bee
burro deer
butterfly
caballine
caddis fly
Caffre cat
camass-rat
campanero
candle fly
canker-fly
cantharis
caparison
carnivore
cart horse
cassowary

cat and dog
catamount
caterwaul
cedarbird
centipede
ceratodus
chaetopod
chaffinch
chameleon
cheese-fly
chessycat
chickadee
chickaree
chihuahua
chinch bug
chrysalis
cicindela
clavicorn
cochineal
cockatiel
cockroach
cock-robin
cocks-comb
coffee-bug
coleopter
columbary
columbine
conger eel
cormorant

corn borer
corncrake
cotton rat
crocodile
crossbill
crossfish
croton bug
cuckoo-fly
currassow
curry comb
dachshund
dairy herd
Dalmatian
damselfly
dark horse
deaf adder
deerhound
deer-mouse
deer-tiger
desert rat
devil-fish
dicky-bird
dimyarian
dinothere
dog collar
dog kennel
dog-salmon
dorsal-fin
dragonfly

dray horse	gaspereau	gyrfalcon
dromedary	gastropod	hawksbill
duck louse	gazehound	heath-cock
dziggetai	gerfalcon	hemiptera
eagle-eyed	ghost crab	herbivore
earth-wolf	gier-eagle	heronshaw
earthworm	gift horse	herpestes
eider duck	ginger tom	high horse
ephemerid	gipsy moth	hippocerf
Eskimo dog	globe fish	hodmandod
feralized	goldcrest	Holly blue
fieldfare	goldeneye	honey bear
fieldlark	goldfinch	hoofprint
fill-horse	goldfinny	horned bug
firecrest	goldsinny	horned owl
fish-eagle	goldspink	hornet fly
fish-garth	goosander	horny-head
fish-louse	grain moth	horse-shoe
flocculus	Great Dane	horse-whip
flour-moth	green-bone	hound-fish
flute-bird	gregarine	Houyhnhnm
flying fox	grey-goose	humble bee
forest-fly	greyhound	ichneumon
frog spawn	grimalkin	ichthyoid
frogmouth	ground-hog	iguanodon
fruit moth	guillemot	Incitatus
gallinazo	guinea-hen	infusoria
gallinule	guinea-pig	jacksnipe
gall-midge	gypsy-moth	jellyfish

Jenny wren	merganser	on the wing
Jersey cow	migration	orange-tip
Judas goat	migratory	orangutan
jungle law	milk snake	ossifrage
Kerry blue	millepede	ostracism
king-cobra	millipede	oviparous
king-eider	monoceros	owl-parrot
king-snake	monotreme	pachyderm
kittiwake	moth borer	pademelon
koala bear	mouldwarp	palm-civet
lake trout	mound-bird	paper-wasp
lamp-shell	mousebird	pariah dog
land-snail	mouse-deer	parrakeet
langouste	mouse-fish	partridge
latration	mousehole	passerine
lemon sole	mud dauber	Pekingese
lion-heart	mule-train	percheron
little auk	musk-shrew	peregrine
livestock	Nandi bear	peripatus
Lowrie Tod	nanny goat	phalanger
mammalian	native cat	phalarope
manticora	neat-house	phytosaur
manticore	neat-stall	pike-perch
March hare	nightbird	pilot fish
mare's nest	night-crow	pine-finch
marsupial	night-fowl	pine-mouse
marsupium	nighthawk	pine-snake
megathere	nocturnal	pinnipede
menagerie	on the hoof	pipistrel

windhover
wolfhound
wolverine
wood-borer
woodchuck
wood-hewer
wood-louse
wood-mouse
woodshock
wood-white
worker ant
worker bee
worm snake
worm-eaten
yellow-dog
youngling
zeuglodon
aberdevine
acorn-shell
actinopoda
Adonis blue
Angora goat
anguifauna
angwantibo
angwartibo
animal life
animalcule
archer-fish
Arctic hare

Arctic loon
Arctic tern
arthropoda
aviculture
babiroussa
Barbary ape
battery hen
bean thrips
bear garden
bêche-de-mer
Bedlington
bell the cat
bellwether
bezoar-goat
billbeetle
bird of Jove
bird of Juno
bird of prey
bird-spider
bitterling
black sheep
black snake
black widow
blister-fly
blood horse
bloodhound
blue pigeon
bluebottle
bluebreast

bluethroat
boll-weevil
Bombay duck
Boston bull
bottle-fish
bottle-nose
brent-goose
brook trout
Brown Argus
brown snake
brown trout
Bucephalus
budgerigar
buffalo bug
bull-roarer
Burmese cat
burnet moth
burrow-duck
bushmaster
bush-shrike
butter-bird
butterfish
cabbage-fly
caddice-fly
caddis worm
calico pony
camel train
camelopard
candlefish

canker worm	cottontail	field-mouse
cannon-bone	cow bunting	fire beetle
canvas-back	crab plover	fishing owl
Cape pigeon	crested jay	fish-ladder
carpet-moth	crio sphinx	flagellata
cattle-grid	crustacean	flea beetle
cephalopod	cuttle fish	flycatcher
chachalaca	dachshound	flying fish
chattering	dapple-grey	fox terrier
cheep cheep	death's-head	freemartin
chevrotain	deathwatch	fritillary
chiff-chaff	deep litter	frog hopper
chimpanzee	demoiselle	galleyworm
chinchilla	dermoptera	gasteropod
chittagong	dickeybird	get the bird
clam shrimp	didunculus	giant panda
Clydesdale	digger wasp	glass snake
coach horse	dog's chance	glossy ibis
cockatrice	drosophila	goatsucker
cockchafer	dumb animal	golden mole
codlin moth	dumb friend	grass snake
coelacanth	dung beetle	green-drake
coleoptera	ember-goose	greenfinch
congo snake	equestrian	green-goose
copperhead	exaltation	greenshank
copper-worm	fallow-chat	green-snake
coral snake	fallow-deer	grey mullet
corn-beetle	fatted calf	grey parrot
cotton worm	*fer-de-lance*	ground dove

ground game
guinea-cock
guinea-fowl
guinea-worm
guitarfish
hairstreak
hammer-fish
hammerhead
hanging fly
harpy eagle
hartebeest
harvest bug
hedge brown
hellbender
henharrier
herald-duck
hermit-crab
herring hog
hessian fly
heterocera
hippogriff
hippogryph
honey-eater
honey-guide
honey-mouse
hooded-crow
hoodie-crow
horned-toad
horn-footed

horseflesh
horse-leech
horse-sense
house finch
hunting dog
Iceland dog
Indian kite
Indian pony
indigo-bird
jack-rabbit
jaguarundi
jigger flea
June beetle
jungle fowl
jungle king
kabeljauer
kingfisher
kitten moth
Kodiak bear
kookaburra
lady beetle
lancet fish
lantern fly
lappet moth
large heath
leaf cutter
leaf hopper
leaf insect
leopardess

lion's share
loggerhead
lumpsucker
Maltese cat
Maltese dog
martingale
meadow lark
megalosaur
missel bird
molluscoid
mossbunker
mousehound
mud-skipper
musk-beetle
mutton bird
neat-cattle
night-churr
night-heron
night-raven
nutcracker
omnivorous
ornithopod
oropendula
otterhound
otter-shrew
ox-antelope
pack of dogs
pack-animal
paddlefish

palaeosaur	Quaker bird	salamander
Pallais cat	rabbit-fish	sand-dollar
palmer-worm	raccoon-dog	sanderling
pantheress	radiolaria	sand-grouse
paradoxure	rat terrier	sand-hopper
parrotbill	red admiral	sand-launce
parrot-fish	red herring	sand-lizard
parson-bird	rhinoceros	sand-martin
periwinkle	ribbon-fish	sand-sucker
Persian cat	ribbon-worm	sausage dog
phyllopoda	right whale	scarabaeus
phylloxera	ring plover	schipperke
pig in a poke	river horse	screech-owl
pigeon hawk	road-runner	sea-blubber
pigeon loft	rock-badger	sea-leopard
pine-beauty	rock-hopper	sea-monster
pine-beetle	rock-pigeon	sea-poacher
pine-carpet	rock-rabbit	sea-serpent
pine-chafer	rock-salmon	sea-surgeon
pine-martin	rock-turbot	sea-swallow
poll parrot	Roman snail	sea-unicorn
pouched rat	rose-beetle	sea-vampire
Pomeranian	rose-chafer	serpentine
prairie-dog	rove-beetle	setting hen
prairie-fox	Russian cat	shearwater
pratincole	sabre-tooth	sheathbill
purple coat	saddleback	sheep-louse
purple-fish	sage-grouse	sheep's eyes
quack quack	sailorbird	Shire horse

short sheep	stone-snipe	turtle-dove
shovelhead	sub-species	vampire bat
shrew-mouse	sucking-pig	vertebrate
Siamese cat	summer-duck	vinegar eel
sickle-bill	summer-teal	vinegar fly
sidewinder	sun-bittern	wading bird
silverfish	Syrian bear	wall-lizard
silver-king	Syrphus fly	water-mouse
small heath	tailor bird	water-ousel
snaffle-bit	tailwagger	water-shrew
social wasp	talk turkey	water-snail
solan-goose	tantony pig	water-snake
soldier ant	tardigrade	weaver-bird
soldierfly	tawny eagle	web spinner
song thrush	thick-knees	Weimaraner
Spanish fly	thill-horse	whale-shark
sperm-whale	*Tiergarten*	wheat-midge
sphinx-moth	tiger-shark	white whale
spider crab	tiger-snake	wild animal
spider's web	timber wolf	wildebeest
spotted ray	tomato worm	willow-wren
springbuck	toy spaniel	winged game
spring-hare	toy terrier	winter-moth
springtail	trace-horse	wolf-spider
squeteague	tree-hopper	wood-grouse
stag-beetle	tropic-bird	woodpecker
stock horse	turkey-cock	wood-pigeon
stone-eater	Turkish cat	wood-shrike
stone-horse	turn turtle	wood-thrush

woolly-bear	bull-terrier	constrictor
wren-thrush	bunny rabbit	corn-ear worm
xiphopagus	Buredan's ass	cosmopolite
yellow-bird	Burmese blue	cotton-mouse
yellowlegs	butcher-bird	cottonmouth
zebra finch	cabbage-moth	crocodilian
accipitrine	cabbage-worm	crown antler
Afghan hound	calling-crab	dairy cattle
assassin bug	Canada goose	daisy-cutter
baleen whale	Cape buffalo	dead as a dodo
banded krait	cardophagus	desert snail
bank swallow	carriage dog	diamondback
barn swallow	carrion crow	Diana monkey
basset hound	cat squirrel	Dolly Varden
bastard-wing	cat's pyjamas	drinker moth
beast of prey	caterpillar	eager beaver
beehawk moth	channel bass	Egyptian cat
Belgian hare	Chanticleer	electric eel
bellows-fish	Cheshire cat	elephantine
black beetle	chickabiddy	emperor-moth
black-cattle	chicken hawk	entire horse
blackgrouse	church mouse	fairy shrimp
black-martin	clothes-moth	fallow-finch
bloodsucker	Cochin-china	fan-tail dove
brine shrimp	cock-a-doodle	fence-lizard
bristletail	cock-sparrow	fishing-frog
brush-turkey	coconut-moth	flickertail
buffalo wolf	codling moth	flour-weevil
bull-mastiff	columbarium	flying lemur

flying-squid	horned snake	meadow-pipit
foraminifer	horned-viper	meliphagous
fox squirrel	hornet's nest	missing link
frigate-bird	horse-collar	mocking bird
game reserve	house martin	moss-cheeper
garter snake	humming-bird	mountain-cat
giant fulmar	ichthyosaur	murmuration
Gila monster	ink-flamingo	muscovy-duck
globigerina	insectarium	muskellunge
gnatcatcher	insectivore	nightingale
golden eagle	Irish setter	orang-outang
golden trout	kangaroo rat	ornithosaur
gopher snake	Kilkenny cat	painted lady
grain beetle	killer whale	painted pony
grasshopper	king-penguin	paper-sailor
green-bottle	king-vulture	Pavlov's dogs
green-linnet	lacewing fly	pearl-oyster
green-turtle	lammergeier	pelican fish
grizzly bear	land spaniel	phantom gnat
ground-robin	lantern fish	pied wagtail
ground-sloth	larch sawfly	pigeon house
heart-urchin	laterigrade	pigeon's milk
hibernation	leatherback	piranha fish
Highland cow	lepidoptera	piscatorial
hippocampus	lion-hearted	plant cutter
hircocervus	lophobranch	plantigrade
honey-badger	Malayan bear	pocket mouse
honey-sucker	man-o'-war bird	prairie wolf
horned horse	meadow-brown	Pretty Polly

pterodactyl
purple-finch
purple-heron
rabbit hutch
rattle-snake
red squirrel
reed-bunting
reed-sparrow
reed-warbler
reservation
rhopalocera
rhynchodont
ringed snake
rock-sparrow
roosterfish
royal walnut
rubber snake
saddle-girth
saddle-horse
salmon trout
sand-skipper
scale insect
scissor-bill
scissor-tail
scolopendra
scorpion fly
Scotch Argus
sea-cucumber
sea-dotterel

sea-elephant
sea-hedgehog
sea-longworm
sea-scorpion
serpent-fish
serpent-head
shepherd dog
shrike vireo
singing bird
sitting duck
Skye terrier
sleuth-hound
small copper
snaffle-rein
snout beetle
snow-bunting
snow-leopard
social whale
soldier crab
song-sparrow
sorrel-horse
Spanish fowl
sparrowhawk
spawning-bed
sporting dog
stick-insect
stickleback
stilt-plover
stone-curlew

stone-falcon
stone-marten
stone-plover
striped bass
sucking-fish
sumpter mule
swallowtail
swamp rabbit
tiger-beetle
titanothere
tobacco worm
tree swallow
trumpet-fish
tussock-moth
Vanga shrike
vine-fretter
water-beetle
wattled crow
weaver-finch
wheel-animal
white ermine
whitethroat
whiting-pout
winged queen
wishtonwish
wolf whistle
wood-fretter
wood-swallow
woodwarbler

xylophagous
yellow grunt
yellow perch
zebra mussel
adjutant bird
American lion
Archangel cat
baby elephant
barndoor fowl
barnyard fowl
basking shark
bay at the moon
beaded lizard
beard the lion
bird's eye view
bonnet monkey
book-scorpion
bottom animal
bramble-finch
branchiopoda
brontosaurus
brown pelican
burrowing-owl
bustard-quail
butterfly dog
buzzard-clock
cabbage-white
Cairn terrier
capercaillie

capercailzie
cardinal-bird
carpenter ant
carpenter bee
carpet python
Cashmere goat
catamountain
Cat's whiskers
cattle market
cecropia moth
chicken house
chimney swift
cinnabar moth
cinnamon bear
cliff swallow
cock-pheasant
congregation
crested swift
crowned eagle
cuckoo roller
cuckoo shrike
cucumber flea
December moth
desquamation
diving beetle
diving petrel
dog in a manger
domestic fowl
dragon-lizard

draught-horse
dumb creature
elephant bird
falcon-gentil
father-lasher
field spaniel
fighting-cock
fighting-fish
flittermouse
flowerpecker
flying dragon
flying lizard
flying marmot
French poodle
fully-fledged
gallinaceous
garden-spider
gazelle hound
Geoffrey's cat
goat antelope
golden oriole
golden plover
golden salmon
goldfish bowl
grey squirrel
ground-beetle
ground-cuckoo
ground-feeder
ground-insect

ground-pigeon	man-of-war fish	rainbow trout
ground-roller	mantis shrimp	ring-dotterel
Guinea baboon	marbled white	rhesus monkey
hare and hound	marine iguana	rifleman-bird
harvest-mouse	marmalade cat	rock squirrel
hellgrammite	marsh-harrier	ruffed grouse
hippopotamus	mating season	Saint Bernard
hedge-sparrow	mealy redpoll	salamandrian
hedge-warbler	merrythought	scarlet tiger
herd instinct	miller's-thumb	scorpion fish
hermit thrush	missel-thrush	sea-butterfly
hippocentaur	mistle thrush	sea-porcupine
homing pigeon	mosquito hawk	sedge warbler
honey-buzzard	mountain goat	sentinel-crab
honey-creeper	mountain hare	sergeant-fish
hoofed animal	mountain lion	serpent-eater
horned lizard	mourning dove	serpentiform
horse blanket	national park	Shetland pony
ichthyopsida	Newfoundland	silver salmon
idiothermous	painted snipe	social insect
Irish terrier	pantophagous	Spanish horse
jumping mouse	paradise fish	Spanish sheep
jumping shrew	pepper shrike	spider-monkey
kettle of fish	platanna frog	spring beetle
king of beasts	pocket gopher	spring-keeper
leopard shark	purple martin	spruce sawfly
lightning bug	quarter horse	standardbred
limnophilous	queen termite	stonechatter
mandarin duck	radish maggot	stormy petrel

streamer tail	trout nursery	wattle turkey
stubble-goose	ugly duckling	Welsh terrier
sucking louse	umbrella bird	whip-poor-will
Suffolk punch	ursine monkey	whip-scorpion
sumpter horse	vapourer moth	white admiral
Sunapee trout	velvet scoter	white herring
swimming crab	Virginia deer	winged insect
thoroughbred	walking-stick	wingless bird
trachypterus	waterboatman	worm's eye view
tree squirrel	water-buffalo	yellow hammer
tropical bird	water-spaniel	yellow jacket
tropical fish	water-strider	yellowthroat
tropical moth	water-wagtail	

MEASUREMENT

This general heading has been divided into two sections, one for Time and the other for Weights, Measures and Coins.

Time

This section includes clocks and clocktime—calendars and calendar time—festivals and holy days—prepositions and adverbs of time—ages—seasons—duration, period and date.

A.D.	era	date	late	soon
am	ere	dawn	Lent	span
B.C.	eve	dial	moon	term
mo'	May	dusk	morn	then
pm	now	even	next	Tib's
age	oft	ever	Noel	tick
ago	old	fall	noon	tide
aye	sec	fast	olam	till
day	ult	fore	once	time
due	yet	ides	over	unto
e'en	aeon	inst.	past	week
e'er	ages	jiff	post	when
eld	anon	June	prox.	Xmas
Eos	ante	July	slow	year

yore	point	August	lately
Yule	prime	Aurora	latest
again	prior	autumn	latish
annum	Purim	Bairam	lustre
April	ready	brumal	*mañana*
as yet	shake	coeval	May day
brief	sharp	coming	midday
clock	short	crisis	minute
cycle	since	curfew	modern
daily	so far	decade	moment
dekad	space	dotage	Monday
delay	spell	during	morrow
diary	still	Easter	new day
early	style	elapse	o'clock
epact	sunup	ere now	of late
epoch	tempo	extant	off-day
fasti	today	ferial	old age
flash	trice	Friday	on time
jiffy	until	future	one day
later	watch	gnomon	period
March	while	heyday	Pesach
matin	years	hiemal	presto
month	young	hourly	prewar
never	youth	Ice age	*pro tem*
night	actual	in time	prompt
nonce	advent	Jet age	pronto
often	always	Julian	rarely
passé	annual	Lammas	recent
pause	at once	lapsed	season

second	bad time	Flag day	morning
seldom	bedtime	for good	New Year
sooner	belated	for life	newborn
spring	betimes	foreday	nightly
sudden	*bientôt*	forever	noonday
summer	boyhood	harvest	October
Sunday	by-and-by	high day	one-time
sunset	calends	history	overdue
timely	century	holiday	pending
to date	chiliad	holy day	pendule
update	current	infancy	pip emma
vernal	dawning	instant	postwar
vesper	daylong	interim	present
weekly	day-peep	Iron Age	proximo
whilst	daytime	January	quarter
winter	diurnal	Jazz age	quondam
yearly	dog days	journal	Ramadan
yester	earlier	jubilee	ripe age
abiding	elapsed	just now	Sabbath
ack emma	endless	kalends	secular
ageless	ephebic	Lady day	shortly
ages ago	epochal	long ago	*sine die*
all over	equinox	long run	someday
almanac	estival	lustrum	stretch
already	evening	manhood	Sukkoth
ancient	exactly	manhour	sundial
anytime	expired	matinal	sundown
archaic	extinct	mid-week	sunrise
at night	Fast day	monthly	teen age

tertian	calendar	fleeting
thereon	calf days	foredawn
this day	cockcrow	forenoon
Tib's eve	Dark Ages	formerly
time was	darkling	frequent
time-lag	date line	gain time
tonight	daybreak	gloaming
too late	daylight	half hour
too soon	deadline	half past
Tuesday	December	Hanukkah
twinkle	Derby day	hereunto
two two's	directly	hibernal
unready	dogwatch	high time
up to now	doomsday	hitherto
usually	duration	Hogmanay
weekday	egg-timer	holy days
weekend	embolism	Holy week
whereon	enduring	horology
whitsun	entr'acte	ill-timed
a long day	Epiphany	in a flash
abruptly	eternity	in a trice
antedate	eventide	in future
as soon as	evermore	in no time
biannual	every day	in season
biennial	evil hour	infinity
birthday	*Fasching*	interval
biweekly	fast time	juncture
blue moon	feast day	keep time
Brumaire	February	kill time

lang syne	not often	Steel Age
last time	November	Stone Age
last week	nowadays	suddenly
lateness	obsolete	take time
latterly	occasion	temporal
leap year	ofttimes	this week
lifelong	Old Style	Thursday
life-span	old times	time-ball
lifetime	on the dot	timeless
livelong	our times	time-worn
long time	pass time	tomorrow
Lord's day	Passover	too early
lose time	postdate	twilight
lunation	postpone	ultimate
make time	previous	until now
mark time	promptly	untimely
mean time	punctual	up-to-date
meantime	recently	weeklong
medieval	right now	whenever
menology	ringtime	Whitweek
meridian	Saturday	year-book
meteoric	seasonal	yearlong
midnight	seedtime	years ago
momently	semester	yoretime
natal day	Shabuoth	Yuletide
New Style	solstice	zone time
next week	sometime	adulthood
noontide	Space Age	after that
noontime	sporadic	after time

afternoon
all at once
antiquity
at present
Atomic Age
bimonthly
Boxing Day
Bronze Age
Candlemas
canicular
centenary
childhood
Christmas
chronicle
civil time
civil year
clepsydra
continual
crepuscle
dawnlight
days of old
dayspring
decennary
decennial
decennium
due season
earliness
early bird
ember days

Empire day
ephemeral
ephemeris
epochally
erstwhile
ever since
every hour
far future
first time
foregoing
forthwith
fortnight
from now on
Gilded Age
Golden Age
great year
Gregorian
Hallowe'en
Hallowmas
happy days
hereafter
honeymoon
hourglass
immediacy
immediate
impromptu
in a second
in due time
in the past

instanter
instantly
interlude
Lammas day
later date
latter day
legal year
light year
local time
long since
long spell
long while
longevity
long-lived
lunar year
Mad decade
many a time
many times
Mardi Gras
Martinmas
mature age
matutinal
meanwhile
mediaeval
menstrual
metronome
middle age
midsummer
midwinter

mistiming	right time	timetable
momentary	St. Tib's Eve	times past
monthlong	Saint's day	to this day
nevermore	salad days	transient
nightfall	sandglass	triennial
nightlong	semestral	twinkling
nighttide	September	two shakes
nighttime	short time	upon which
nocturnal	short-term	vicennial
octennial	solar time	waste time
oftentime	solar year	Wednesday
opportune	sometimes	well-timed
out of date	space time	wherefore
overnight	spare time	whereunto
Pentecost	spend time	whereupon
perennial	stop watch	wrong time
permanent	Swiss plan	yesterday
postcenal	temporary	after which
preceding	temporize	afterwards
precisely	therewith	alarm clock
premature	these days	all the time
presently	till death	Allhallows
prolepsis	time being	anno Domini
quarter to	time check	ante-bellum
quarterly	time clock	at all times
quotidian	time flies	at that time
recurrent	time limit	at this time
regularly	time of day	before long
remote age	timepiece	beforehand

beforetime	frequently	Middle Ages
behind time	futuristic	middle-aged
behindhand	generation	midmorning
better days	Good Friday	millennium
break of day	half a jiffy	moratorium
by the clock	half a shake	Mother's day
bygone days	half an hour	near future
centennial	hardly ever	nick of time
childermas	hebdomadal	now or never
chronogram	Hebrew year	occasional
chronology	henceforth	of the clock
close of day	here and now	olden times
common time	heretofore	on occasion
consequent	historical	on the eve of
constantly	immemorial	one fine day
continuous	in good time	post-bellum
cosmic time	incidental	posthumous
crepuscule	incunabula	prehistory
days gone by	invariably	present day
days of yore	isochronon	previously
Easter Time	Julian year	proper time
Eastertide	just in time	repeatedly
evanescent	Lammastide	retrospect
eventually	last chance	ripe old age
Father Time	last minute	Sabbath day
Father's day	Lententide	seasonable
fiscal year	lunar month	semiweekly
fleetingly	Methuselah	septennial
flow of time	Michaelmas	sextennial

short spell	wristwatch	day and night
small hours	years on end	day in, day out
soon enough	yesteryear	dead of night
springtide	a woman's year	Dominion Day
springtime	adjournment	duskingtide
subsequent	adolescence	endless time
summertide	after-dinner	ever and a day
summertime	against time	ever and anon
thereafter	ahead of time	everlasting
this minute	All Fool's Day	every moment
time signal	All Soul's day	Feast of Lots
time-keeper	anachronism	*fin de siècle*
time to come	anchor watch	flower of age
time to kill	anniversary	forevermore
timeliness	at intervals	former times
transitory	bicentenary	fortnightly
tricennial	bygone times	Gay Nineties
triple time	ceaselessly	golden hours
ultimately	chronograph	good old days
very seldom	chronometer	halcyon days
vespertime	chronoscope	half a second
water clock	coincidence	hebdomadary
wedding day	concurrence	hereinafter
whensoever	continually	hush of night
Whitmonday	contretemps	ides of March
Whitsunday	crack of dawn	immediately
wintertide	crepuscular	in an instant
wintertime	cuckoo clock	in due course
with the sun	day after day	incessantly

inopportune	perennially	time to spare
interregnum	perfect year	*tout à l'heure*
Judgment day	perpetually	turret clock
lapse of time	play for time	twelvemonth
leisure time	point of time	ultramodern
little while	present time	waiting time
livelong day	prime of life	White Sunday
long overdue	prochronism	Whitsuntide
long-lasting	promptitude	with the lark
march of time	punctuality	Year of Grace
Mauve decade	quadrennial	a long time ago
microsecond	quarter past	all of a sudden
middle years	sands of time	All Saint's day
millisecond	semimonthly	Allhallowmas
modern times	shining hour	ancient times
momentarily	short notice	Annunciation
morning time	some time ago	ante meridiem
morningtide	split second	antediluvian
never-ending	straightway	antemeridian
New Year's day	synchronize	apparent time
New Year's eve	synchronism	Armistice day
night and day	*tempus fugit*	Ascension day
on the morrow	the other day	Ash Wednesday
once or twice	thenceforth	auld lang syne
opportunely	this morning	bide one's time
opportunity	this very day	calendar year
out of season	time and tide	Candlemas day
Passion week	time drags by	Christmas day
penultimate	time machine	Christmas eve

consequently	many a long day	sidereal time
contemporary	metachronism	sidereal year
course of time	nychthemeron	simultaneous
decisive hour	occasionally	stall for time
decline of day	old-fashioned	standard time
donkey's years	on the instant	still of night
eleventh hour	once in a while	stitch in time
Feast of Asses	one's born days	synodic month
Feast of Fools	parachronism	tercentenary
Feast of Weeks	periodically	the dawn of day
following day	Platonic year	the year round
fourth of July	post meridiem	then and there
from that time	postdiluvian	time and again
Greek calends	postmeridian	time will tell
Holy Thursday	postponement	time-honoured
in days of yore	postprandial	timelessness
in olden times	Quadragesima	turning point
Indian summer	quinquennial	Twelfth-night
Innocents' Day	quinquennium	twelve o'clock
intermission	rare occasion	unseasonable
late in the day	red letter day	witching hour
long-standing	sempiternity	without delay

Weights, Measures, Coins

This section includes list of weights and measures, dry and liquid—length and breadth—volume and area—instruments for measuring—coins, past and present, foreign and slang terms.

A.U.	ohm	cash	kyat	pony
as	pai	cent	link	quid
lb	pie	chip	lira	real
oz	rad	coin	mark	reis
amp	rem	dime	mass	rial
are	rep	doit	merk	rood
B.T.U.	rod	dram	mile	rule
bit	sen	duit	mill	ryal
bob	sol	dyne	mint	size
cab	sou	écus	mite	spit
cwt	ton	foot	mole	step
écu	yen	gill	norm	tape
ell	acre	gram	pace	thou
erg	anna	gros	peck	volt
kip	area	hand	peso	watt
log	atom	hour	phon	week
mag	B.Th.U.	inch	phot	yard
meg	barn	iota	pint	year
mil	bean	kilo	plum	angel
mph	buck	knot	pole	angle

asper	gross	pound	bawbee
asses	henry	quart	besant
belga	hertz	ruble	bovate
broad	homer	ruler	bushel
carat	joule	rupee	calory
chain	krona	saiga	cental
chera	krone	scale	chopin
colon	level	sceat	copack
conto	libra	score	copper
crown	litre	semis	cupful
cubit	livre	soldo	decade
curie	louis	stere	decare
cycle	lumen	stone	décime
daric	massa	styca	degree
depth	medal	sucre	denier
dinar	meter	tanka	dirhem
dozen	metre	therm	dollar
ducat	minim	third	drachm
eagle	mohur	toise	escudo
farad	month	toman	fathom
fermi	noble	tonne	finger
fiver	obang	uncia	florin
folio	paolo	unite	follis
franc	pence	ampere	gallon
gauge	penny	armful	gramme
gerah	perch	arpent	guinea
grain	piece	aureus	gulden
grand	plumb	azteca	height
groat	point	barrel	kilerg

kopeck	solidi	dry pint	pfennig
league	specie	exergue	piastre
length	square	furlong	poundal
lepton	stater	gilbert	quarter
linear	stiver	granule	quintal
magnum	tanner	guilder	red cent
megohm	tenner	ha'penny	reverse
micron	tester	hectare	röntgen
minute	teston	hundred	rouleau
monkey	thaler	iron man	sawbuck
myriad	triens	jillion	sceatta
net ton	volume	Kai-yuan	scruple
nickel	billion	kiloton	section
nonius	breadth	lambert	sextans
oxgang	calibre	leopard	sextant
oxgate	calorie	log line	sixfold
oxland	centava	long bit	smacker
parsec	centime	long ton	solidus
peseta	centimo	maximum	T square
photon	centner	maxwell	ten spot
proton	century	millier	tenfold
radian	chiliad	milreis	testoon
rouble	compass	minimum	tonneau
scudos	cordoba	modicum	transit
second	crusado	moidore	two bits
sector	déciare	neutron	twofold
sequin	decibel	*numisma*	umpteen
shekel	denarii	nummary	vernier
siglos	drachma	obverse	virgate

zillion	keration	spoonful
angström	kilogram	standard
assay ton	kilovolt	teaspoon
base coin	kilowatt	ten cents
calipers	land mile	thousand
carucate	louis d'or	tuppence
centiare	magneton	twopence
cruzeiro	marigold	watt-hour
decagram	megavolt	zecchino
decigram	megawatt	barometer
denarius	microbar	board-foot
didrachm	milliard	bracteate
distance	molecule	callipers
dividers	napoleon	cart-wheel
doubloon	new pence	centesimo
dry quart	new penny	centigram
electron	ninefold	cistorphi
farthing	particle	cubic foot
fivefold	picayune	cubic inch
fourfold	planchet	cubic mile
fraction	quadrans	cubic yard
gold coin	quadrant	decalitre
gram atom	roentgen	decametre
groschen	semissis	decastere
gross ton	semuncia	decilitre
half-life	shilling	decimetre
hogshead	short bit	dekameter
inch tape	short ton	dupondius
inchmeal	sixpence	eightfold

9–10

fluid dram	plumb line	decagramme
fourpence	pound mole	decigramme
fourpenny	pound tray	dry measure
gold crown	quinarius	elevenfold
gold penny	rose-noble	Fahrenheit
gold piece	schilling	fluid ounce
half-crown	set square	foot pounds
half-eagle	sevenfold	gold florin
half-noble	size stick	gradometer
halfpenny	slide rule	half a crown
hectogram	sovereign	half dollar
kilocycle	thickness	half solidi
kilolitre	threefold	hectolitre
kilometre	tremissis	hemidrachm
light year	troy ounce	horse power
long-cross	try square	kilogramme
medallion	umpteenth	liquid pint
megacurie	vicesimal	megaparsec
megacycle	vigesimal	*mètre carré*
metric ton	yardstick	microcurie
microbarn	yellow boy	micrometer
milestone	zwanziger	millicurie
millenary	carat grain	millilitre
millibarn	centennial	mint legend
milligram	Centigrade	multicurie
myriagram	centilitre	myriameter
nonillion	centimetre	nanosecond
ounce troy	centistere	planimeter
pistareen	decadrachm	protractor

reichsmark	double eagle	thermal unit
Rutherford	foot poundal	thermometer
sestertius	George noble	undecennary
sexagenary	hundredfold	undecennial
short-cross	kilocalorie	antoninianus
siege-piece	liquid quart	base shilling
silver joey	long million	electronvolt
square feet	magic number	golden guinea
square foot	mean calorie	gram molecule
square inch	metric carat	Gunter's scale
square mile	microsecond	hairsbreadth
square yard	milligramme	imperial coin
tablespoon	millimicron	imperial pint
theodolite	millisecond	kilowatt-hour
thimbleful	pennyweight	large calorie
threepence	piece of gold	measured mile
troy weight	quadrillion	metric system
twelvefold	sexagesimal	miles per hour
volt-ampere	silver crown	milliröntgen
avoirdupois	silver penny	nautical mile
baker's dozen	sixpenny bit	piece of eight
bonnet-piece	spirit level	piece of money
cable-length	square metre	quarter-noble
candle power	statute mile	silver dollar
centigramme	tape measure	small calorie
cool million	teaspoonful	straightedge
decimal point	tetradrachm	thousandfold

PEOPLE AT HOME, WORK AND PLAY

This general heading includes sections for People and Jobs; Sports, Games and Pastimes; Clothing and Household, Food and Drink.

People and Jobs

This section includes list of jobs, professions, occupations, crafts and trades—payment—criminals —sportsmen—scholars and students—relatives— musicians—clerics—literary men—soldiers and rank —racial types.

A.B.	Mr.	doc	lad	rip	beak
B.A.	ma	don	Mrs.	sir	bear
C.A.	P.A.	dux	man	son	beau
CO.	P.M.	fan	mum	sot	bore
D.D.	pa	fop	N.C.O.	spy	boss
Dr.	ace	guy	nun	tar	bull
G.I.	ass	hag	oaf	vet	Celt
G.P.	B.Sc.	ham	P.R.O.	wit	chap
M.A.	boy	hex	pal	aide	char
M.C.	C.I.D.	job	pay	aunt	chef
M.D.	cad	kid	R.S.M.	babe	chum
M.O.	dad	kin	rat	baby	cook
M.P.	deb	L.D.S.	rep	bard	cove

crew	lass	twin	caddy	dummy
curé	lead	twit	cadet	dunce
dean	liar	tyro	canon	dutch
demy	lout	wage	caser	elder
dick	magi	ward	chair	enemy
diva	maid	whip	cheat	envoy
doll	mate	wife	chief	exile
dolt	mime	work	child	extra
doxy	minx	abbot	chips	fakir
drip	miss	actor	chore	felon
dude	monk	ad-man	chump	fence
dupe	ogre	adult	clerk	fiend
dyer	page	agent	clown	fifer
feed	peer	aider	coach	flirt
firm	peon	alien	comic	fraud
fool	poet	angel	crank	freak
girl	pope	aunty	crier	friar
G-man	prig	baboo	crone	Galen
gull	rake	baker	crony	ghost
hack	sage	belle	crook	gipsy
hand	salt	bigot	cynic	grass
head	seer	blade	daddy	groom
heel	serf	blood	dandy	guard
heir	silk	boots	decoy	guest
hero	sire	bosun	devil	guide
hick	snob	boxer	diver	hewer
hobo	star	bride	donor	hussy
host	task	bully	doyen	idler
kith	toff	buyer	drone	in-law

issue	nanny	saver	twins
joker	navvy	sawer	uhlan
Judas	Negro	scamp	uncle
judge	niece	scion	usher
juror	nomad	scold	valet
knave	nurse	scout	vicar
laird	odist	sewer	viner
limey	owner	shrew	vixen
local	padre	siren	wages
locum	party	slave	wench
loser	pater	smith	widow
lover	pilot	sneak	witch
luter	pin-up	sonny	woman
madam	piper	sower	yokel
major	posse	spark	youth
maker	prior	sport	abbess
Maori	proxy	staff	ad-mass
mason	prude	stoic	agnate
mater	pupil	tenor	air ace
mayor	puppy	thief	airman
medic	quack	tiler	albino
mimic	quill	toady	alumna
miner	rabbi	tommy	Amazon
minor	racer	toper	apache
miser	rider	trade	archer
model	rival	tramp	artist
moron	rogue	trier	*au pair*
mouse	rover	tuner	auntie
mummy	saint	tutor	aurist

author	bursar	cousin	escort
backer	busker	coward	Eskimo
bandit	butler	cowboy	etcher
banker	cabbie	Creole	expert
barber	caddie	critic	fabler
barfly	cadger	curate	factor
bargee	caller	cutter	faggot
barker	camper	damsel	fantod
barman	canter	dancer	father
Basque	cantor	deacon	fawner
batman	captor	dealer	feeder
batter	career	debtor	fellow
beadle	carper	deputy	fiancé
bearer	carter	divine	fibber
beater	carver	docker	fictor
beggar	casual	doctor	fitter
beauty	censor	dodger	flunky
beldam	chaser	dotard	flyman
Berber	cleric	double	forger
bibber	codist	dowser	frater
bishop	con man	draper	friend
blonde	consul	drawer	fuller
boffin	coolie	driver	gaffer
bomber	cooper	drudge	gagman
bookie	copier	duenna	ganger
bowman	copper	duffer	gaoler
brewer	co-star	editor	*garçon*
broker	coster	egoist	gasbag
bugler	couper	ensign	gaucho

gay dog	hymner	living	musico
genius	ice-man	loafer	mystic
German	infant	lodger	nannie
gigolo	inmate	looter	native
gillie	intern	lutist	nephew
glazer	jailer	lyrist	nobody
glover	jester	madman	Norman
golfer	jet set	maiden	notary
gossip	jobber	marine	novice
graver	jockey	marker	nudist
grocer	joiner	martyr	nuncio
grouch	jumper	master	nuncle
grower	junior	matron	oboist
gunman	junker	medico	odd job
gunner	junkie	medium	office
hatter	keeper	member	ogress
hawker	killer	menial	oilman
healer	lackey	mentor	old boy
helper	lancer	mercer	optime
hep-cat	lascar	mikado	oracle
herald	lawyer	miller	orator
hermit	layman	minion	orphan
hetman	leader	mister	ostler
high-up	lector	moiler	outlaw
hippie	legate	monger	packer
hosier	lender	moppet	parent
humbug	lessee	mortal	pariah
hunter	Levite	mother	parson
hussar	limner	mummer	pastor

patron	regius	sentry	sutler
pedant	rhymer	sexton	tailor
pedlar	rigger	shadow	talent
penman	ringer	sheila	tanner
pen-pal	rioter	shower	Tartar
picket	roamer	singer	taster
pieman	robber	sinner	tatter
pirate	Romany	sister	teller
pitman	rookie	skater	tenant
plater	rotter	skivvy	Teuton
player	rouper	skyman	tiller
Pommie	runner	slater	tinker
porter	rustic	slavey	tinner
potter	sadist	slayer	toiler
prater	sailor	sleuth	trader
priest	sapper	smoker	truant
pundit	sartor	sniper	turner
punter	savage	soaker	tycoon
puppet	savant	soutar	typist
purist	sawyer	souter	tyrant
purser	scorer	sowter	umpire
rabbin	scouse	sparks	urchin
ragman	scribe	spouse	usurer
ranger	sea-dog	square	valuer
rascal	sealer	squire	vandal
rating	seaman	status	vanman
reader	second	stoker	vendor
reaper	seller	stooge	verger
rector	senior	suitor	victor

Viking	almoner	big name	caveman
virago	also-ran	big shot	'cellist
voyeur	alumnus	bit-part	Charlie
waiter	amateur	blender	charmer
walk-on	analyst	boarder	chauvin
warden	ancient	boaster	cheater
warder	apostle	boatman	chemist
Watson	arbiter	bookman	chindit
weaver	artisan	bouncer	chorist
welder	artiste	bounder	citizen
whaler	ascetic	breeder	cleaner
winner	assayer	brigand	climber
wizard	athlete	brother	clippie
worker	attaché	bucolic	coalman
worthy	auditor	buffoon	cobbler
wretch	avenger	builder	cockney
wright	aviator	bumpkin	cognate
writer	babbler	burglar	colleen
yeoman	bailiff	bushman	collier
zealot	ballboy	butcher	colonel
zombie	bandman	buttons	commère
abetter	barmaid	callboy	company
abigail	bassist	calling	compère
acolyte	beatnik	cambist	comrade
acrobat	Bedouin	captain	consort
actress	beldame	captive	convert
actuary	bellboy	carrier	convict
admiral	bellhop	cashier	co-pilot
adviser	best man	caulker	copy cat

copyist	devotee	escaper	gambler
copyman	diehard	esquire	gate-man
coroner	dilutee	fall-guy	general
corsair	diviner	famulus	ghillie
Cossack	dominie	fanatic	glazier
counsel	doorman	farcist	gleaner
courier	doubter	farrier	glutton
cowherd	dowager	fathead	gourmet
cowpoke	dragoon	fiancée	grown-up
coxcomb	drapier	fiddler	grummet
creator	drayman	fighter	gun moll
crofter	dreamer	filcher	gymnast
crooner	dresser	fireman	haggler
cropper	drifter	fish-fag	half-wit
cry baby	driller	flagman	handler
cuckold	drinker	*flâneur*	hangdog
culprit	drummer	flapper	hangman
curator	dullard	flesher	hard man
custode	dustman	florist	harpist
cuttler	egghead	flutist	has-been
cyclist	eggmass	footboy	haulier
dabbler	egotist	footman	head boy
dallier	elogist	footpad	headman
danseur	embassy	foreman	heckler
darling	entrant	founder	heiress
daysman	epicure	frogman	hellcat
debater	equerry	furrier	hellier
denizen	eremite	gabbler	heretic
dentist	escapee	gallant	heroine

hipster	learner	modiste	patriot
histrio	liberal	monitor	patroon
hoodlum	lie-abed	moulder	Paul Pry
hostess	lineman	mourner	peasant
hothead	linkboy	Mr Right	pianist
hotspur	linkman	mud-lark	pierrot
husband	lockman	navarch	pilgrim
hustler	look-out	Negress	pioneer
hymnist	lorimer	Negrito	planner
imagist	lounger	newsboy	planter
in-crowd	lowbrow	newsman	playboy
inditer	lunatic	oarsman	plumber
infidel	maestro	oculist	poacher
invalid	magnate	oddball	poetess
Jack-tar	mailman	officer	pollman
janitor	magnate	old fogy	poloist
jemedar	manager	old maid	pontiff
Jezebel	mankind	old salt	poor man
Joe Soap	man's man	omnibus	pop idol
juggler	mariner	oratrix	pop star
junkman	marshal	orderly	post-boy
justice	masseur	outcast	postman
kindred	matador	page-boy	prefect
kingpin	matelot	painter	prelate
kinsman	meatman	paragon	premier
knacker	meddler	partner	presser
knitter	midwife	parvenu	primate
know-all	milkman	passman	printer
know-how	mobsman	patient	privado
	mobster		

private	routine	show-off	taborer
proctor	ruffian	shyster	tapster
prodigy	runaway	sibling	teacher
progeny	sad sack	skinner	thinker
proofer	saddler	skipper	tippler
prophet	sagaman	slacker	tipster
protégé	samurai	soldier	tosspot
provost	sandman	soloist	tourist
prowler	saviour	sophist	trainee
puddler	scalper	soprano	trainer
punster	scenist	sparrer	traitor
puritan	sceptic	speaker	trapper
pursuer	scholar	spinner	trawler
radical	scraper	sponger	tripper
railman	Scrooge	sponsor	trooper
rancher	sea-cook	spotter	trouper
rat race	sea-king	stand-by	trueman
realtor	sea-lord	starlet	tumbler
recluse	sea-wolf	starman	turfman
redhead	seminar	station	twister
redskin	senator	stepson	upstart
referee	servant	steward	veteran
refugee	service	stipend	viceroy
regular	sharper	student	villain
remover	shearer	supremo	vintner
rescuer	sheriff	surgeon	visitor
reserve	shopman	suspect	vulture
retinue	shopper	swagman	warrior
rich man	showman	swinger	wastrel

webster	alter ego	benefice	castaway
welcher	altruist	betrayer	cenobite
welsher	ambivert	big noise	ceramist
whipcat	ancestor	bigamist	chairman
whipper	anchoret	blackleg	chambers
widower	anti-hero	blighter	champion
windbag	antipope	blind man	chandler
wise guy	apostate	blowhard	chaperon
wiseman	armorist	bluenose	chaplain
witness	armourer	boardman	children
wolf cub	arranger	Bohemian	choirboy
woodman	assassin	bondsman	cicerone
woolman	assessor	boniface	cicisbeo
workman	*assoluta*	borrower	civilian
workshy	attacker	botanist	claimant
wrecker	attorney	bowmaker	clansman
abductor	axemaker	boxmaker	class man
adherent	bachelor	boy scout	clerkess
adjutant	bagmaker	braggart	clothier
advocate	banjoist	brunette	co-author
aeronaut	bankrupt	bunkoman	comedian
aesthete	banksman	business	commando
aetheist	banterer	busybody	commoner
agitator	bargeman	cabin boy	compiler
agnostic	baritone	calendar	composer
alarmist	beadsman	call-girl	conjurer
alderman	bedesman	canoness	convener
alienist	bedmaker	cardinal	corporal
allopath	beginner	carouser	coryphée

cottager	dogsbody	fanfaron
courtier	domestic	fanmaker
coxswain	dragoman	farm hand
crackpot	druggist	feminist
creditor	drunkard	ferryman
criminal	duettist	figurant
croupier	educator	film idol
cupmaker	elegiast	filmstar
cutpurse	embalmer	finalist
dairyman	emeritus	fine lady
danseuse	emigrant	finisher
daughter	emissary	fishwife
deceiver	employee	flatfoot
deck hand	engineer	flautist
defector	engraver	floorman
delegate	epic poet	folk-hero
derelict	essayist	follower
deserter	eulogist	forester
designer	everyman	forgeman
detainee	evildoer	freshman
dictator	examinee	front man
diet cook	examiner	fugitive
diocesan	executor	funnyman
diplomat	explorer	fusilier
director	exponent	gadabout
dirty dog	exporter	gamester
disciple	fabulist	gangsman
divorcee	factotum	gangster
do-gooder	falconer	gaolbird

gardener	henchman	investor
garroter	herdsman	islander
gendarme	highbrow	jabberer
goatherd	hijacker	jailbird
gourmand	hired gun	jawsmith
governor	hired man	jet pilot
gownsman	hireling	jeweller
graduate	home help	jingoist
grandson	hooligan	John Bull
great man	horseman	jongleur
guardian	hotelier	juvenile
guerilla	houseboy	knife-boy
gunmaker	houseman	labourer
gunsmith	hula girl	lame duck
ham actor	humorist	land-girl
handmaid	huntsman	landlady
handyman	identity	landlord
hanger-on	idolater	landsman
hatmaker	idyllist	lapidary
hawkshaw	imbecile	law agent
haymaker	importer	lawgiver
head cook	impostor	law-maker
head girl	inceptor	layabout
headship	informer	laywoman
Hebraist	initiate	lecturer
hectorer	inkmaker	licensee
hedonist	innocent	life-peer
helmsman	intruder	life-work
helpmeet	inventor	linesman

linguist	millhand	observer
listener	milliner	occupant
livewire	minister	occultist
logician	ministry	offender
loiterer	minstrel	official
lone wolf	mistress	old Dutch
long hair	mittimus	onlooker
looker-on	modeller	op artist
lowlifer	moralist	operator
lumberer	motorist	opponent
luminary	muleteer	optician
lyricist	muralist	optimist
macaroni	murderer	oratress
magician	musician	organist
mandarin	Napoleon	outsider
man-hater	narrator	overlord
mapmaker	naturist	overseer
marauder	neophyte	pacifist
marksman	nepotist	paleface
martinet	netmaker	paramour
masseuse	newcomer	parasite
mayoress	news-hawk	pardoner
mechanic	nightman	parodist
mediator	nihilist	partisan
melodist	Norseman	party-man
mercator	novelist	passer-by
merchant	nuisance	patentee
milkmaid	numskull	penitent
millgirl	objector	penmaker

perfumer	purveyor	rugmaker
perjurer	quackery	saboteur
picaroon	quarrier	salesman
pilferer	quisling	salvager
pillager	radar man	satirist
plagiary	rag-trade	saucebox
plebeian	ragwoman	sawbones
poetling	rakehell	sawsmith
poisoner	receiver	scalawag
polisher	recorder	sciolist
poltroon	reformer	scullion
pontifex	relation	sculptor
poor soul	relative	seacunny
popinjay	renegade	seafarer
position	reporter	seedsman
potmaker	research	selector
practice	resident	sentinel
prattler	retailer	sergeant
preacher	retainer	servitor
pressman	reveller	shepherd
prioress	revenant	shipmate
prisoner	reviewer	shopgirl
prizeman	rewriter	showgirl
producer	rifleman	side-kick
promoter	rivetter	silk gown
prompter	road-gang	sinecure
psychist	romancer	sketcher
publican	romantic	sky-scout
pugilist	rotarian	slattern

small fry	swagsman	underdog
smuggler	swindler	union man
solitary	sybarite	unionist
somatist	tallyman	vagabond
somebody	taxpayer	valuator
songster	teddy boy	vanguard
son-in-law	teen-ager	virtuoso
sorcerer	tell-tale	vocalist
sorehead	thatcher	vocation
spaceman	theorist	waitress
spearman	Thespian	ward maid
speed cop	thurifer	wardress
spinster	tightwad	watchman
spitfire	tin miner	waterman
sprinter	tinsmith	wayfarer
stageman	Tom Thumb	wet nurse
star turn	tone poet	wheelman
stockman	top brass	whiphand
storeman	toreador	whipjack
stowaway	torturer	whittler
stranger	townsman	whizz-kid
stripper	trainman	wigmaker
stroller	tripeman	wise fool
stunt man	triplets	wiseacre
superior	truchman	woodsman
superman	truckler	workfolk
supplier	tunester	workgirl
surveyor	turncoat	workhand
survivor	two-timer	wrangler

wrestler	attendant	bootblack
yodeller	authoress	bootmaker
aborigine	authority	boy friend
absconder	automaton	boy wonder
accessory	axlesmith	brass-hats
admiralty	bacchanal	brigadier
adulterer	balladist	buccaneer
adversary	ballerina	bus driver
aerialist	barbarian	bush pilot
alchemist	bargainer	bystander
alcoholic	barrister	cab driver
anatomist	barrow boy	cabin crew
anchoress	battle-axe	café-owner
anchorite	beefeater	cakemaker
annotator	bee-keeper	calendrer
announcer	beermaker	cameraman
antiquary	beggarman	candidate
apologist	bellmaker	canvasser
applicant	big talker	cardsharp
appraiser	biologist	career man
arch-enemy	bit player	careerist
architect	Bluebeard	caretaker
archivist	blusterer	carpenter
art critic	boatswain	casemaker
art dealer	bodyguard	celebrity
artificer	bodymaker	cellarman
assistant	boilerman	centurion
associate	boltsmith	chain-gang
astronaut	bookmaker	character

charlatan
chartered
charterer
charwoman
chatterer
chauffeur
chiseller
choralist
chorus boy
churchman
clergyman
clinician
clogmaker
coadjutor
coal miner
coenobite
colleague
collector
columnist
combatant
comforter
commander
commodore
companion
concierge
concubine
conductor
confessor
confidant

conqueror
conscript
consenter
constable
contender
contralto
cornerboy
cosmonaut
cost clerk
costumier
coughdrop
court fool
couturier
covergirl
crackshot
cracksman
craftsman
crayonist
cricketer
cupbearer
custodian
cutthroat
cymbalist
daily help
dark horse
day-labour
deaconess
dean of men
debutante

decorator
defeatist
defendant
defrauder
demagogue
dependent
desert rat
designate
desk clerk
desperado
detective
dialogist
dietician
dignitary
dispenser
dissenter
dogmatist
dog-walker
dollmaker
dramatist
drum major
drysalter
early bird
eccentric
ecologist
economist
Edwardian
embezzler
emolument

enamelist
enchanter
engrosser
entourage
errand boy
espionage
estimator
exchanger
exchequer
exciseman
executive
exploiter
exquisite
extravert
extrovert
eye doctor
family man
favourite
fieldwork
figurante
film actor
film extra
film-maker
financier
fire-eater
fire-guard
first mate
firstborn
fisherman

flag waver
forebears
foreigner
fossicker
foundling
free agent
freelance
freemason
fruiterer
furnisher
garreteer
garrotter
gas-fitter
gazetteer
gem-cutter
gentleman
geologist
girl guide
gladiator
gluemaker
go-between
godfather
godmother
goldsmith
gondolier
good mixer
governess
grand-aunt
grape-vine

great-aunt
greenhorn
grenadier
guarantor
guardsman
guerrilla
guest star
guitarist
gun-runner
hand sewer
harbinger
harbourer
hard graft
harebrain
harlequin
harmonist
harpooner
harvester
head clerk
Hellenist
hello girl
herbalist
hill-billy
hired hand
hired help
historian
hold-upman
home-maker
homeopath

honest man	kinswoman	liveryman
honour man	lacemaker	loan agent
Hottentot	lady's maid	lockmaker
house dick	ladies' man	locksmith
housemaid	lampmaker	log-roller
husbandry	lampooner	lord mayor
hypnotist	land-agent	lost sheep
hypocrite	land-force	loud-mouth
ignoramus	land-owner	lowlander
immigrant	landreeve	lumberman
in service	land-shark	machinist
inamorata	larcenist	major domo
increment	late riser	major poet
incumbent	launderer	make-up man
inebriate	laundress	male model
innkeeper	lawmonger	male nurse
inscriber	lay-figure	man-at-arms
inside man	lay-reader	man Friday
inspector	lay-sister	man of mark
interview	lazybones	man of note
introvert	legionary	man-slayer
ironminer	lensmaker	masochist
ironsmith	libertine	matriarch
jay-walker	librarian	medallist
jitterbug	lifeguard	mendicant
jobholder	life's work	mercenary
key worker	linotyper	mesmerist
kid sister	liontamer	messenger
kidnapper	lip-reader	middleman

minor poet	pacemaker	pitwright
modelgirl	panellist	plaintiff
monitress	pantomime	plasterer
moon-raker	part-owner	ploughboy
mortician	passenger	ploughman
muscle-man	patriarch	plunderer
musketeer	patrician	plutocrat
mythmaker	patrolman	poetaster
navigator	patroness	poison pen
neighbour	paymaster	policeman
newsagent	paysagist	pop artist
newshound	Pecksniff	pop singer
next of kin	peculator	portrayer
nonentity	pedagogue	portreeve
non-smoker	pen-friend	possessor
nursemaid	pen-pusher	postilion
nut doctor	pensioner	postulant
occultist	performer	postwoman
odd job man	personage	poulterer
odd man out	personnel	precentor
office boy	persuader	precursor
offspring	pessimist	prelector
old master	phone girl	presbyter
old stager	physician	president
ombudsman	physicist	pretender
operative	picksmith	priestess
osteopath	Pierrette	principal
otologist	pistoleer	privateer
outfitter	pit-sawyer	professor

profiteer	sackmaker	simpleton
proudling	sacristan	situation
prud'homme	safemaker	skin-diver
publicist	sailmaker	skylarker
publisher	sales team	slowcoach
puppeteer	salesgirl	smatterer
racketeer	Samaritan	soapmaker
raconteur	sassenach	sob-sister
rainmaker	scapegoat	socialist
ransacker	scarecrow	socialite
ranzelman	scavenger	solicitor
ratefixer	scenarist	songsmith
ratepayer	scientist	sonneteer
recordist	scoundrel	sophister
reference	scrapegut	sophomore
registrar	screwball	sorceress
reprobate	scribbler	soubrette
residency	scrivener	space crew
rhymester	sea-lawyer	speedster
ringsider	secretary	spider-man
roadmaker	seneschal	spokesman
rocket man	sentryman	sportsman
rocketeer	seraskier	stage idol
roisterer	serenader	stagehand
ropemaker	sermonist	star pupil
roughneck	servitude	star-gazer
roundsman	shoemaker	statesman
rum-runner	signaller	stationer
rural dean	signalman	steersman

stevedore	tribesman	zoologist
strangler	troubador	able seaman
strike-pay	trumpeter	accomplice
strongman	tympanist	accountant
subaltern	undergrad	adventurer
sub-editor	underling	advertiser
suffragan	usherette	aeronomist
sundowner	Victorian	aficionado
suppliant	vigilante	agrologist
swaggerer	violinist	agronomist
swellhead	visionary	aide-de-camp
swineherd	volunteer	air hostess
sycophant	wanted man	air steward
tablemaid	warmonger	amanuensis
tactician	wassailer	ambassador
tailoress	waxworker	anglophile
tap dancer	week-ender	anglophobe
tax-evader	wheelsman	Anglo-Saxon
tentmaker	winemaker	antecedent
termagant	womanizer	antagonist
test pilot	womenfolk	anvilsmith
therapist	wood-reeve	apothecary
timberman	workwoman	apprentice
toolsmith	wrongdoer	arbitrator
town clerk	xenophobe	archbishop
towncrier	yachtsman	archdeacon
tradesman	youngster	archpriest
traveller	zitherist	aristocrat
treasurer	zookeeper	assignment

astrologer
astronomer
auctioneer
audit clerk
au pair girl
babe in arms
baby-sitter
ballet girl
ballplayer
bandmaster
bank robber
baseballer
bassoonist
bear-leader
beautician
bell-ringer
benefactor
best friend
Big Brother
bill-broker
billposter
biochemist
biographer
black sheep
blackguard
blacksmith
bladesmith
blockmaker
bludgeoner

bluebottle
blue-jacket
boatwright
bobbysoxer
bogtrotter
bombardier
bonesetter
bonus clerk
bookbinder
bookdealer
book-folder
bookholder
bookkeeper
bookseller
bookwright
bootlegger
bootlicker
brain-child
brain drain
brakemaker
brass-smith
brazenface
breadmaker
bricklayer
brickmaker
bridegroom
bridesmaid
broom-maker
brushmaker

bulbgrower
bumbailiff
bureaucrat
burlesquer
camera team
campaigner
career girl
cartoonist
cat breeder
cat-burglar
catechumen
cavalryman
ceramicist
chainmaker
chairmaker
chancellor
changeling
chargehand
charity boy
chatterbox
chauffeuse
chauvinist
cheesecake
chorus girl
chronicler
church-goer
cider-maker
cigar-maker
Cinderella

claim agent
clapper boy
cloakmaker
clockmaker
clocksmith
clog dancer
cloisterer
cloistress
clothmaker
clubmaster
coachmaker
coastguard
co-director
collar-work
coloratura
colporteur
comedienne
commandant
commission
competitor
compositor
concertist
confidante
consultant
contestant
contractor
controller
copyreader
copywriter

corn doctor
cornettist
coryphaeus
councillor
counsellor
country boy
countryman
couturière
cover agent
crackbrain
crosspatch
crown agent
cultivator
customs man
cytologist
daydreamer
day-tripper
dead ringer
delinquent
demoiselle
dilettante
dirty nurse
disc-jockey
discounter
discoverer
dishwasher
dispatcher
dog breeder
Don Quixote

donkey work
doorkeeper
dramatizer
dramaturge
dressmaker
drug addict
drug pusher
drummer boy
dry cleaner
Dutch uncle
duty-roster
early riser
empiricist
employment
enthusiast
equestrian
evangelist
experience
eye-witness
fabricator
faith curer
farmer's boy
fellmonger
fictionist
film editor
firemaster
fire-raiser
fishmonger
flag bearer

flight crew	goalkeeper	highlander
flower girl	gold-beater	highwayman
fly-by-night	gold-digger	hitch-hiker
folk singer	goldworker	holy orders
foot doctor	goody-goody	Home Office
footballer	grammarian	honorarium
forecaster	grand prior	horn player
forefather	grandchild	horologist
forerunner	grandniece	house agent
forty-niner	granduncle	human wreck
frame-maker	grass widow	husbandman
freebooter	great-uncle	impresario
fuddy-duddy	grindstone	incendiary
fund raiser	groceryman	incumbency
gamekeeper	gubernator	inhabitant
game-warden	gun-slinger	inquisitor
garage-hand	half-sister	instructor
gastronome	hall porter	ironmaster
gatekeeper	handmaiden	ironmonger
gatewright	handshaker	ironworker
geisha girl	hatchet man	jackanapes
geneticist	head porter	jewel thief
gentlefolk	head waiter	job printer
geochemist	headhunter	job-hunting
geographer	headmaster	journalist
girl Friday	hedgesmith	journeyman
girl friend	henchwoman	junk-dealer
glassmaker	high priest	kennelmaid
glossarist	highjacker	kid brother

kitchen-boy	loom-worker	ministress
kitchenman	lotus-eater	misogynist
kith and kin	lumberjack	missionary
knifesmith	machineman	modelmaker
lady-killer	magistrate	monopolist
land-holder	maiden aunt	moonshiner
land-jobber	mail robber	moral agent
land-lubber	malefactor	motley fool
land-pirate	malingerer	mountebank
land-waiter	man of straw	mouthpiece
lapidarist	management	naturalist
laundryman	manageress	nautch girl
lawbreaker	manicurist	naval cadet
law-officer	manservant	ne'er-do-well
lay brother	mastermind	negotiator
leading man	matchmaker	neutralist
left-winger	medical man	news editor
legislator	medicaster	newscaster
liberty-man	merrymaker	news-vendor
librettist	message boy	news-writer
licentiate	Methuselah	next friend
lieutenant	middlebrow	night float
lighterman	midshipman	night nurse
lime-burner	militarist	non-starter
linotypist	militiaman	notability
livelihood	millwright	nurseryman
lobsterman	mind-curist	obituarist
lock-keeper	mind-healer	occupation
loggerhead	mind-reader	oil painter

old soldier
pall-bearer
pantomimic
pantry maid
paper-maker
park-keeper
park-ranger
past master
pastry-cook
pathfinder
pawnbroker
peacemaker
pearl-diver
pearly king
pedestrian
pediatrist
pedicurist
peeping Tom
penologist
perruquier
petitioner
pharmacist
philistine
piano tuner
piccoloist
pickpocket
piermaster
plagiarist
platelayer

playbroker
playwright
playwriter
poet-artist
poet-farmer
poet-priest
politician
postmaster
pragmatist
prebendary
priesthood
prima donna
private-eye
procurator
profession
programmer
prolocutor
proprietor
prospector
proveditor
psychiater
psychopath
questioner
quiz-master
railwayman
raw recruit
recidivist
recitalist
researcher

retirement
revenue man
revivalist
rhapsodist
ringleader
ringmaster
roadmender
ropedancer
ropewalker
safeblower
sales clerk
sales force
saleswoman
saltworker
sand-dancer
schoolma'am
scrub nurse
scrutineer
sculptress
sea-captain
seamstress
second mate
secularist
seminarian
sempstress
serologist
serviceman
session man
seventh son

shanghaier
shipwright
shopfitter
shopkeeper
shoplifter
signwriter
sinologist
smart aleck
sneak thief
social lion
son and heir
songstress
sound-mixer
spacewoman
specialist
speculator
spoilsport
spy-catcher
squanderer
staff nurse
starmonger
steelmaker
step dancer
stepfather
stepmother
stepsister
stewardess
stick-up man
stockrider

stocktaker
stonemason
storesmith
strategist
street arab
submariner
subscriber
substitute
sugar-daddy
supercargo
supervisor
supplicant
sweetheart
swordsmith
symphonist
syncopator
tally clerk
tallywoman
taskmaster
taxi-dancer
technician
technocrat
televiewer
tenderfoot
theatreman
third party
tilewright
timekeeper
time-server

trafficker
translator
triphound
tripe-woman
troglodyte
trombonist
tub-thumper
tweedledee
tweedledum
typesetter
typing pool
underagent
understudy
undertaker
upper crust
utopianist
vacillator
vegetarian
versemaker
versesmith
veterinary
vice-consul
vice-master
victualler
vine-grower
wage-earner
wageworker
wainwright
wallflower

watchmaker	appointment	braggadocio
water-guard	army officer	breadwinner
well-wisher	astrologist	bridgemaker
wharfinger	astronomist	broadcaster
wholesaler	atomologist	bronzesmith
winebibber	audio typist	bull-fighter
wine-waiter	backroom boy	bushfighter
wireworker	bag snatcher	businessman
woman-hater	bank cashier	callow youth
wood-carver	bank manager	candlemaker
woodcutter	barge-master	car salesman
woodworker	basketmaker	cat's pyjamas
wool-carder	beachcomber	cattle thief
wool-comber	beauty queen	centenarian
wool-sorter	bell-founder	chamberlain
wool-winder	beneficiary	chambermaid
work-fellow	Bible reader	charcoalist
working man	bill-sticker	cheer-leader
workmaster	bingo caller	cheese-maker
workpeople	bird-fancier	cheese-parer
worshipper	bird-watcher	chiropodist
young blood	blackmailer	choirmaster
abecedarian	blood sister	clairvoyant
academician	blue-eyed boy	clergywoman
accompanist	board-member	close friend
actor's agent	body servant	coachwright
adventuress	bodybuilder	co-authoress
animal lover	boilermaker	coffinmaker
antiquarian	boilersmith	cognoscenti

commentator
common scold
condisciple
congressman
connoisseur
conspirator
contributor
conveyancer
co-ordinator
coppersmith
country girl
court jester
crane driver
crimewriter
cross-cousin
crown lawyer
cub reporter
cypher clerk
day-labourer
deadly enemy
dean of women
delivery man
demographer
dipsomaniac
distributor
domestician
double agent
draughtsman
drug peddler

duty officer
eager beaver
electrician
embroiderer
enlisted man
entertainer
estate agent
etymologist
executioner
extortioner
factory hand
faith healer
father-in-law
femme fatale
field-worker
fifth column
fighting man
filing clerk
fingersmith
fire-brigade
fire-watcher
first cousin
flag-captain
flag-officer
flat-dweller
flying squad
foot soldier
foster child
francophile

francophobe
freethinker
fruit picker
funambulist
functionary
galley slave
gallows bird
games master
gate-crasher
gentlewoman
ghostwriter
ginger group
glass-blower
glass-cutter
gouvernante
grandfather
grandmother
grandnephew
grandparent
grave digger
grave robber
greengrocer
gunman's moll
guttersnipe
haberdasher
hair stylist
hairdresser
half brother
half scholar

hammersmith	lamplighter	merchantman
handservant	land-grabber	mercy killer
hard drinker	landscapist	merry-andrew
hardwareman	land-steward	metalworker
head teacher	laundrymaid	method actor
helping hand	leading lady	military man
high sheriff	ledger clerk	millionaire
high society	lickspittle	mimographer
home-crofter	lifeboatman	miniaturist
homo sapiens	lifemanship	misanthrope
horse doctor	line-shooter	money-lender
horse trader	living image	moonlighter
housekeeper	*locum tenens*	mother-in-law
housemaster	lollipop man	mother's help
housemother	Lord Provost	mountaineer
housewright	lorry driver	music critic
human nature	madrigalist	name-dropper
ice-cream man	maidservant	nationalist
illuminator	man of genius	naval rating
illusionist	mandolinist	needlewoman
illustrator	manipulator	neurologist
imperialist	masquerader	night-hunter
infantryman	master baker	night-porter
internuncio	materialist	night-sister
interpreter	matinee idol	night-worker
interviewer	mechanician	nosey-parker
iron-founder	medicine man	novelettist
kitchenmaid	memorialist	office party
knucklehead	mental giant	onion Johnny

opportunist	portraitist	safebreaker
optometrist	predecessor	safecracker
ornamentist	prize-winner	sandwich man
orthopedist	probationer	saxophonist
palaestrian	prodigal son	scaremonger
pamphleteer	proof-reader	scenarioist
panel-beater	protagonist	school nurse
panel-doctor	purse-holder	scorekeeper
papal nuncio	quacksalver	scoutmaster
paper-hanger	questionist	scrap dealer
paragrapher	quill-driver	scrimshoner
parish clerk	radiologist	scythesmith
parlourmaid	rag merchant	search party
pathologist	rank and file	secret agent
pearlfisher	rapscallion	self-made man
pearly queen	rationalist	semanticist
penny-a-liner	reactionary	semaphorist
personality	rear admiral	semi-skilled
petrologist	relic-monger	senior clerk
philanderer	reparteeist	sharebroker
philatelist	research man	sheep farmer
philologist	resignation	shepherdess
philosopher	rhetorician	shipbuilder
phonologist	right-winger	ship's cooper
piece worker	river keeper	ship's tailor
pillar saint	road-sweeper	ship's writer
poet-patriot	rocket pilot	shop steward
police cadet	rugby player	silversmith
policewoman	Sabbatarian	simple Simon

sister tutor
sister-in-law
slaughterer
slave-labour
slave-trader
sleep-walker
smallholder
sociologist
soliloquist
space doctor
space-writer
speechmaker
spendthrift
stage-player
stagewright
stallholder
steeplejack
stenotypist
stepbrother
stereotyper
stipendiary
stockbroker
stockfarmer
stockjobber
stonecutter
stool pigeon
storekeeper
storyteller
straight man

strip-teaser
subordinate
suffragette
surrebutter
swordmaster
sympathizer
talent scout
taxidermist
teacher's pet
telegrapher
telepathist
telephonist
terpsichore
testimonial
the ministry
ticket agent
toastmaster
tobacconist
Tommy Atkins
tooth doctor
toothdrawer
town-dweller
town-planner
toxopholite
train robber
train-bearer
transcriber
travel agent
trendsetter

truck-farmer
typographer
upholsterer
van salesman
versemonger
vice-admiral
vine-dresser
viola player
Walter Mitty
war criminal
war reporter
washerwoman
water-doctor
water-finder
welfare work
whalefisher
wheelwright
white hunter
white-collar
witch doctor
woodchopper
wool-stapler
working girl
workmanlike
xylophonist
youth leader
actor-manager
advance party
air commodore

aircraftsman	brother-in-law	Colonel Blimp
air-sea-rescue	cabinet-maker	commissioner
ambulance man	calligrapher	confectioner
anaesthetist	camp-follower	conquistador
archeologist	candlewright	conservative
armour-bearer	caricaturist	contemporary
artful dodger	carpet-bagger	corn-chandler
artilleryman	carpet-fitter	cosmopolitan
awkward squad	carpet-knight	costermonger
backwoodsman	cartographer	cousin-german
ballad singer	casual labour	customs clerk
balladmonger	cattle lifter	Darby and Joan
ballet dancer	cerographist	deep-sea diver
bible-thumper	chicken thief	demonstrator
bibliologist	chief cashier	desk-sergeant
bibliopegist	chief mourner	doctor's round
blood brother	chief of staff	*doppelgänger*
blue stocking	chief-justice	dramaturgist
board meeting	chimney sweep	drill-master
bobby-dazzler	chirographer	eavesdropper
body snatcher	chiropractor	ecclesiastic
booking-clerk	churchwarden	electrotyper
bookstitcher	circuit rider	elocutionist
border sentry	civil servant	entomologist
bottlewasher	civil service	entrepreneur
boulevardier	clarinettist	equestrienne
bridgemaster	clerk of works	escapologist
brigade major	coachbuilder	exhibitioner
brinkmanship	collaborator	experimenter

ex-service man
exterminator
family doctor
father figure
featherbrain
field-marshal
field-officer
figure dancer
filibusterer
film director
film producer
first officer
first reserve
flying column
flying doctor
footplateman
foster-father
foster-mother
foster-parent
foster-sister
garret-master
general agent
geriatrician
globe-trotter
grandstander
grease-monkey
grey eminence
group captain
guest speaker

gynecologist
hair-splitter
headmistress
head-shrinker
heir apparent
high official
hockey player
holidaymaker
hotel manager
housebreaker
house-painter
humanitarian
hydropathist
immunologist
impersonator
improvisator
in conference
inseparables
instructress
intermediary
investigator
jazz musician
junior rating
juvenile lead
king's counsel
kitchen staff
kleptomaniac
knife grinder
knife-thrower

lady superior
land surveyor
landed gentry
law-stationer
lay-out artist
leader writer
leathernecks
legal adviser
letter writer
lexicologist
line sergeant
literary hack
literary lion
lithographer
longshoreman
loss adjuster
lounge-lizard
maid of honour
maître d'hôtel
major-general
make-up artist
man of letters
man of science
man-about-town
manual worker
manufacturer
mass-producer
master-at-arms
mastersinger

metallurgist	pastoral poet	quarrymaster
metropolitan	patent office	racing driver
mezzo soprano	pediatrician	radiodontist
mid-Victorian	penitentiary	radiographer
mineralogist	petty officer	receptionist
modest violet	photographer	remuneration
money-changer	physiologist	restaurateur
moneygrubber	plant manager	retaining fee
monographist	ploughwright	right-hand man
motorcyclist	plumber's mate	rodomontader
musicologist	poet laureate	rolling stone
natural child	poor relation	sales manager
naval officer	postgraduate	salvationist
near relation	postmistress	scatterbrain
newspaperman	practitioner	scene-painter
notary public	press officer	scene-shifter
nutritionist	prevaricator	schoolmaster
obstetrician	prince-bishop	screenwriter
office bearer	principal boy	scriptwriter
office junior	prison warder	scullery maid
one-upmanship	prison worker	second cousin
orchestrator	private clerk	second fiddle
organ-grinder	prize-fighter	set decorator
organization	professional	sharecropper
orthocousins	propagandist	sharpshooter
orthodontist	psychiatrist	sheep-shearer
paper-marbler	psychologist	sheriff-clerk
paper-stainer	public figure	show business
parish priest	publicity man	silk-gownsman

single person	stonedresser	**trichologist**
sister german	stormtrooper	trick-cyclist
site engineer	street-trader	troublemaker
snake-charmer	street-urchin	troutbreeder
social worker	stuffed shirt	truce-breaker
soil mechanic	Sunday driver	ugly customer
sole occupant	swashbuckler	ugly duckling
somnambulist	tax-collector	undermanager
special agent	technologist	vaudevillist
speechwriter	telegraph boy	vice-director
spiritualist	telephone man	vice-governor
sports master	tennis player	warehouseman
sportscaster	test engineer	water-diviner
sportswriter	theatre nurse	wind musician
staff officer	theatre staff	wine merchant
stage manager	ticket holder	wood-engraver
statistician	ticket writer	wool-gatherer
steel erector	top executive	worker priest
stenographer	trained nurse	working party
stepdaughter	transgressor	workmistress
stereotypist	transvestite	works manager

Sport, Games, Pastimes

This section includes lists of sports, indoor and outdoor—sportsmen and players—indoor games, including names of card games and terms used—children's games and popular toys—sports equipment—sports grounds—sporting terms—popular dances and dance steps—athletics and gymnastics —hobbies, except art and photography which are included under Art.

K.O.	fan	par	bail	chip
P.T.	fun	peg	bait	chop
T.T.	gin	pin	ball	club
ace	gym	Pit	bank	coup
aim	hit	pot	base	crew
bat	hop	run	beat	dart
bet	jab	set	bend	dash
bid	*jeu*	shy	bias	deal
bow	jig	ski	bike	deck
box	kit	tag	bind	dice
bye	l.b.w.	tie	blow	dive
cap	lap	ton	blue	doll
cat	leg	top	bout	drag
cox	let	toy	bowl	draw
cue	lie	try	brag	duck
cup	lob	win	buck	duel
dan	loo	ante	calx	épée
die	net	away	card	fall

fare	I spy	meld	rule	wing
file	iron	mile	sail	wire
fish	jack	nock	seat	wood
fist	jape	Oaks	seed	yo-yo
foil	jess	oars	shot	alley
fore	jest	odds	side	angle
form	jive	Oval	skat	apron
foul	joke	over	skid	arena
gaff	judo	pace	skip	arrow
gala	jump	pack	skis	baffy
game	kail	pass	slam	bathe
gate	keno	pawn	slip	baths
gear	kill	play	snap	baton
goal	king	polo	solo	bingo
golf	kite	pool	spin	blade
grid	lane	port	spot	blind
grip	lark	puck	suit	bluff
hand	leap	punt	sumo	board
hank	lido	putt	swim	bogey
heat	lift	quiz	tack	bound
hike	lock	race	team	bower
hipe	loom	raft	tice	bowls
hold	loop	reel	toss	boxer
hole	lose	ring	trap	break
home	love	rink	trot	bully
hook	ludo	roll	turf	caber
hoop	lure	rook	walk	caddy
hunt	mall	ruck	whip	cadge
hype	meet	ruff	wide	canoe

caper	dormy	Jenny	ouija	samba
cards	drill	jetty	pairs	scent
carom	drive	joker	parry	score
catch	dummy	joust	pilot	screw
cavel	eagle	kails	pique	scrum
chase	evens	kayak	pitch	scull
check	event	kendo	piton	serve
chess	eyass	kevel	pivot	shaft
chips	fault	kitty	point	shogi
chute	feint	knave	poker	shoot
cleek	field	lance	polka	sight
climb	fight	links	pools	skier
clubs	final	lists	prank	skiff
coach	fives	loops	punto	slice
congé	fling	loose	quart	slide
count	flush	loser	queen	slips
coupé	frame	lotto	racer	smash
court	gaper	lunge	rally	spear
craps	going	mambo	range	spoon
crawl	grass	march	relay	sport
cycle	green	match	rouge	stake
dance	guard	medal	rough	stalk
darts	guide	mid-on	round	steer
début	gully	miler	rover	strip
decoy	halma	monte	rugby	sweep
Derby	heave	morra	rules	swing
deuce	hobby	no bid	rumba	sword
diver	horse	notch	rummy	tally
divot	inner	ombre	sabre	tango

217

taroc	bishop	cinema	gallop
tarot	bisque	circus	gambit
title	blocks	conker	gaming
ton-up	bookie	corner	glider
touch	borrow	course	goalie
track	boston	cradle	gobang
trick	bowled	crambo	gobble
trump	bowler	crease	go-kart
twist	bowman	crosse	golfer
valse	boxing	cruise	googly
venue	bracer	cup tie	ground
wager	bricks	curler	gutter
waltz	bridge	dealer	hammer
wedge	bulger	dedans	hand-in
whist	bumper	discus	hazard
widow	bunker	diving	header
abseil	caddie	dog-leg	hearts
akimbo	can-can	dormie	helmet
anchor	cannon	driver	hiking
angler	canter	dry fly	hockey
anorak	car-run	eleven	honour
archer	casino	*équipe*	hooker
ascent	castle	*espada*	hookey
at ease	centre	euchre	hoop-la
attack	cestus	fencer	hurdle
bailer	cha-cha	fisher	hurley
banker	chassé	*flèche*	ice-axe
bidder	cherry	flight	jesses
birdie	chukka	flying	jigsaw

jockey	paddle	result	sports
jostle	peelee	rhumba	sprint
joujou	pelota	riddle	squash
jumper	penché	riding	stakes
karate	period	roll-in	stance
knight	piquet	roquet	sticks
lariat	player	rowing	stilts
leader	plunge	rubber	strike
leg-bye	pocket	rugger	stroke
mallet	pommel	runner	stroll
manège	popgun	safari	stumps
marble	puppet	savate	stymie
marina	putter	scorer	*suerte*
mascot	puzzle	sculls	sweeps
mashie	quarry	séance	swivel
maxixe	quarte	second	TT race
merils	quinze	seesaw	tackle
mid-off	quiver	shimmy	target
minuet	quoits	shinny	tarots
misère	rabbit	shinty	tennis
morris	racing	shorts	the leg
mud pie	racket	skater	threes
muleta	raffle	skiing	thrust
murder	ramble	slalom	thwart
Nassau	rapids	sledge	tickle
nelson	rapier	soccer	tipcat
no ball	record	spades	tiptoe
opener	remise	spikes	tivoli
pad boy	replay	spiral	*torero*

touché	balloon	charter	descent
toy gun	bar-bell	Chicago	diamond
trophy	bathing	chicane	dicebox
truant	batsman	chimney	discard
umpire	beguine	chipper	dogfall
versus	bézique	chukker	doubles
volley	bicycle	circuit	drawing
wicket	bidding	classic	dribble
willow	big game	compass	driving
winger	bivouac	*corrida*	*en prise*
winner	bladder	*couloir*	end game
yoicks	blaster	counter	end play
yorker	boating	crampon	entrant
ace high	bonfire	creases	*estoque*
acrobat	bowling	cricket	fairway
address	box-kite	croquet	fan club
also-ran	bracing	cue ball	fencing
amateur	bran tub	curb bit	fielder
angling	brassie	curling	fifteen
apex pin	bubbles	cushion	fine leg
archery	camp bed	cutlass	finesse
arm hold	camping	cutover	fishing
arm lock	captain	cycling	fixture
assault	capture	cyclist	fly half
athlete	carioca	dancing	foot bow
back row	cassino	day trip	forehip
bad calx	catcher	decider	formula
balance	century	declare	forward
ballast	charade	defence	fox hunt

220

foxtrot	infield	netball	potshot
free hit	innings	niblick	press-up
frogman	jackpot	ninepin	prowess
funfair	*j'adoube*	no trump	pyramid
gallery	javelin	oarsman	quarter
gavotte	joy-ride	off-side	rackets
gliding	ju-jitsu	old maid	rag doll
goggles	keep fit	on guard	rambling
golf tie	kick-off	one-step	rebound
golf-bag	knock-up	over par	referee
golfing	lancers	overarm	regatta
good fun	landing	paddock	reserve
Gossima	last lap	pallone	ripcord
grounds	leg-hold	partner	riposte
guy rope	leg-side	*passade*	rockers
gymnast	let ball	*passado*	rosette
hacking	line-out	pastime	rowlock
hairpin	long bow	penalty	rubicon
hand-off	long-hop	picador	running
harpoon	long-leg	picquet	sailing
harrier	lottery	pin high	sand pie
hawking	marbles	pinball	sand pit
holster	matador	pinfall	scooter
honours	maypole	pinocle	scratch
hunting	mazurka	pitcher	service
hurdler	meccano	pit-stop	seven-up
hurling	melding	play-off	shot-put
ice-pick	midiron	poloist	shuffle
ice-rink	net cord	pontoon	shuttle

singles	The Oval	backhand	catapult
singlet	throw-in	backheel	cat-stick
skating	tie game	backspin	champion
skid-lid	tilting	bail-ball	charades
snaffle	toe-hold	balk line	checkers
snooker	tombola	ball game	chequers
snorkel	Torpids	baseball	chessman
society	tourney	baseline	chess-set
soft toy	trainer	beagling	chin hold
sparrer	tumbler	biathlon	chip-shot
squails	twosome	blocking	climbing
St Leger	two-step	boat race	coasting
stadium	vantage	body blow	contract
stamina	vaulter	boloball	cottabus
starter	walking	bonspiel	counters
stirrup	war-club	boundary	coursing
striker	war-game	brackets	coxswain
stumped	workout	bull-ring	crap game
sub-aqua	wrestle	bull's eye	cribbage
sun bath	ziganka	bully off	crossbar
tacking	all-fours	cakewalk	cross-bat
tactics	approach	camp site	cruising
take-off	après-ski	campfire	cup final
tally ho	aqualung	canoeing	dark blue
tangram	aquatics	car rally	dead ball
tantivy	armguard	card game	dead heat
tenpins	away game	carnival	dead shot
tent peg	baby doll	carousel	deadlock
The Oaks	baccarat	castling	delivery

diamonds	flippers	golf-club
dominoes	floating	golliwog
doubling	foilsman	good calx
dragster	foot race	good shot
draughts	football	gridiron
draw lots	foot-hold	guarding
dressage	footwork	gym shoes
drop goal	forehand	gymkhana
drop kick	forfeits	habanera
drop-shot	foul goal	halfback
dumb-bell	foul line	half-ball
en rappel	foul play	half-blue
estocada	foursome	half-mile
even keel	foxhound	half-shot
even odds	free kick	half-time
exercise	frescade	handball
face card	fretwork	handicap
fair play	front row	hat trick
falconer	full back	haymaker
falconry	full draw	headlock
fandango	full toss	helmsman
fast ball	gambling	high dive
field day	gamester	high jump
finalist	garrocha	hole high
firework	gauntlet	holed out
fistiana	gin rummy	home game
fivepins	goal-kick	hornpipe
flapping	goalpost	horseman
flat race	golfball	how's that

hula hoop	love game	pinochle
hula-hula	lucky bag	pin-table
huntsman	lucky dip	playmate
hurdling	mah-jongg	playroom
ice yacht	marathon	plunging
Irish jig	marksman	polo ball
iron shot	marriage	polo pony
jiu-jitsu	monopoly	pony trek
joystick	motorist	pool room
knock out	napoleon	port tack
korfball	natation	pugilism
lacrosse	ninepins	pugilist
lawn game	no trumps	pushball
leapfrog	nose-dive	pyramids
left back	off break	quintain
left half	off drive	quiz game
left hook	Olympiad	racegoer
left wing	open file	radio ham
leg break	opponent	reaching
leg-guard	outfield	recovery
life-line	outsider	red cloak
linesman	oval ball	redouble
long game	paddling	ricochet
long jump	pall-mall	rink polo
long odds	pass roll	rope ring
long rush	pass-line	roulette
long shot	patience	rounders
long stop	pike dive	rucksack
lost ball	ping-pong	runner-up

Ruy Lopez
sack race
sand iron
sand trap
saraband
sardines
Scrabble
scramble
scrum-cap
sculling
selector
set point
shell out
shooting
short leg
side line
side-blow
ski slope
skin-game
ski-stick
skittles
sledging
slow ball
snap ring
snapshot
snowball
snow line
softball
south paw

speedway
sparring
spoon-oar
sporting
sprinter
stalking
stand pat
stand-off
stations
stoccado
stock-car
stop shot
straddle
straight
tap-dance
team game
tent-pole
The Ashes
the field
third man
thole-pin
toreador
Totopoly
tracking
trailing
train set
training
tug-of-war
under par

underarm
undercut
upper cut
vaulting
venation
walk-over
wall game
wing area
wood club
wood shot
wrestler
yachting
acey-deucy
advantage
all square
all-comers
anchor man
arabesque
arrow-shot
astrodome
athletics
Aunt Sally
back court
back edges
back swing
badminton
bagatelle
bandalore
bandy-ball

barn dance
baulk line
beach ball
best bower
big dipper
billiards
black belt
black jack
black pawn
blackjack
bladework
boarhound
boar-spear
bob-sleigh
body check
body punch
bolo punch
bossa nova
bowstring
broad jump
bull fight
caddie car
camel spin
card trick
cartwheel
cavalcade
cha-cha-cha
chair-lift
challenge

checkmate
chess-game
clock golf
clog dance
closing in
club house
collector
combatant
conjuring
contender
cotillion
court card
crackshot
cricketer
crossjack
crossword
cycle race
cycle tour
dance step
dartboard
decathlon
decoy duck
disengage
dog racing
doll's pram
drawn game
dribbling
en passant
en tout cas

enclosure
equalizer
exercises
extra time
face-guard
favourite
field game
fieldsman
first half
first seed
first slip
fisherman
fisticuff
five-a-side
fletching
flight bow
flyweight
foot fault
fore court
fore royal
forty-love
free reach
freestyle
freewheel
full house
galleries
game point
gardening
gladiator

goalposts
go-karting
gold medal
golf widow
golf-links
golf-range
golf-shoes
good loser
good sport
grand prix
grand slam
gum shield
gymnasium
handstand
hard court
high jinks
hill climb
hit wicket
hitch-hike
hopscotch
horse race
horseback
horseplay
ice hockey
ice skates
infielder
jackknife
joshiyori
judo throw

karabiner
kennelman
king's rook
lawn bowls
left bower
left inner
leg before
leg spread
light blue
Long Jenny
long loser
long tacks
loose ball
loose maul
loose rein
love forty
love-match
low volley
match play
matrimony
medal play
medallist
mid mashie
music hall
Newmarket
Nuts in May
pacemaker
palaestra
panel game

pantomime
paper doll
parachute
party game
paso doble
passepied
Paul Jones
pelmanism
pen friend
penthouse
philately
pickaback
pilot ball
pinch draw
pirouette
pitch camp
plaything
pogo stick
poker dice
pole vault
polonaise
pot-holing
punch-ball
push parry
quadrille
quickstep
race track
racing car
relay race

relay team
reverse Qs
right back
right half
right hook
right wing
ringsider
rock climb
round game
round trip
roundelay
rover hoop
safety net
sand-yacht
sauna bath
schnorkel
schwingen
score card
scrapbook
screw dive
scrimmage
scrum half
scrummage
second row
semi-final
shaftment
shamateur
shin-guard
short game

short leat
short odds
shortstop
shrimping
signal gun
silver cup
singleton
skiamachy
skijoring
skin-diver
sky-diving
small bore
snow climb
solitaire
solo whist
spectator
speedboat
spin parry
split shot
sports day
sportsman
spot-dance
square leg
stable boy
stalemate
starboard
steersman
step dance
stopwatch

stud poker
surfboard
sweatband
swordplay
swordsman
teddy bear
tennis net
terracing
test match
the sticks
thirty-one
three-jump
threesome
three-turn
tight rein
tip-and-run
torch race
touch down
touch goal
touchline
track suit
trump-card
trump-suit
turnstile
twenty-one
twist dive
vingt-et-un
water polo
whirligig

white pawn
wristlock
yacht club
yacht race
yachtsman
York round
youth club
acrobatics
aerobatics
agility mat
agonistics
back marker
back stroke
backgammon
baggataway
balneation
banderilla
basketball
battledore
bee-keeping
betting man
binoculars
bird-skiing
blind poker
blood sport
booby prize
Boston crab
boxing ring
catch a crab

cat's-cradle
centre half
challenger
change-over
charleston
checkpoint
chessboard
Chinese box
chuck-a-luck
clay pigeon
coconut shy
competitor
contestant
contractor
counted out
cover-point
cricket bat
cricket net
crown green
daily dozen
deck quoits
deck tennis
discobolus
diving bell
doll's house
dolly-catch
double axle
double game
double peel

draw stumps
drop cannon
drop volley
equitation
Eskimo roll
fairground
fantoccini
fast bowler
feathering
fianchetto
field event
field sport
first blood
fishing-net
fishing-rod
flat racing
fly fishing
flying mare
flying shot
footballer
forced move
forecaddie
foundation
fox hunting
free-for-all
full nelson
gambit-pawn
ghost train
glaciarium

goal circle
goal crease
goal tender
goalkeeper
golf course
grandstand
gymnastics
half bisque
half nelson
half volley
halieutics
halved hole
handspring
hard tackle
Harrow game
haute école
hazard side
headhunter
health club
health farm
heel-and-toe
high diving
hitch-hiker
hobby-horse
hockey team
hog-hunting
horseshoes
horsewoman
hunting bow

ice dancing
ice skating
in the rough
in training
Indian club
Indian file
indoor golf
injury time
inside home
inside lane
inside left
inside lock
instructor
isometrics
jackstones
jackstraws
Jockey Club
jump the gun
karate chop
kewpie doll
kite-flying
kriegspiel
lansquenet
lawn tennis
league game
little slam
loaded dice
loose scrum
love-thirty

maiden over
marionette
marker buoy
mashie iron
match point
middle spot
minor piece
non-starter
object ball
off the hook
open season
open target
opening bat
ouija-board
outfielder
pancration
pancratium
paper chase
par contest
pari-mutuel
passed pawn
penalty try
pentathlon
philatelic
pigeon loft
planchette
playground
point-of-aim
poker chips

polo ground
potato race
prize fight
prize money
punch-drunk
puntilléro
push stroke
queen's pawn
queen's rook
racecourse
racing cars
ratcatcher
real tennis
recreation
relaxation
relegation
rifle-range
right bower
right inner
right swing
ring-o'-roses
rod and reel
round dance
roundabout
rowing boat
royal flush
rubber ball
rubber duck
rugby union

rumpus room
run-through
rush stroke
sand castle
scoreboard
second half
second slip
second wind
seconds out
seven-a side
short tacks
show jumper
side stroke
sidesaddle
silly mid-on
silly point
single file
single game
ski-jumping
skin diving
ski-running
sky-jumping
slow bowler
somersault
speed trial
spike shoes
spin bowler
sportswear
spot stroke

square odds
square ring
stamp album
stock cards
stop thrust
strathspey
strike camp
stroke play
submission
substitute
sun-bathing
surf-riding
suspension
sweepstake
switchback
sword dance
take a trick
tarantella
team spirit
tennis ball
tennis shoe
tetherball
thirty-love
thrown goal
tiger badge
time thrust
timekeeper
tin soldier
title fight

toe scratch
tour skiing
tournament
toy soldier
track event
trampoline
trial match
triple jump
triple peel
true to form
tumble turn
turkey trot
twelfth man
vantage set
Vardon grip
volleyball
water wings
whippers in
whist drive
wilful foul
willow wand
win by a head
winning gun
Yarborough
young entry
accumulator
baseball bat
bear-baiting
bell-ringing

Bengal spear
betting ring
biased bowls
big game hunt
blackbottom
boating pond
Bombay spear
bow and arrow
boxing match
bridge whist
bronze medal
bull-baiting
casual water
Channel swim
chariot race
cheer-leader
cinder track
class racing
close season
close tennis
corps-à-corps
country walk
county match
coup de grâce
court tennis
crash helmet
crawl stroke
cricket ball
cricket pads

croquet arch
croquet ball
croquet hoop
croquet lawn
cross swords
curling pond
curling rink
cycle racing
daisy-cutter
deck of cards
deep fine leg
direct parry
diving board
diving dress
double check
double fault
downhill run
driving iron
egg and-spoon
envelopment
eurhythmics
false attack
fencing mask
Ferris wheel
field events
fifteen-love
figure eight
first attack
first eleven

fishing line
flick stroke
flying start
football fan
forced error
forward line
forward pass
fox and geese
free skating
fun and games
gambit-piece
gambling man
gaming house
gaming table
garden party
glove puppet
gone fishing
good innings
Graeco Roman
grand salute
groundsheet
hairpin bend
half passage
heavyweight
hide-and-seek
hitch-hiking
hockey match
hockey stick
home and away

horse racing
horse riding
ice yachting
inside right
judge-of-play
jumping bean
king's bishop
king's knight
lap of honour
league table
lightweight
lock forward
loop-the-loop
love-fifteen
modern waltz
morris dance
motor racing
mountaineer
mystery tour
nailed boots
neck and neck
offside rule
Olympic team
out of bounds
outside home
outside left
pack of cards
pair skating
palaestrian

pancake race
pancratiast
parasailing
parlour game
pawn and move
penalty area
penalty goal
penalty kick
penalty line
photo finish
picture card
pillow fight
pigeon timer
pigeon-flier
pigeon-house
pig sticking
piscatology
pitch-and-run
play the game
playing card
playing line
pole vaulter
prize-winner
prop forward
public games
punto dritto
pyramid spot
quarterback
rabbit punch

race meeting
racing craft
racing shell
racket court
record break
riddle-me-ree
Roman candle
rouge et noir
round of golf
royal tennis
rugby league
Schottische
seam bowling
self-defence
serendipity
service grip
service line
service side
shinty stick
shovelboard
show-jumping
shuttlecock
sightseeing
silver medal
simple parry
singing-game
skating rink
skiing field
sleeping bag

slot machine
slow foxtrot
snow glasses
snowshoeing
soft landing
spade mashie
speculation
spinning top
sportswoman
spreadeagle
springboard
square dance
square tango
squash court
staghunting
starting gun
straight bat
striker ball
sudden death
swallow dive
sweep rowing
table tennis
target arrow
tennis court
tennis match
tent-pegging
Terpsichore
the Olympics
third player

three-legged
tiddlywinks
tobogganing
totalisator
touring club
toxopholite
training run
transfer fee
triple crown
Turkish bath
waiting game
walking race
water hazard
water skiing
water sports
Western roll
win on points
wine tasting
wing forward
winning post
winning time
wooden horse
world record
youth hostel
anchor cannon
approach shot
back straight
banderillero
bantamweight

batting order	cockfighting	first reserve
beachcombing	consequences	first service
Becher's brook	country dance	flat foot spin
billiard ball	cradle cannon	flying tackle
billiard hall	crapshooting	foursome reel
billiard room	cricket boots	free wheeling
billiard spot	cricket pitch	French boxing
bingo session	croquet court	fruit machine
bird-watching	cross-country	game of chance
body building	curling stone	game of points
bowling alley	cut and thrust	gamesmanship
bowling green	dead ball line	gone to ground
boxing gloves	deep-sea-diver	ground stroke
break the bank	direct cannon	guessing game
breast stroke	directors' box	halfway line
bull-fighting	disqualified	handicap race
butterfly net	do-it-yourself	head scissors
callisthenic	double sculls	hill climbing
captain ball	double threes	home straight
century break	doubles match	homing pigeon
championship	dressing room	horsemanship
change of ends	earth stopper	housey housey
change-bowler	Eton wall game	hundred yards
changing room	fast-and-loose	hunting groom
checkerboard	field glasses	in the running
classic races	figure skater	infringement
climbing boot	final whistle	jack-in-the-box
climbing rope	first defence	jigsaw puzzle
coarse fisher	first innings	kaleidoscope

knucklebones	parallel bars	referee's hold
lampadedromy	penalty bully	return crease
landing stage	penalty throw	ride to hounds
level-pegging	physical jerk	riding school
London Bridge	picture house	rock climbing
long distance	pigeon-flying	rocking horse
loose forward	ping-pong ball	roller skates
losing hazard	pitch and putt	running strip
maiden stakes	pitch and toss	sand-yachting
marathon race	playing cards	scissors jump
medicine ball	playing field	second attack
melding score	*plaza de toros*	second eleven
merry-go-round	pleasure trip	second player
mincing steps	point-to-point	secular games
mixed doubles	pony trekking	service hold
National Hunt	primary loose	shadow boxing
nature ramble	prize fighter	sharpshooter
noble science	professional	shove ha'penny
nursery slope	Punch and Judy	short pinocle
obstacle race	punto reverso	shrimping net
old-time dance	putting green	shuffleboard
Olympic games	quarter-final	side chancery
Olympic title	queen's bishop	simple attack
Olympic torch	queen's knight	single combat
opposing side	racing season	single sculls
ordinary foul	raffle ticket	singles match
orienteering	receiving end	skating boots
outside right	record-holder	skipping rope
paddling pool	redoublement	slice service

slippery pole
soap-box derby
speed skating
sport of kings
sporting life
stabbing blow
stand-off half
starting grid
starting post
steeplechase
sticky wicket
stilt-walking
straddle jump
stranglehold

strong finish
suit of lights
Sunday driver
sweep oarsman
swimming gala
swimming pool
sword fencing
table turning
tennis player
tennis racket
tennis stroke
three quarter
toss the caber
train spotter

trapshooting
treasure hunt
treble chance
trick cyclist
trigger happy
tunnel of love
umpire's chair
vantage point
Virginia reel
weightlifter
welterweight
wicket keeper
winter sports

Clothing

This section includes articles of clothing, male, female and children's, modern and historical—fashions—headgear—footwear—underwear—hairstyles and cosmetics—accessories—colours—fabrics and materials—uniform and vestments—gems and jewellery—dressmaking terms.

alb	nap	bias	duds	hoop
bag	net	blue	élan	hose
bib	pin	boot	fano	huke
boa	rag	brim	fawn	hyke
bob	red	buff	felt	hype
bra	rig	*capa*	fold	jade
bun	sox	cape	frog	jean
cap	tab	clog	gamp	jupe
dun	tag	coat	garb	kepi
fan	tan	coif	gear	kilt
fez	tie	comb	gilt	knot
fob	wig	cope	gimp	lace
fop	zip	cord	gold	lake
fur	alba	cowl	gore	lamé
gem	bags	cuff	gown	lawn
hat	band	curl	grey	list
hem	bang	dart	haik	lock
kid	bead	drag	heel	mask
mac	belt	duck	hood	maud

238

maxi	saxe	wool	cameo	flame
mini	seal	wrap	carat	flare
mink	seam	yarn	chain	flash
mitt	shoe	yoke	chaps	frill
mode	silk	agate	charm	frock
muff	skip	A-line	check	fucus
mule	slip	amber	clasp	gauze
navy	sock	amice	cloak	get-up
onyx	sole	apron	clogs	gipon
opal	stud	array	cloth	glove
peak	suit	azure	coral	green
pink	talc	badge	cotta	grego
poke	tick	baize	crape	guimp
puce	tile	bands	crash	guise
pump	toga	bangs	cream	gunny
rags	togs	batik	crêpe	habit
ring	torc	beads	crown	helio
robe	tuck	beard	cymar	henna
rose	tutu	beige	dandy	ivory
ruby	vamp	beret	denim	jabot
ruff	veil	beryl	derby	jeans
rust	vent	bijou	dhoti	jewel
sack	vest	black	drape	jupon
saga	warp	blond	dress	khaki
sage	wear	blues	drill	lapel
sard	weft	boots	ducks	lapis
sari	welt	braid	ephod	lemon
sark	wine	brown	fanon	Levi's
sash	woof	busby	fichu	lilac

linen	pleat	skirt	twill	biggin
lisle	plume	smock	umber	bikini
lungi	plush	snood	upper	blazer
lurex	point	spats	V-neck	blonde
manta	print	specs	voile	blouse
manto	pumps	stays	waist	boater
mauve	purse	stock	wamus	bodice
model	queue	stole	watch	bodkin
moire	rayon	stuff	weave	bolero
motif	robes	style	white	bonnet
mufti	romal	suede	wigan	bootee
mules	rouge	tabby	woven	bouclé
nappy	rumal	tails	achkan	bow tie
Nylon	sable	talma	afghan	bowler
ochre	sabot	tammy	albert	braces
Orlon	sagum	taupe	almuce	briefs
paint	satin	tawny	alnage	brogan
pants	scarf	terry	alpaca	brogue
parka	scrim	tiara	angora	brolly
paste	sepia	toile	anklet	bronze
patch	serge	topaz	anorak	brooch
patte	shako	topee	armlet	buckle
peach	shawl	toque	attire	burlap
pearl	sheer	train	auburn	buskin
perse	shift	tress	bangle	bustle
piqué	shirt	trews	basque	button
pixie	shoes	tulle	bauble	byssus
plaid	simar	tunic	beaver	caftan
plait	skein	tweed	bertha	calash

240

6

calico	diadem	garter	madder
camise	diaper	gewgaw	madras
canvas	dickey	girdle	magyar
capote	dimity	goatee	make-up
casque	dirndl	greave	mantle
castor	dittos	gusset	mantua
cerise	dolman	hairdo	marcel
cestus	duffel	hankie	maroon
chimer	ermine	hat box	melton
chintz	fabric	hatpin	minium
chiton	facial	helmet	mitten
choker	facing	indigo	mob cap
chopin	faille	infula	modena
cilice	fallal	insole	modius
cloche	fannel	jacket	mohair
coatee	fascia	jargon	moreen
cobalt	fedora	jasper	murrey
collar	feeder	jemima	muslin
collet	fibula	jerkin	nankin
colmar	fillet	jersey	needle
copper	finery	jumper	nylons
corset	fox fur	kaftan	orange
cotton	frills	kimono	outfit
cravat	fringe	kirtle	panama
curler	gaiter	lappet	parure
Dacron	galoon	lining	pastel
damask	galosh	livery	patent
dapper	gamash	locket	patten
denier	garnet	lustre	pearls

241

peplos	sarong	tissue	woolly
peplum	sateen	titian	yellow
peruke	scarab	toecap	zircon
plasma	semmit	tongue	zoster
pocket	sequin	top hat	*à la mode*
pomade	serape	topper	abraxas
pompom	sheath	torque	Acrilan
poncho	shoddy	toupee	adamant
pongee	shorts	tricot	alamode
poplin	shroud	trilby	annato
powder	sienna	trunks	apparel
purple	silver	T-shirt	apricot
raglan	ski cap	tucker	argyles
rebato	slacks	turban	armband
redder	sleeve	tussah	armhole
reefer	slip-on	Tuxedo	baboosh
reseda	spinel	tweeds	baldric
revers	sun hat	ulster	bandana
ribbon	switch	unisex	bandbox
rigout	tabard	uppers	bandeau
rinker	talcum	velure	bath oil
rochet	tartan	velvet	batiste
roller	tassle	violet	beading
rubine	tettix	waders	belcher
ruffle	thread	wallet	biretta
russet	tiepin	wampus	bombast
sacque	tights	waspie	brocade
samite	tin hat	whites	buckram
sandal	tippet	wimple	bunting

burdash	compact	fitting	hip boot
burnous	coronet	flannel	homburg
bycoket	corsage	flounce	hosiery
calotte	costume	foulard	iron red
cambric	couture	fourche	jacinth
capuche	coxcomb	freckle	jaconet
carmine	crewcut	frocked	jaegers
casheen	crimson	frogged	jargoon
cassock	crochet	fur coat	kilt pin
casuals	cuculla	fustian	layette
cat's eye	culotte	gaiters	leather
cat suit	diamond	gamboge	leghorn
chamois	doeskin	garment	leotard
chapeau	doublet	gingham	loafers
chaplet	dress up	girasol	long bob
chéchia	drawers	glasses	Mae West
chemise	droguet	grogram	magenta
cheviot	drugget	G-string	malines
chevron	earring	guipure	maniple
chiffon	elastic	gumboot	manteau
chignon	emerald	gym slip	manteel
chimere	falsies	hair cut	mascara
chlamys	fashion	hairnet	Mechlin
chopine	feather	hairpin	modesty
citrine	felt hat	handbag	modiste
civvies	ferrule	hatband	monocle
clobber	fig leaf	hemline	mozetta
clothes	filemot	hessian	mudpack
cockade	filibeg	high hat	muffler

nankeen	pelisse	sautoir	tea gown
necktie	pendant	scarlet	textile
new blue	Percale	sea blue	texture
New Look	perfume	selvage	ticking
nightie	peridot	shampoo	tiffany
oil silk	periwig	shingle	tile hat
oilskin	petasus	silk hat	tile red
old blue	pigskin	singlet	tonsure
old gold	pigtail	skimmer	top boot
olivine	pillbox	sky blue	top hose
organdy	pin curl	slicker	topcoat
organza	pith hat	soft hat	topknot
orphrey	porceau	soutane	torchon
outsize	porkpie	spangle	tricorn
overall	puttees	spencer	trinket
Oxfords	pyjamas	sporran	tunicle
padding	raiment	stammel	turn-ups
paenula	redhead	stetson	twinset
page-boy	ringlet	sun suit	undress
paisley	rompers	surcoat	uniform
pajamas	rosette	surtout	Vandyke
paletot	rubbers	swaddle	veiling
pallium	ruby red	sweater	velours
panache	rug gown	tabaret	webbing
pannier	sacking	taffeta	worsted
panties	saffron	taffety	yashmak
parasol	sagathy	tarbush	aigrette
partlet	sandals	tatters	amethyst
pegtops	sarafan	tatting	appliqué

Ascot tie	bustline	crush hat
ash-blond	calyptra	culottes
babouche	camisole	dalmatic
baby blue	capeline	dark blue
Balmoral	capuchin	day dress
barathea	carcanet	diamanté
basquine	cardigan	disguise
bath cube	cashmere	dove grey
bathrobe	Celanese	dress-tie
bearskin	chaperon	drilling
bedsocks	chasuble	drop curl
berretta	chenille	dunce cap
black tie	chestnut	dust-coat
blood red	cheverel	Dutch cap
bloomers	churinga	duvetine
boat neck	ciclaton	eau-de-nil
bobbinet	cincture	ear-muffs
bongrace	cingulum	elflocks
boot-lace	cloth cap	en brosse
bouffant	clothing	ensemble
bracelet	coiffure	Eton crop
braiding	cold wave	Eton suit
brass-hat	corduroy	eye-shade
breeches	corselet	face-lift
brocatel	cosmetic	face-pack
brunette	creepers	fairisle
buckskin	cretonne	fastener
burberry	crew neck	fatigues
Burgundy	crucifix	filigree

fillibeg	half-boot	manicure
fire opal	half-hose	mantelet
fish-tail	hand-knit	mantevil
flannels	hat-guard	mantilla
fob watch	headband	material
fontange	headgear	moccasin
fool's cap	headwear	moleskin
footwear	high heel	mourning
frippery	himation	mulberry
froufrou	hipsters	muscadin
fur stole	homespun	mustache
furbelow	inch tape	nail file
galoshes	iron grey	nainsook
gamashes	jackboot	navy blue
gambados	Jacquard	near-silk
gambeson	jodhpurs	neckband
gauntlet	kerchief	necklace
gemstone	kiss curl	neckline
girasole	knickers	negligée
glad rags	knitwear	nightcap
gold lamé	lavender	nose-ring
gossamer	leggings	off-white
grey hair	leotards	oilcloth
gridelin	lingerie	oilskins
gym pants	lip brush	opera hat
gym shoes	lip rouge	overalls
gym tunic	lip salve	overcoat
hair band	lipstick	pabouche
hairline	mackinaw	paduasoy

pea green	sap green	snub nose
pedicure	sapphire	sombrero
peignoir	sardonyx	spit curl
pelerine	saxe blue	stickpin
perruque	scanties	stocking
philabeg	scapular	straw hat
pinafore	sea green	streamer
play suit	sealskin	subucula
plimsoll	seamless	sunstone
pochette	Shantung	surplice
polka dot	shirring	swaddled
polo neck	shirting	swim suit
pomander	shirt-pin	taglioni
pony tail	shoehorn	tail coat
ponyskin	shoelace	tapestry
poppy red	shoe-tree	tarboosh
postiche	short bob	tarlatan
primrose	shot silk	Terylene
pullover	side vent	Thai silk
pure silk	sideburn	toilette
quilting	siege cap	top boots
rag trade	ski-boots	trimming
raincoat	ski-pants	trot-cozy
raw umber	skullcap	trousers
red ochre	slipover	tweezers
red sable	slippers	two-piece
reticule	smocking	umbrella
sandshoe	snap brim	vestment
sanguine	sneakers	viridian

wardrobe	Breton hat	cocked hat
war paint	brilliant	cold cream
whiskers	broadloom	comforter
white tie	burnt lake	corduroys
wig block	burnt rose	cornelian
woollens	bush shirt	cosmetics
wristlet	cadet blue	crinoline
xanthein	cadet grey	Cuban heel
zoot suit	cairngorm	cuff-links
Alice band	calamanco	décolleté
astrakhan	camel hair	demob suit
azure blue	camel coat	deodorant
baby linen	cameo pink	djellabah
balaclava	cap in hand	dog-collar
baldachin	cap sleeve	drape suit
ball dress	caparison	dress coat
bath salts	carbuncle	dress ring
bed jacket	carnelian	dress suit
billycock	cassimere	drop black
black onyx	champagne	duck green
black opal	chantilly	duffel bag
blue black	cherry red	dungarees
blue jeans	chevelure	Dutch pink
bobbin net	China silk	epaulette
bombasine	chinstrap	erminette
bone black	chrome red	eye shadow
bowler hat	claret red	face cream
brassiere	coat-frock	false-face
breast pin	coat-tails	farandine

filoselle
fingering
floss silk
forage cap
frock coat
full dress
full skirt
gabardine
gaberdine
georgette
gold watch
great coat
Greek lace
green-eyed
grenadine
grey agate
grosgrain
hair cloth
hair shirt
hair-brush
hairpiece
hand cream
headdress
headpiece
high stock
hip pocket
hoop skirt
horsehair
housecoat

huckaback
in fashion
Indian red
Inverness
jade green
jadestone
jewellery
jockey cap
Juliet cap
kick pleat
kid gloves
kirby grip
knee-socks
lambswool
le smoking
leaf green
light blue
lime green
linenette
livid pink
loincloth
longcoats
longcloth
lorgnette
Louis heel
madder red
massaline
millinery
mini-skirt

model gown
moonstone
morganite
moss agate
moss green
mouse grey
moustache
muckender
mustachio
Naples red
nauticals
neckcloth
neckpiece
nightgown
nightwear
Nile green
nun's habit
off the peg
olive drab
opera pink
overdress
overshoes
overskirt
Panama hat
pantalets
Paris doll
pea jacket
peaked cap
pearl grey

percaline
persienne
petticoat
phillibeg
pinstripe
pixie hood
plus-fours
point lace
polo shirt
pompadour
pourpoint
press stud
raw sienna
ready-made
redingote
reticella
Roman lace
round neck
royal blue
sack dress
safety pin
sailcloth
sailor hat
school cap
school hat
scoop neck
seed pearl
separates
shadbelly

sharkskin
sheepskin
shirt-band
shirt-stud
shirt-tail
shovel hat
shower cap
sideburns
silver grey
siren suit
ski-jacket
ski-jumper
skin-tight
sloppy Joe
slouch hat
smoke grey
snowshoes
solferino
solitaire
soot black
sou'wester
sphendone
spun rayon
steel blue
steel grey
stitching
stockinet
stomacher
strapless

sun bonnet
sun helmet
swansdown
sweatband
swing curl
tangerine
tarpaulin
terra rosa
toilet bag
towelling
towheaded
track suit
tremblant
tricotine
trousseau
tube dress
Turkey red
turquoise
undervest
underwear
urchin cut
velveteen
vermilion
victorine
waistband
waistcoat
waistline
war bonnet
wedge heel

whalebone

wrap-round

wristband

zucchetto

acid yellow

adder stone

after-shave

all the rage

ankle socks

apple green

aquamarine

astringent

Balbriggan

ballet shoe

bathing cap

beauty spot

Berlin blue

Berlin wool

beryl green

black dress

black pearl

black sable

bloodstone

bobbed hair

bobbin lace

bobbysocks

boiler suit

boudoir cap

broadcloth

brown ochre

bubble bath

burnt umber

bushjacket

buttonhole

button-hook

camel's hair

cap and gown

carmagnole

chalcedony

chaparajos

chartreuse

chatelaine

Chemstrand

chevesaile

chinchilla

Chinese red

chrysolite

Claude tint

claw-hammer

coat hanger

coat of mail

cobalt blue

collarette

collar-stud

college cap

cossack hat

cotton wool

court shoes

court-dress

covert-coat

cummerbund

curling pin

dentifrice

déshabillé

dinner gown

direct blue

dishabille

double chin

drainpipes

dress shirt

dressing up

dressmaker

duster coat

embroidery

emery board

empire-line

Eton collar

Eton jacket

evening bag

eye-glasses

face-powder

false teeth

fancy dress

fascinator

fast yellow

fearnought

feather boa

fitted coat
flake white
foundation
fourchette
French blue
French grey
French knot
French navy
fustanella
Geneva gown
goldilocks
grass green
grass skirt
Greek point
green ochre
habit-cloth
hair ribbon
half-kirtle
halter neck
hand lotion
headsquare
heliotrope
hook and eye
hop sacking
hugmetight
Irish green
Janus green
jersey silk
jersey wool

lappet-head
life-jacket
lounge suit
lover's knot
lucky charm
mackintosh
madder blue
madder lake
madder pink
mantellone
maquillage
marcel wave
marine blue
marquisite
marseilles
masquerade
mess jacket
Milan point
monk's cloth
monk's habit
mousseline
nail polish
needlecord
nightdress
nightshirt
old clothes
olive brown
olive green
overblouse

Oxford bags
Oxford grey
Oxford ties
pantaloons
Paris green
Paris model
party dress
paste jewel
Persian red
picture hat
pillow lace
pin cushion
pith helmet
plastic mac
poke bonnet
powder blue
powder puff
print dress
Psyche knot
puff sleeve
Quaker grey
rabbitskin
raven black
rhinestone
riding hood
ring-brooch
Roman point
romper suit
roquelaure

rose madder	steenkirk	watchstrap
rose quartz	suede shoes	water opal
rubber sole	Sunday best	waterproof
sailor suit	sunglasses	Wellington
salmon pink	suspenders	widow's peak
scalloping	sweat shirt	Windsor tie
scatter pin	tailor-made	wing collar
scratch-wig	terra cotta	wrap-around
seersucker	terry cloth	wraprascal
shaving kit	the cap fits	wrist watch
shirtdress	threadbare	aiguillette
shirt-frill	tight skirt	alexandrite
shirtfront	toilet soap	barrel dress
shoe-buckle	toiletries	bathing suit
signet ring	toothbrush	beauty sleep
silhouette	toothpaste	bellbottoms
silver lamé	tourmaline	best clothes
ski sweater	trench coat	bishop's ring
sleeveless	trypan blue	black patent
smock-frock	turtle neck	black velvet
smoking cap	underlinen	Blucher boot
solar topee	underpants	blue clothes
spectacles	undershirt	boiled shirt
spinel ruby	underskirt	bottle green
sport shirt	upper-stock	boutonnière
sports coat	vanity case	boxer shorts
sports suit	virgin knot	brown madder
sportswear	wampum belt	burnt orange
square neck	watch-chain	burnt sienna

button shoes	dressmaking	Japanese red
campaign hat	dress-shield	kilted skirt
candy stripe	English pink	king's yellow
canvas shoes	evening gown	lacing shoes
cap and bells	farthingale	lapis lazuli
cardinal red	fine feather	lawn sleeves
carmine lake	flannelette	leatherette
casual shoes	flared skirt	leg-of-mutton
cheesecloth	flesh colour	lemon yellow
Chinese silk	flying panel	leopardskin
chrome green	formal dress	mantelletta
chrome lemon	full feather	marquisette
chrysoberyl	Geneva bands	matinee coat
chrysoprase	Geneva cloak	Mechlin lace
clodhoppers	grease paint	middy blouse
cloth of gold	guipure lace	morning coat
cobalt green	hand-me-downs	morning gown
contact lens	Harris tweed	mortar-board
crash helmet	herringbone	mutton chops
crimson lake	high fashion	nail varnish
cutaway coat	hobble skirt	neckerchief
cyanine blue	houppelande	needle point
dark glasses	hummel-bonnet	orange-stick
décolletage	hunting pink	overgarment
deerstalker	incarnadine	Oxford shoes
dinner dress	Indian shawl	panty girdle
dreadnought	isamine blue	Paris yellow
Dresden blue	Italian blue	peacock blue
dress-length	Italian pink	Persian blue

Persian lamb
Phrygian cap
pilot jacket
Prussian red
ready to wear
regimentals
riding habit
Russian jade
school dress
set-in sleeve
shaving soap
shawl collar
shell jacket
shirt-button
shock-headed
shoe leather
shoulder bag
slave bangle
smoky quartz
Spanish comb
spatterdash
stiff collar
subcingulum
suede gloves
Sunday black
swagger coat
swallowtail
tailor tacks
tam-o'-shanter

tennis dress
tennis shoes
terra sienna
toilet water
tooth powder
torchon lace
trencher cap
trouser-suit
ultramarine
Venetian red
Vienna green
walking shoe
wash leather
watch-pocket
watered silk
wedding ring
white collar
widow's weeds
windbreaker
windcheater
Windsor knot
wooden shoes
work clothes
woven fabric
yellow ochre
airforce blue
antigropelos
apron strings
bathing-dress

bespectacled
bib and tucker
bicycle clips
birthday suit
blue-stocking
body stocking
Bohemian ruby
brass buttons
breast pocket
brilliantine
burnt carmine
business suit
canary yellow
cap of liberty
cardinal's hat
cavalry twill
cerulean blue
chastity belt
chesterfield
chin whiskers
Chinese white
chrome orange
chrome yellow
clothes-brush
clothes-horse
collar and tie
college scarf
combinations
crêpe-de-Chine

crewel needle
curling tongs
dinner jacket
divided skirt
donkey jacket
double jersey
dress uniform
dressing-case
dressing-gown
dressing-room
dropped waist
duchesse lace
duffel jacket
Easter bonnet
eau-de-Cologne
electric blue
emerald green
eternity ring
evening cloak
evening dress
evening shoes
fashion-house
fashion-plate
fatigue-dress
flaxen-haired
football boot
full mourning
galligaskins

glass slipper
golden yellow
golden-haired
gun-metal grey
haberdashery
hair dressing
hair-restorer
half mourning
handkerchief
haute couture
Hessian boots
hyacinth blue
if the cap fits
knee breeches
knitting wool
lavender blue
lightning zip
link bracelet
lumberjacket
madder orange
madder violet
madder yellow
magyar sleeve
midnight blue
monkey jacket
morning dress
mourning ring

mousquetaire
nail clippers
nail scissors
national blue
night clothes
old-fashioned
orange madder
out of fashion
Paisley shawl
palladium red
Paris fashion
pastel colour
pedal-pushers
Penang-lawyer
pillar-box red
plain clothes
pressure-suit
Prince Albert
Princess line
Prussian blue
quince yellow
raglan sleeve
rayon casheen
sapphire blue
scarlet ochre
semi-precious
set one's cap at

Household, Food and Drink

This section includes articles of furniture, furnishings and ornaments—fixtures and fittings—linen and cutlery—crockery, drinking vessels, vases and containers—list of foods including fruit, vegetables, pasta, cheeses, confectionery—meats and cuts of meat—drinks including wines and spirits—cooking implements, utensils and terms—meals—eating places.

ade	fry	nut	sup	boil
ale	gas	oil	tap	bolt
bar	gin	ort	tea	bowl
bed	ham	pan	tin	bran
bib	hob	pea	tot	brew
bin	ice	peg	tyg	bulb
box	inn	pie	urn	café
bun	jam	pig	vat	cake
can	jar	poi	yam	carp
cod	jug	pop	bath	case
cos	key	pot	beam	cask
cot	leg	pub	bean	chop
cup	log	roe	beef	chow
den	mat	rue	beer	clam
eel	mop	rug	beet	coal
egg	mug	rum	bell	coke
fig	nip	soy	bite	corn

257

crab	grog	meat	rump	tuna
crib	grub	menu	rusk	vase
curd	hake	milk	sack	veal
date	hall	mint	safe	wall
desk	hash	must	sage	whet
diet	herb	nook	*sake*	whey
dill	hi-fi	nosh	saki	wine
dine	hock	oats	salt	wing
dish	hose	okra	sash	yolk
door	iron	olio	seat	zarf
dram	jamb	olla	sink	zest
duck	kale	ouzo	slaw	acorn
duff	kola	oven	soap	ambry
eats	lamb	pail	soda	anise
Edam	lamp	pâté	sofa	apple
ewer	lard	pear	sole	apron
fare	leek	peas	soup	arras
feed	lees	peel	soya	ashet
fish	lift	pipe	spit	aspic
flan	lime	plug	spud	attic
flip	loaf	plum	stew	bacon
flue	lock	pork	suet	basil
food	loft	port	tank	basin
fool	loin	puff	tart	bench
fork	mace	rare	tidy	berry
fowl	malt	rice	tile	besom
fuel	mash	rock	Toby	bidet
game	mead	roll	tray	blind
gong	meal	roof	tuck	board

boeuf	couch	frame	ladle	pecan
booze	cover	fruit	lager	perch
bread	cream	fudge	latch	piano
bream	cress	gigot	lemon	pilaf
broil	crisp	*glacé*	light	pilau
broom	crock	glass	linen	pilaw
broth	cruet	goody	liver	pizza
brush	crumb	goose	lobby	plate
bully	cruse	gorge	lunch	poach
cacao	crust	Gouda	maize	poker
caddy	cubeb	grain	mango	porch
candy	curds	grape	manna	poult
caper	curry	grate	Médoc	prawn
capon	décor	gravy	melon	press
carte	dicer	grill	mince	print
chair	diner	gruel	mixer	prune
chard	diota	gumbo	mocha	pulse
cheer	divan	hinge	mural	punch
chest	doily	honey	offal	purée
chips	dough	hotel	olive	quaff
chive	drain	icing	onion	quail
chore	dregs	jelly	paint	quilt
chuck	drink	joint	panel	radio
cider	duvet	jorum	papaw	roast
cigar	farce	juice	*pasta*	round
clock	feast	julep	paste	salad
cloth	flank	kebab	pasty	salmi
clove	flask	knife	patty	salon
cocoa	flour	kraut	peach	sauce

sauté	table	ananas	bureau
savoy	taffy	ash-bin	burner
scone	T-bone	ash-can	butter
scrag	tench	awning	cachou
shank	thyme	banana	canapé
sheet	timer	bar-fly	candle
shelf	toast	barley	carafe
sieve	toddy	basket	carpet
skate	tongs	batter	carrot
slops	torch	beaker	carver
snack	*torte*	Beigal	cashew
spice	towel	bibber	cassis
spoon	treat	biggin	caster
sprat	tripe	bisque	castor
squid	trout	bistro	catsup
steak	trunk	bleach	caviar
stein	tunny	blintz	celery
stock	vegan	bluing	cellar
stool	vodka	boiler	cereal
stout	wafer	bonbon	cheese
stove	water	borage	cherry
straw	wheat	borsch	chilli
study	whelk	bottle	citron
sugar	whisk	brandy	citrus
suite	yeast	breast	claret
swede	addled	brunch	closet
sweet	aerial	bucket	cockle
swill	alcove	buffet	coffee
syrup	almond	bunker	coffer

cognac	entrée	hamper	lentil
collop	farina	handle	lintel
comfit	fender	hearth	liquid
compot	fennel	heater	liquor
cooker	fiasco	hominy	litchi
cookie	fingan	hostel	locker
cornet	flacon	hot dog	log bin
course	flagon	hot-pot	lounge
cradle	flitch	humbug	louvre
croute	fodder	ice-box	lowboy
cutlet	fondue	imbibe	luxury
dainty	forage	jam-jar	lychee
damper	frappé	jam-pot	magnum
day-bed	fridge	jujube	mangle
dining	frieze	jumble	marrow
dinner	galley	junket	medlar
dishes	gammon	kaross	ménage
dolium	garage	kernel	mincer
dormer	garlic	kettle	mirror
dragée	garret	kidney	mobile
drawer	gas jet	kipper	morsel
duster	gas tap	kirsch	mousse
eat out	*gâteau*	kumiss	muffin
éclair	geyser	kümmel	muscat
edible	giblet	ladder	mussel
egg-box	ginger	lagena	mutton
egg-cup	goblet	larder	napkin
egg-nog	grater	leaven	nectar
endive	grouse	*légume*	noggin

noodle	porter	savory	tea-bag
nougat	posada	scales	teacup
nutmeg	posset	scampi	teapot
omelet	*potage*	sconce	teapoy
orange	potato	Scotch	teaset
oxtail	pouffe	screen	tea-urn
oyster	*poulet*	settee	tiffin
paella	pulley	settle	tipple
panada	quiche	shandy	titbit
pantry	quince	sherry	toffee
papaya	rabbit	shovel	tomato
parkin	radish	shower	tongue
pastry	ragout	shrimp	toybox
patina	raisin	skewer	trifle
pawpaw	rasher	spirit	trivet
pea pod	ration	sponge	tucker
peanut	recipe	spread	tuck-in
pelmet	relish	sprout	turbot
pepper	remove	squash	tureen
Pernod	repast	starch	turkey
pickle	rhyton	string	turnip
picnic	rocker	subric	umbles
pigeon	ruelle	sundae	veneer
pilaff	rummer	supper	vessel
pillow	saddle	sweets	viande
plaice	salami	switch	viands
plaque	salmon	tamale	waffle
polish	salver	tamara	walnut
pomato	saucer	tavern	washer

whisky	beer mug	*cantina*	commons
window	beeswax	car port	compote
wiring	bellows	caramel	cookery
a bad egg	bibelot	caraway	cooking
absinth	big feed	carouse	cordial
adaptor	biscuit	catchup	cracker
al dente	bitters	caviare	cricket
albumen	blanket	cayenne	crumpet
alcohol	boiling	ceiling	crystal
aliment	bologna	chalice	cuisine
almirah	bolster	chamber	cupcake
amphora	borscht	chamois	curaçao
anchovy	boudoir	charpoy	currant
aniseed	bouquet	charqui	curtain
antique	bourbon	chervil	cushion
apricot	boxroom	chianti	custard
armoire	bramble	chicken	cutlery
ashtray	brisket	chicory	deed box
avocado	brittle	chimney	deep fry
Bacardi	broiler	chopper	dessert
bannock	bunk bed	chowder	dine out
banquet	buttery	chutney	dinette
Bath bun	cabbage	cistern	dish mop
bath mat	cabinet	cleaner	doormat
bathtub	cake tin	cleaver	doorway
bay leaf	cake-mix	coconut	draught
bedding	calorie	codfish	dredger
bedroom	candies	cold cut	dresser
beef tea	canteen	commode	dry wine

dustbin	glutton	lacquer	pabulum
dust-pan	goulash	lagging	padella
edibles	gourmet	landing	pancake
egg-flip	griddle	lantern	paprika
egg-plum	grocery	lattice	parfait
egg-yolk	Gruyère	lettuce	parlour
element	gumdrop	library	parquet
épergne	haddock	limeade	parsley
epicure	halibut	liqueur	parsnip
essence	Hamburg	lobster	pass-key
faience	hammock	lozenge	philtre
fig roll	haricot	Madeira	picture
filbert	heating	malmsey	pie-dish
fitting	helping	martini	pikelet
fixture	herring	matches	pimento
fondant	hickory	matzoth	pitcher
fritter	high tea	meat pie	platter
furbish	hip bath	Moselle	play-pen
furnace	holdall	mustard	plumcot
furnish	hot cake	new wine	poisson
fuse-box	ice cube	nursery	popcorn
game-pie	iced tea	nurture	popover
garnish	ingesta	oatcake	pork pie
gas ring	jam roll	oatmeal	potable
gelatin	jam tart	octopus	potherb
gherkin	ketchup	oil lamp	pottage
giblets	keyhole	oregano	pottery
gin fizz	kitchen	ottoman	poultry
glucose	knuckle	overall	praline

pretzel	shelves	tea-tray	wine gum
protein	sherbet	tequila	work-top
pudding	shoebox	thermos	wringer
pumpkin	sirloin	thimble	yoghurt
ramekin	skillet	ticking	à la carte
ratafia	sloe gin	toaster	absinthe
rations	soufflé	Toby jug	acid drop
ravioli	soupçon	tool kit	Adam's ale
red wine	spatula	transom	agar-agar
rhubarb	spinach	treacle	*al fresco*
risotto	spirits	trellis	allspice
rissole	sprouts	trolley	ambrosia
roaster	spy-hole	truffle	angelica
romaine	stamnos	tumbler	anisette
rum baba	steamer	utensil	antepast
salsify	stewpot	valance	ante-room
samovar	strudel	vanilla	apéritif
sanctum	succory	varnish	appetite
sardine	sultana	venison	apple pie
sausage	sundial	vinegar	armagnac
saveloy	sweeper	vintage	armchair
savoury	tabasco	vitamin	atomiser
scallop	tallboy	vitrail	audit ale
seafood	tankard	washday	back door
seakale	tapioca	wash-tub	baked egg
seltzer	teacake	wassail	ballcock
service	tea-cosy	whatnot	ballroom
serving	tea-leaf	whiskey	banister
shallot	tearoom	whiting	barbecue

Bar-le-Duc	canister	corridor
barstool	capsicum	coverlet
basement	cardamon	crawfish
bassinet	cardamum	crayfish
bath soap	caryatid	cream jug
bed linen	casement	crockery
bedcover	cassolet	cross bun
bedstead	cauldron	*croûtons*
beef cube	cellaret	cucumber
beetroot	chair-bed	cupboard
bell-pull	chair-leg	cuspidor
betel nut	chapatty	cut glass
beverage	chestnut	daiquiri
bilberry	china tea	date roll
billy can	chop suey	decanter
bird-bath	chow mein	déjeuner
bog apple	cigar box	delicacy
bookcase	cinnamon	demijohn
bookends	citrange	dillseed
Bordeaux	cocktail	doorbell
bouillon	cocoanut	doorknob
bread tin	colander	door-post
broccoli	cold meat	door-step
bull's eye	coleslaw	doorstop
Burgundy	collards	doughboy
cache-pot	confetti	doughnut
calabash	conserve	Drambuie
camomile	consommé	dressing
caneloni	*coq au vin*	dried egg

8

dripping	flounder	home-spun
driptray	flour bin	hot drink
dry sherry	fly paper	hot toddy
Dubonnet	food-mill	hot-plate
duckling	fried egg	hydromel
dumpling	frosting	ice cream
egg-apple	fruit-cup	ice water
egg-fruit	fruit-gum	immerser
egg-plant	fruit-pie	infusion
egg-shell	full wine	jalousie
egg-slice	fuse-wire	jellybag
egg-spoon	gallipot	jewel-box
egg-timer	gas meter	julienne
egg-whisk	gelatine	kedgeree
egg-white	gin and It	kickshaw
Emmental	gin sling	kindling
emulsion	gourmand	kohlrabi
escalope	green tea	lamb chops
escargot	grilling	lassagne
escarole	handbell	lemonade
fanlight	handrail	libation
filament	hangings	licorice
fireside	hangover	linoleum
firewood	hard tack	loin chops
fixtures	hatstand	lollipop
flan case	hazelnut	love seat
flapjack	highball	luncheon
flat iron	hip flask	macaroni
flesh pot	Hollands	macaroon

267

mackerel	omelette	pot plant
mad apple	ornament	pot roast
main dish	out-house	potation
marinade	ovenware	potherbs
marinate	painting	preserve
marjoram	pannikin	quenelle
marzipan	paraffin	radiator
matchbox	pastille	rice soup
mattress	pastrami	rice-beer
meat ball	patty pan	Riesling
meat loaf	pembroke	rock cake
meat roll	pemmican	rock salt
meat stew	pendulum	roly-poly
meat-safe	pheasant	root beer
meringue	pigs' feet	rose-bowl
mess hall	pig-swill	rosemary
mild soap	pilchard	ruby port
mince pie	pimiento	rum punch
molasses	pink lady	rutabaga
monogram	pipe-rack	rye bread
moth ball	plantain	salt beef
moulding	playroom	salt pork
moussaka	plum cake	sandwich
mulberry	polisher	saucepan
muscatel	pope's eye	Sauterne
mushroom	pork chop	scallion
new broom	porridge	schnapps
night-cap	port wine	schooner
olive oil	portrait	scissors

scrag-end	soybeans	thin wine
scramble	spice jar	tortilla
scraps bag	spittoon	trap-door
scrubber	split pea	trencher
scullery	squeezer	trotters
sea trout	stairway	tuna fish
semolina	stock-pot	turmeric
shoehorn	strainer	turnover
shoulder	stuffing	underlay
shredder	sturgeon	upstairs
shutters	sun-blind	vargueno
side-dish	supplies	verjuice
side-door	surf food	vermouth
sink unit	surround	viaticum
sitz bath	syllabub	victuals
skylight	table-leg	wainscot
slop-bowl	table-mat	wall-safe
slop-pail	table-top	wardrobe
small ham	tamarind	water ice
snack-bar	tantalus	water jug
snuffbox	tapestry	water-tap
soap-dish	tarragon	wig-block
soapsuds	teabread	wild duck
soft soap	tea-break	wireless
solarium	tea-caddy	wishbone
solecism	tea-chest	wood shed
souvenir	tea-cloth	Yale lock
soy flour	teaspoon	yoghourt
soy sauce	tea-table	zucchini

zwieback
acid drops
Adam's wine
addled egg
aitchbone
angel cake
antipasto
apartment
appetiser
aqua vitae
arrowroot
artichoke
asparagus
aubergine
bake blind
baking tin
banquette
barmbrack
barometer
bath salts
bath towel
bay window
bean feast
bed-settee
bedspread
beefsteak
beer glass
birch beer
bite to eat

blank door
boiled egg
bookshelf
brasserie
Brazil nut
breakfast
bric-à-brac
bubble gum
bully beef
butter pat
cafeteria
cakestand
calf's head
Camembert
cane chair
cantharus
capuccine
card table
carpeting
carpet-rod
cashew nut
casserole
champagne
charlotte
chick-peas
chinaware
chocolate
chophouse
cigarette

clear soup
clepsydra
cloakroom
club chair
club steak
cochineal
coffee cup
coffee pot
Cointreau
colcannon
cold drink
collation
condiment
confiture
container
cookhouse
coriander
corkscrew
corn bread
cornflour
cough drop
crab apple
crackling
cranberry
cream cake
cream horn
cream puff
croissant
croquette

crossbeam
croustade
Cuba libre
cubby-hole
cullender
dark bread
davenport
deck chair
demitasse
desk light
detergent
diet-sheet
directory
dish-cloth
dish-towel
dishwater
distemper
dog-basket
doorframe
door-plate
double bed
Dover sole
drain pipe
dried eggs
dried peas
drop scone
drum table
drumstick
dust-sheet

Dutch oven
Dutch tile
Dutch wife
easy-chair
egg-beater
egg-powder
egg-slicer
eiderdown
elevenses
entremets
epicurean
epulation
estaminet
etiquette
face towel
facecloth
fire-alarm
fireguard
fire-irons
firelight
fireplace
firewater
fish knife
fish slice
flageolet
flower pot
foodmixer
foodstuff
footstool

forcemeat
foretaste
French bed
fricassee
fried rice
fried sole
front door
fruit bowl
fruit cake
fruit dish
frying pan
furniture
galantine
garden hut
gas burner
gas cooker
Georgiana
ginger ale
ginger pop
girandole
glass door
glory-hole
gold plate
gravy boat
gravy soup
green peas
green soap
grillroom
groceries

groundnut
guest room
half a loaf
hallstand
hamburger
hand towel
heavy wine
highchair
hope chest
hourglass
household
house-room
housewife
housework
humble-pie
inglenook
Irish stew
jackfruit
japanning
jelly baby
jewel-case
joss-stick
lamb fries
lamplight
lampshade
lampstand
layer cake
leaf-table
left-overs

leg of lamb
lemon curd
lemon sole
letterbox
light bulb
light wine
Lima beans
liquorice
loaf sugar
log-basket
love apple
loving-cup
lump sugar
lunchroom
macédoine
maid's room
marchpane
margarine
marmalade
marquetry
master-key
meat paste
metheglin
mezzanine
middlings
milk-shake
mincemeat
mint julep
mint sauce

monkey nut
mousetrap
muscadine
music room
muskmelon
navy beans
neat drink
nectarine
new potato
nutriment
objet d'art
onion soup
orangeade
panelling
paper knife
parquetry
partition
partridge
passe-vite
patchwork
patty-cake
peanut bar
persimmon
phone book
phosphate
picnic ham
pie-funnel
pierglass
pier-table

piggy-bank	rye whisky	soft drink
pineapple	safety pin	soup plate
piping bag	salad bowl	soup spoon
piping hot	Sally Lunn	soya beans
pistachio	salt bacon	spaghetti
place-card	sapodilla	spare room
porcelain	sauce-boat	spareribs
porringer	Scotch egg	spearmint
pot-pourri	seasoning	spin-drier
pound cake	secretary	sponge-bag
preserves	serviette	spun sugar
provender	shakedown	staircase
provision	shellfish	statuette
punch bowl	shoeblack	steam iron
rabbit pie	short ribs	steel wool
radiogram	shortcake	still wine
raspberry	shot glass	storm door
reception	show piece	stovepipe
red pepper	shower cap	sugar beet
refection	side light	sugar bowl
refectory	side table	sugar lump
Rhine wine	sideboard	sugar plum
rice paper	single bed	sun lounge
ringstand	slop-basin	sweet corn
roadhouse	small beer	sweet wine
roast beef	snap beans	sweetmeat
rock candy	soda bread	swing door
Roquefort	soda scone	Swiss roll
rump steak	soda water	table lamp

tableware	water-cock	blackberry
tangerine	wax polish	blancmange
tasty dish	wheat germ	Bloody Mary
tawny port	white meat	blue cheese
teakettle	white wine	boiled fish
tea-leaves	whitebait	boiled meat
tea-waggon	whitewash	Bombay duck
telephone	wild honey	*bon appetit*
tête-à-tête	window box	boot-polish
threshold	wine glass	brandy snap
tiger milk	wing chair	bread board
timepiece	yard of ale	bread sauce
tinder box	abstergent	bread stick
tin-opener	alarm clock	breadcrumb
toast-rack	anthracite	breadfruit
toilet bag	apple sauce	breadknife
top drawer	apple-cover	Brie cheese
underfelt	aristology	broad beans
vegetable	baked beans	brown sugar
vol-au-vent	baking bowl	brown trout
wall-clock	baking tray	bucket seat
wall-light	balustrade	butter dish
wallpaper	Bath oliver	buttermilk
washbasin	Beaujolais	*café au lait*
washboard	bedclothes	candelabra
washstand	bedsprings	candy floss
water butt	bell pepper	cantaloupe
water pipe	bellarmine	caper sauce
water tank	bill of fare	cappuccino

cassolette	cooking fat	Edam cheese
celery salt	cooking oil	elderberry
chafing pan	corned beef	escritoire
Chambertin	corned meat	fatted calf
chandelier	cornflakes	featherbed
Chartreuse	cos lettuce	finger bowl
chaudfroid	curtain rod	fire-basket
cheese dish	custard pie	fire-escape
cheesecake	daily bread	firescreen
Chelsea bun	Danish blue	fish kettle
chewing gum	darning egg	flank steak
chiffonier	deep-freeze	floor-cloth
chocolates	devil's food	folding bed
chopsticks	dill pickle	food supply
chou pastry	dining hall	forcing bag
chuck roast	dining room	fork supper
clothes peg	dinner gong	four-poster
clothes pin	dinner roll	frangipane
coal-bucket	dishwasher	French cake
coal-bunker	dog biscuit	French sash
coal-cellar	doorhandle	fresh cream
coat-hanger	double loin	fricandeau
coddled egg	downstairs	frozen food
coffee bean	drawing pin	fruit juice
coffee cake	dried fruit	fruit salad
coffee mill	dropped egg	fruit-knife
coffee shop	dry measure	funeral ham
concoction	dumb waiter	garden path
confection	Dutch clock	garden peas

garden shed	ingredient	meal ticket
garlic salt	intoxicant	Melba toast
gastronome	Jamaica rum	milk bottle
ginger beer	*jardinière*	minestrone
ginger snap	jugged hare	mint humbug
glass-cloth	kidney bean	mixed drink
gooseberry	knick knack	mixing bowl
Gorgonzola	lamb cutlet	mock turtle
gramophone	lamp socket	mortedella
granadilla	lemon juice	Moscow mule
grand piano	letter-rack	mozzarella
grape juice	light lunch	mulled wine
grapefruit	liquid diet	Munich beer
greedyguts	liverwurst	music stool
green beans	living room	musical box
green salad	loganberry	mustard pot
ground rice	loose cover	mutton chop
half-bottle	love-potion	napkin ring
ham and eggs	lumber room	night-light
headcheese	malt whisky	nutcracker
hearty meal	malted milk	on the rocks
hickory nut	mangosteen	on the shelf
Holland gin	manzanilla	oven gloves
hollow ware	maple syrup	paint-brush
honey crisp	maraschino	passageway
horse-brass	marble cake	pastry case
hot and cold	marrow bone	pâtisserie
iced coffee	matchstick	peach melba
icing sugar	mayonnaise	pepper mill

peppermint
percolator
periwinkle
Persian rug
persiennes
photograph
piano stool
piccalilli
pickled egg
pillow slip
pillowcase
pilot bread
pilot light
pin cushion
pinto beans
plat du jour
plate glass
plate piece
poached egg
provisions
pot scourer
pot scraper
potted meat
power point
public room
puff pastry
rain barrel
ration book
red cabbage

red currant
red herring
regalement
restaurant
rice polish
rock salmon
rolled lamb
rolled oats
rolled pork
rolling pin
rose-window
round steak
royal icing
rumpus room
Russian tea
saccharine
salmagundi
salt cellar
sauce-alone
sauerkraut
scatter rug
sea biscuit
sealing-wax
secretaire
shallow fry
sheep's head
shirred egg
shish-kebab
shortbread

shortcrust
silverside
silverware
Simnel cake
slivowitza
smooth wine
soap flakes
soap powder
soda syphon
sour grapes
sour pickle
space-saver
spatchcock
spirit lamp
sponge cake
spotted dog
square meal
squeteague
staple diet
step ladder
stiff drink
stirrup cup
storage jar
strawberry
strip-light
stroganoff
stuffed egg
sucking pig
sugar candy

sugar mouse	trust house	whole wheat
sun parlour	turtle soup	wicker-work
sweet stuff	upholstery	window-pane
sweet tooth	usquebaugh	window-sash
sweetbread	vanilla pod	window-seat
swing chair	vanity lamp	window-sill
Swiss chard	veal cutlet	wine basket
Swiss steak	vegetarian	wine cellar
table d'hôte	ventilator	wine cooler
tablecloth	vermicelli	wine-bottle
table-knife	Vichy water	wooden ware
table-linen	Victoriana	work basket
tablespoon	Victory gum	yacht chair
tea biscuit	Vienna loaf	zabaglione
tea service	Vienna roll	airtight jar
television	waffle-iron	almond icing
tenderloin	wall-socket	almond paste
thermostat	warming pan	amontillado
time-switch	washbasket	apple brandy
tobacco jar	water clock	avocado pear
toilet roll	water cress	baking sheet
toilet soap	water icing	banana split
Tom Collins	water lemon	barley broth
tomato soup	watermelon	barley sugar
tonic water	wet measure	barley water
toothbrush	whisk broom	basket chair
toothpaste	whisky sour	bead curtain
transistor	white bread	beef extract
trinket box	white sauce	beef sausage

below stairs
Benedictine
black butter
black coffee
black pepper
blank window
bonne bouche
bonne femme
bookshelves
brandy sauce
brandy smash
breadcrumbs
broom handle
burnt almond
butter beans
butter-knife
cabriole leg
calf's brain
candelabrum
candlestick
caster sugar
Castile soap
celery stick
centrepiece
chafing dish
cheese board
chicken feed
chicken soup
chilli sauce

china figure
Chinoiserie
chipped beef
Chippendale
chokecherry
citrus fruit
clam chowder
clothes line
clothes pole
clove pepper
coal scuttle
coffee table
coffee-break
coffee-house
comestibles
cookery book
cooking wine
cooling tray
cottage loaf
counterpane
cover charge
cowslip wine
cream cheese
cuckoo clock
curry powder
curtain hook
curtain rail
curtain ring
custard tart

dessert fork
devilled egg
devilled ham
dining table
dinner party
door-knocker
double cream
draught beer
drawing room
dressed crab
Dutch carpet
Dutch cheese
earthenware
eating apple
eating house
eating irons
eiffel tower
elbowgrease
Eve's pudding
family album
festal board
fillet steak
firelighter
fireside rug
first-aid box
flank mutton
floor polish
fold-away bed
frankfurter

French beans	invalid fare	oil painting
French bread	Irish coffee	olla-podrida
French chalk	Irish potato	orange juice
French toast	iron rations	oriel window
French wines	Italian iron	Oriental rug
fresh butter	jam turnover	oyster plant
furnishings	jellied eels	paperweight
gammon steak	kitchen sink	Parma violet
garden chair	kitchen unit	parson's nose
garden-hose	kitchenette	peach brandy
garden party	laundry room	period piece
garden swing	leg of mutton	Petit Suisse
ginger punch	light repast	*petits fours*
gingerbread	light switch	picture rail
Gouda cheese	linen basket	pig's trotter
green pepper	link sausage	plant-holder
griddlecake	loaf of bread	player piano
ground spice	loving spoon	plum pudding
health foods	Madeira cake	pocket flask
hearth brush	mantelpiece	poached fish
Hepplewhite	marshmallow	pomegranate
Hollandaise	meat chopper	pork sausage
hors d'oeuvre	meat cleaver	potato crisp
horseradish	metal polish	potato salad
hot cross bun	milk pudding	preparation
hot luncheon	morning roll	pressed beef
huckleberry	morning room	prickly pear
ice lollipop	non-stick pan	primus stove
incinerator	nourishment	profiterole

public house
pudding bowl
pumice stone
quince jelly
reading lamp
record album
refreshment
rice pudding
roast grouse
roast potato
roasting tin
roll-top desk
room service
room-divider
rotary whisk
runner beans
salmon trout
sauce bottle
sausage roll
Scotch broth
scouring pad
scratch feed
self-service
service lane
service lift
serving dish
ship biscuit
shopping bag
shower-cloth

side of bacon
silver plate
silver spoon
single cream
sitting room
skeleton key
sliced bread
sliding door
smörgasbord
spotted Dick
spring clean
spring onion
staff of life
storm-window
string beans
strong drink
studio couch
suet pudding
summer-house
sweet almond
sweet pickle
sweet pepper
sweet potato
sweet sherry
Swiss cheese
swivel chair
table napkin
tagliatelle
tape measure

tea-strainer
thermometer
toffee apple
tomato juice
tomato sauce
tossed salad
treacle tart
trencherman
tutti-frutti
utility room
vacuum flask
Vienna steak
vinaigrette
vintage wine
washing line
washing soap
washing soda
wassail bowl
water closet
water heater
wedding cake
Welsh rabbit
wheaten loaf
white coffee
white pepper
white potato
wicker chair
wienerwurst
window blind

window frame	bottled fruit	clothes-brush
window-light	bottle-opener	clothes-drier
winter cress	bottom drawer	clothes-horse
wintergreen	bouquet garni	clotted cream
wonderberry	breast of lamb	codfish balls
wooden spoon	breast of veal	companion set
work-surface	brewer's yeast	console-table
writing-desk	butcher's meat	contour chair
wrought iron	butterscotch	convex mirror
adhesive tape	*café espresso*	cooking apple
Admiralty ham	candleholder	cooking range
afternoon tea	candle-sconce	corn on the cob
antimacassar	caraway seeds	Cornish pasty
apple crumble	carpet beater	*coupe Jacques*
apple fritter	carriage lamp	crust of bread
apple strudel	carving-knife	cupboard love
apron-strings	chaise longue	curds and whey
asparagus tip	cheese-grater	custard apple
bacon and eggs	chesterfield	custard sauce
bakewell tart	chilli pepper	Danish pastry
ball of string	chiming clock	Danzig brandy
bedside light	chimney piece	delicatessen
bedside table	chimney-stack	dessert spoon
birthday cake	chitterlings	disinfectant
bitter almond	chocolate bar	Dormer window
black currant	chocolate box	double boiler
Black Hamburg	choice morsel	dressing room
black pudding	cigarette box	Dutch courage
blood pudding	cinnamon ball	Dutch dresser

electric fire	ice-cream cone	pastry cutter
electric iron	ice-cream soda	peanut butter
electric lamp	inner sanctum	pease pudding
emergency bed	Irish whiskey	Persian melon
extractor fan	ironing board	pickled onion
fillet of sole	ironing table	picnic basket
finnan haddie	Italian paste	picnic hamper
firelighters	kettle-holder	picture frame
fireside seat	kitchen table	pigs' knuckles
fish and chips	kneehole desk	Pilsener beer
fish dressing	labour-saving	pistachio nut
fitted carpet	*langue de chat*	place-setting
flower holder	Leyden cheese	planked steak
Forfar bridie	library table	pork and beans
French pastry	light fitting	potato crisps
French polish	looking-glass	pudding basin
french window	lunch counter	pumpernickel
gate-leg table	luncheon meat	radiant plate
grated cheese	magazine rack	rainbow trout
grilled steak	mangel-wurzel	record-player
ground almond	marrowfat pea	reel of cotton
ground ginger	mineral water	reel of thread
ground pepper	mulligan stew	refrigerator
Hamburg steak	mulligatawny	regency chair
haricot beans	nest of tables	reproduction
hasty pudding	non-alcoholic	rocking chair
haute cuisine	paraffin lamp	Russian salad
hot chocolate	passe-partout	sage and onion
hot water tank	passion fruit	salted peanut

sarsaparilla	spare bedroom	thermos flask
scarlet beans	spirit of wine	toasting fork
Scotch kisses	sponge finger	trestle table
scrambled egg	spring greens	turkish towel
serving hatch	stain remover	upright piano
serving spoon	standard lamp	vegetable oil
sewing needle	streaky bacon	visiting card
sheepskin rug	supernaculum	Waldorf salad
sherry trifle	sweet and sour	washing board
shopping list	swizzle stick	washing cloth
short commons	tobasco sauce	water biscuit
shoulder clod	table lighter	Welsh dresser
silver polish	table service	Welsh rarebit
sirloin steak	talcum powder	whipped cream
smoked salmon	tape-recorder	writing-table
Spanish onion	tartare sauce	yellow mombin

SCIENCE AND TECHNOLOGY

This general heading includes sections for General Science, Natural History, Machinery, Medicine, Warfare and Geography.

General Science

This section includes a list of the sciences—botany, biology, chemistry, physics, nuclear physics, zoology and dietetics—chemical elements and compounds—scientific instruments, vessels and equipment—mathematics—algebra, trigonometry—geometry—arithmetic and numbers.

AU	ion	sum	axis	cone
pH	lab	tan	base	core
pi	lac	wow	beam	cosh
add	law	acid	bion	cube
amp	nil	acme	bios	cusp
arc	ova	alar	bomb	cyte
cos	PVC	alum	buna	data
cot	ray	amyl	calx	dyad
dye	sac	apex	cell	echo
erg	sec	atom	CERN	etna
gas	sin	axes	coil	flex
gel	sol	axil	coke	flux

foam	rule	anode	ester
foci	rust	argon	ether
foil	sine	assay	ethyl
fuse	sinh	attar	fauna
gene	soda	basic	fibre
germ	sums	bevel	field
half	surd	bifid	flame
heat	tank	borax	flask
lees	tone	boron	flora
lens	trig	brass	fluid
line	unit	bursa	focus
load	volt	chord	force
lune	wane	class	gauge
mass	watt	clone	gauss
muon	wave	conic	gemma
neon	X-ray	cosec	genes
node	zein	count	genus
norm	zero	cubed	glass
otto	acute	cubic	graph
ovum	agene	cupel	group
phon	agent	curie	helix
pile	algae	curve	henry
pion	alkyl	cycle	hertz
plot	alloy	cyton	hexad
plus	alpha	datum	hypha
pole	amide	delta	index
rake	amine	digit	inert
rays	angle	dregs	laser
root	anion	equal	latex

leach	poise	tenth	alkali
lemma	polar	tithe	amoeba
light	power	tongs	ampere
linin	prime	toxin	amylum
locus	prism	triad	anneal
lymph	radar	uredo	apogee
lysin	radii	U-tube	atomic
maths	radix	value	baffle
meson	radon	vinyl	barium
minus	ratio	virus	baryta
monad	relay	wedge	beaker
mucin	resin	xenon	binary
nitre	rhomb	X-rays	binate
nylon	rider	xylem	biogen
octad	robot	yeast	biotin
octet	rosin	zooid	bisect
optic	ruler	abacus	boffin
orbit	salts	A-blast	bolide
order	slide	acetic	borate
ottar	solid	action	botany
ovate	solve	adding	bronze
ovoid	sound	aerial	bunsen
ovule	spark	aerobe	calcar
oxide	spore	agamic	calxes
ozone	steam	air gap	camera
petri	still	air gas	carbon
phase	style	albedo	carboy
plane	table	albose	casein
point	taxis	alidad	cation

cerate	embryo	inulin	mortar
cerium	energy	iodide	necron
charge	enzyme	iodine	niacin
circle	erbium	ionium	nickel
citric	Euclid	isobar	nonary
cloaca	eureka	isomer	nought
cobalt	factor	kation	nozzle
coccus	fibrin	ketone	nuclei
cohort	figure	labile	number
colony	filter	lacuna	oblong
cosine	finite	lambda	octane
cosinh	fluent	lamina	octant
cuboid	fluent	lanate	opaque
cuneus	foment	litmus	optics
curium	funnel	lipase	oroide
cyclic	fusion	loglog	osmium
cytode	galena	lutein	ovisac
damper	gamete	lysine	oxygen
decane	gas jar	magnet	patina
decant	G-clamp	matrix	pectin
degree	Geiger	matter	pentad
denary	gluten	megohm	pepsin
dilute	halide	methyl	pestle
diplon	H-blast	metric	petrol
dipole	helium	micron	pewter
divide	heptad	minute	phenol
dry ice	hybrid	mirror	photon
dynamo	ignite	module	phylum
emanon	indium	moduli	plasma

poison	stress	zymase	ampoule
potash	symbol	abaxial	amylase
proton	syphon	acetate	analogy
quasar	system	acetone	anatomy
radian	tables	acetose	anaxial
radium	target	acid-dye	aneroid
radius	tetrad	acidity	angular
radome	theory	acrylic	aniline
retort	thoron	actinon	anodize
ribose	thrust	acyclic	anomaly
ripple	tissue	adaptor	antacid
runner	torque	aerator	antenna
saline	trigon	aerobic	aphotic
secant	tripod	aerosol	aquaria
sector	ullage	air pump	arsenic
senary	uncate	airlock	atavism
sensor	ungula	albumen	atomics
series	uv lamp	albumin	atomism
serine	vacuum	alchemy	atom-sub
sesqui	vapour	alcohol	aureole
sinter	vector	alembic	azimuth
sodium	versed	algebra	balance
solder	versin	alidade	bascule
sphere	vertex	aliquot	battery
spirit	volume	allobar	bearing
square	vortex	amalgam	bell jar
stable	weight	amidase	benthos
staple	xylose	ammeter	benzene
starch	xygote	ammonia	beta-ray

binocle	coal-tar	dibasic	fission
biology	colloid	digital	fistula
bipolar	compass	diluent	flaccid
bismuth	complex	dioxide	flexure
bitumen	conduit	diploid	fluxion
blubber	congeal	dissect	forceps
boiling	control	divisor	formula
booster	cordate	Doppler	freezer
bracket	corrode	dry cell	fulcrum
brazier	counter	eclipse	furnace
brazing	crystal	ecology	gallium
breeder	cubical	egg-cell	gametes
bromide	culture	elastic	genesis
bromine	cuneate	element	geodesy
burette	cuprite	ellipse	geogony
cadrans	current	emitter	geology
caesium	cyanide	enation	gilbert
calomel	cycloid	entropy	gimbals
calorie	decagon	essence	gliadin
capsule	decibel	EURATOM	glucose
carbide	decimal	eutropy	gravity
cascade	decuple	excited	habitat
cathode	deltoid	exhaust	hafnium
cell sap	density	fall-out	halogen
chamber	dentine	fatigue	haploid
chemism	deposit	ferment	heating
chemist	dextrin	fertile	hexagon
circuit	diagram	figures	hexapod
citrate	dialyse	fissile	histoid

holmium	lipoids	nonacid	peptone
hot atom	lithium	nonuple	percent
hydrate	maltose	nothing	PH meter
hydride	Martian	nuclear	PH value
hyperon	matrass	nucleon	physics
igniter	megaton	nucleus	pig iron
impulse	melanin	nuclide	pigment
indices	mercury	numeral	pincers
inertia	mesoton	numeric	pipette
integer	metamer	oblique	plastic
iridium	methane	obovate	plastid
isochor	micelle	obovoid	polygon
isotone	microbe	octagon	positon
isotope	minuend	octuple	potable
isotopy	missile	off-peak	primary
isotron	mitosis	ohmeter	primate
isotype	mixture	ordinal	problem
keratin	modulus	osmosis	process
kiloton	monitor	oxalate	product
krypton	muonium	oxidant	project
lacquer	myology	oxidase	propane
lactase	nascent	oxidose	protein
lactate	negaton	oxonium	protium
lactose	network	oxyacid	pyramid
lamella	neutron	paracme	quantum
lanolin	niobium	pedicel	quinary
lateral	nitrate	pennate	quinine
lattice	nitride	pentose	radiant
leucine	nitrite	peptide	radical

radicle	spirits	tinfoil	acceptor
radions	Sputnik	titrate	accuracy
rare gas	squared	toluene	acicular
reactor	stimuli	torsion	acid bath
reagent	stirrer	totient	acid salt
re-entry	stopper	trapeze	acid test
rhenium	subacid	trigger	actinism
rhodium	sublime	tritium	actinium
rhombic	sucrose	trypsin	actinoid
rhombus	sulphur	unitary	activate
röntgen	sun-spot	uranide	activity
rotator	synapse	uranium	addition
sagitta	synergy	vaccine	additive
saltant	syringe	valence	adhesion
scalene	tabular	valency	adhesive
scanner	tangent	vascula	aerology
science	tarnish	vernier	aerostat
sebacic	Telstar	vinegar	agar-agar
section	tensile	vitamin	alcahest
segment	tension	vitriol	aldehyde
sextant	terbium	voltage	algorism
shellac	ternary	wolfram	aliquant
sigmoid	ternion	yolk sac	alkahest
silicon	terpene	yttrium	alkaline
solvent	theorem	zoology	alpha ray
sounder	thermal	zootomy	amandine
spatula	thorite	zymurgy	amitosis
species	thorium	abrasive	ammonium
spireme	thulium	absorber	anabatic

analogue	beta-rays	centroid
analyser	betatron	centuple
analysis	bevatron	cesspool
analytic	binomial	charcoal
angle bar	bioblast	chemical
angström	biochemy	chemurgy
anode ray	biometer	chlorate
antimony	biophore	chloride
antinode	bivalent	chlorine
aquarium	blastema	chlorite
argument	blowpipe	chromate
armature	body cell	chromium
arsenate	Bohr atom	cleveite
arsenite	brackets	cobalite
asbestos	buoyancy	co-enzyme
astatine	calculus	cohesion
asteroid	calipers	cold bend
atmology	capacity	cold weld
atomizer	carbonyl	collagen
autobomb	cardinal	compound
autology	carotene	computer
autunite	cassette	conchate
Avogadro	cast-iron	constant
avometer	catalyze	copperas
Bakelite	catalyst	cosecant
barnacle	catolyte	counting
basicity	cavitron	coupling
basidium	cell wall	crescent
benzoate	centrode	cruciate

crucible	division	filtrate
cube root	docimasy	fineness
cubiform	drip tray	fistular
cucurbit	dye-stuff	fluoride
cyanogen	dynamics	fluorine
cyclosis	ectogeny	fluxions
cylinder	effluent	follicle
cytology	electron	formulae
decimate	emulsion	fraction
delta ray	enthalpy	francium
demersal	entozoon	free pole
dendrite	epiblast	freezing
detector	epivisor	friction
deuteron	equation	fuel cell
dew-point	esterase	function
dextrose	ethylene	gamma ray
diagonal	eugenics	gapmeter
dialysis	europium	gas laser
dialytic	eutectic	gas meter
diameter	euxenite	gasoline
diastase	excitant	gelatine
diatomic	exhalant	genetics
dihedral	exit beam	genotype
dilution	exit dose	geometer
diplogen	exotoxin	geometry
diplosis	exponent	geotaxis
divalent	fast pile	globulin
divided	figurate	glutelin
dividers	filament	**glutenin**

glycogen	isobaric	Mohr clip
gradient	isogonic	molecule
gram-atom	isomeric	momentum
graphite	isoteric	monomial
guidance	isotopic	monoxide
half-life	isotropy	multiple
hard soap	karyotin	multiply
harmonic	kerosene	mutation
heat sink	klystron	mycology
helicoid	laser gun	negative
heptagon	laudanum	negatron
hexagram	leaching	neutrino
homogamy	leak tube	nicotine
honey-dew	lecithin	nitrogen
hotplate	lenticel	nobelium
hydracid	levulose	nonenary
hydrogen	litharge	non-metal
ignition	lutetium	nucleate
impeller	magic eye	nucleole
inductor	mantissa	nucleons
infinity	marsh-gas	numerary
infra-red	matrices	octonary
injector	mean life	odometer
inositol	melamine	ohmmeter
integral	meniscus	one-sided
involute	mercuric	organism
ion drive	mesotron	overload
ionizing	miniscus	oxidizer
iriscope	miscible	oximeter

parabola	pure line	samarium
paradigm	pure tone	sand bath
parallax	pyroxene	saxicola
parallel	quadrant	scandium
particle	quadrate	scanning
peak load	quantity	scissile
pedology	quotient	sediment
pentagon	radiable	selenium
pentosan	radiator	septimal
peroxide	rational	septuple
phenolic	reactant	sequence
phosgene	reaction	sex ratio
physical	reactive	sextuple
pinacoid	real time	silicate
pioscope	receiver	silicone
plankton	recorder	sine wave
plastics	repetend	sitology
platinum	research	skin dose
plotting	resinoid	slow pile
plumbago	resistor	smelting
polarity	retarder	soft soap
polonium	reticule	solarium
polyacid	rheology	solation
positive	rheostat	solution
positron	rhomboid	sounding
power cut	roentgen	Space Age
pressure	rubidium	spagyric
prismoid	rudiment	specimen
prophase	sabulose	spectrum

sphenoid	trioxide	xenogamy
spheroid	trochoid	X-ray tube
spot test	truncate	zoetrope
stimulus	tryosine	zoom lens
subatoms	tungsten	zoospore
sub-order	unciform	zygotene
subtract	unit cell	absorbent
sulphate	unstable	acoustics
sulphide	uric acid	actinides
sulphite	vanadium	activated
sum total	variable	activator
synapsis	variance	adiabatic
syndesis	vascular	advection
tantalum	velocity	aggregate
tartrate	viagraph	air pocket
taxonomy	viameter	alchemist
test-tube	vicenary	algebraic
tetragon	vinculum	algorithm
thallium	virology	allotropy
thiamine	vitamin A	altimeter
thruster	vitamin B	aluminium
tincture	vitamin C	ambergris
titanium	vitamin D	americium
totitive	vitamin E	amino acid
traction	vitellus	amplitude
transect	volatile	anabolism
triangle	watt-hour	anaerobic
tribasic	wave form	anamorpha
trigonal	wet steam	angle iron

anglesite	basic salt	cellulose
anhydride	beet sugar	chemiatry
annealing	berkelium	chemistry
aperiodic	beryllium	chemurgic
apparatus	beta decay	chiliagon
aqua regia	bifarious	chill bath
archetype	bigeneric	chromatin
arrowroot	bilateral	clinostat
aspirator	binocular	cochleate
astrolabe	bionomics	coelostat
astrology	bipyramid	coenobium
astronaut	bisulcate	cold short
astronomy	bivalence	colloidal
atavistic	bivariant	compasses
atmolysis	blast wave	condenser
atmometer	blood bank	conductor
atom blast	bolometer	conjugate
atomic gas	boric acid	converter
atomicity	Boyle's law	convolute
atomology	callipers	co-polymer
atom-plane	canal-rays	cork borer
attenuate	cane-sugar	corrosion
autoclave	capacitor	cosmic ray
autoflash	capillary	cosmogony
automaton	carbonate	cosmology
barograph	carbonize	cosmonaut
barometer	catalysis	cosnotron
baroscope	catalytic	cotangent
base metal	celluloid	countdown

covalence	discharge	fadometer
covalency	dispenser	field coil
cryogenic	distiller	figure out
cryoscope	desimeter	flame test
cuneiform	desimetry	flash burn
curvature	duodenary	flash test
cyclotron	duplicate	flotation
cytoplasm	dust cloud	flow lines
dead point	Early Bird	flow meter
decade box	eccentric	fluxional
decagonal	ectoplasm	focimeter
decaploid	effluvium	folic acid
deflector	eidograph	frequency
deionizer	elastance	fulminate
depth dose	elastomer	fungicide
desiccant	electrode	galactose
detergent	elemental	galvanize
detonator	ellipsoid	gamma rays
deuteride	emanation	gemmology
deuterium	endoplasm	geobiotic
deuterous	endosperm	geodesist
developer	endospore	geography
dial gauge	entelechy	germanium
dichotomy	equipoise	gestation
dietetics	erythrite	glucoside
dimension	erythrose	glutinous
dimorphic	Euclidean	glycerine
dineutron	evolution	graticule
directrix	explosion	guard-ring

gyroscope	inhibitor	magnesium
halophily	initiator	magnetism
hard water	injection	magnetron
heat index	inventory	magnifier
heliostat	inversion	malic acid
hemicycle	isinglass	malt sugar
herbarium	isocyclic	manganese
heterosis	isomerism	manometer
hexagonal	isosceles	mass ratio
histidine	isosteric	mechanics
histogram	isotropic	megacurie
histology	klinostat	megacycle
hodometer	lactation	megascope
homocycle	lanthanum	mesic atom
hydration	laser beam	mesotrons
hydrazine	lead glass	metalloid
hydrology	Leyden jar	metameric
hydrolyst	libration	metaplasm
hydrolyte	life-cycle	microbarn
hydrostat	light wave	microfilm
hydroxide	light year	microsome
hygrostat	limnology	microtome
hyperacid	lithology	microtron
hyperbola	logarithm	microwave
increment	long waves	milk sugar
incubator	lubricant	millibarn
indicator	luciferin	minometer
induction	Mach front	moderator
inelastic	macrodome	molecular

monatomic	path range	polygonal
morphosis	peak value	polythene
multiplet	pedometer	potassium
multipole	perimeter	potential
museum jar	petri dish	potometer
myography	petroleum	power pack
neodymium	petrology	processed
neptunium	phenology	prolamine
Newtonian	phenotype	protamine
nilpotent	phonemics	protogyny
nitration	phosphate	proton gun
normality	phosphide	protosome
notations	phosphite	prototype
numbering	photocell	pyramidal
numerator	photogene	pyridoxal
numerical	phycology	pyrogenic
nutrition	physicist	pyrolysis
occlusion	phytotron	pyrometer
octagonal	pinchbeck	quadruple
osmometer	pîtot tube	quasi-star
Otto cycle	planetoid	quintuple
ovulation	plumb-line	radiation
oxidation	plural gel	radiology
palladium	plutonium	radio rays
pantothen	pneumatic	raffinose
paralyser	polar axis	rare gases
parameter	polar body	reckoning
paraplasm	polybasic	recording
passivate	polyester	rectangle

reduction	sulphacid	univalent
re-entrant	summation	uranology
reflector	surveying	verdigris
reservoir	symbiosis	video tape
resonance	synthesis	virginium
rhombical	synthetic	viscosity
ruthenium	tabulator	vitelline
saccharin	telemeter	voltmeter
saltpetre	telemetry	wattmeter
satellite	teleology	wave guide
scientist	telephony	wire gauge
scintilla	telescope	wirephoto
separator	tellurite	yolk stalk
set square	tellurium	ytterbium
short wave	telophase	zirconium
side-chain	tempering	zoobiotic
slide rule	tetragram	zoogamete
soft water	tetroxide	zygophase
sound wave	threomine	aberration
spaceship	threshold	absorption
spacesuit	thyristor	acetic acid
spacewalk	time-clock	achromatin
stability	titration	acidimeter
still-room	tolerance	actinic ray
stop clock	trapezium	activation
strontium	trapezoid	acute angle
subatomic	triatomic	admittance
subdivide	trinomial	aero-engine
sub-weight	unguentum	aeruginous

air-cooling	baffle tube	catabolism
albuminoid	balance pan	catenation
algebraist	ballistite	cathode ray
alkalinity	bathometer	cavitation
alpha decay	battery jar	cell tissue
amal burner	biochemics	cellophane
amphoteric	biochemist	centesimal
amylaceous	biogenesis	Centigrade
anemometer	biometrics	centrifuge
anhydrides	biophysics	centrosome
anisotropy	biquadrate	chloroform
antecedent	bisulphate	chromatics
antibodies	bisulphide	chrome-alum
antifreeze	blastoderm	chromosome
antimatter	blastomere	cine-camera
antiproton	bleep-bleep	citric acid
antitoxins	Bohr theory	clinometer
aqua fortis	box furnace	coalescent
arithmetic	brinometer	cobalt bomb
astrograph	cacogenics	coconut oil
asymmetric	calcareous	collimator
atmosphere	calciferol	combustion
atomic bond	calcimeter	comparator
atomic mass	calculator	complement
atomic pile	calorifier	complicant
atomic unit	cancellate	compressor
atom-rocket	carbon atom	concentric
atom-tagger	carbonated	consequent
audiometer	carcinogen	control rod

controller	double-pole	Fahrenheit
convection	Dreyer tube	fibrinogen
co-ordinate	drying tube	filter pump
corrugated	duodecimal	filter tube
cross-staff	dysprosium	final state
cryogenics	efficiency	flight time
culture jar	egg albumen	fluorotype
curiescopy	elasticity	formic acid
cyanic acid	electronic	foursquare
cyclometer	elementary	fractional
decahedron	elongation	gadolinium
decinormal	embryology	gallic acid
decompound	emulsifier	gamma decay
deep freeze	energetics	generation
degaussing	entomology	geocentric
delay timer	enzymology	geophysics
demography	ephemerist	glass basin
denaturant	epithermal	goniometer
densimeter	equivalent·	goniometry
depilatory	estimation	gravimeter
depth gauge	etiolation	growth ring
desiccator	eudiometer	half circle
Dewar flask	eupotamous	Hall effect
dichromate	evaporator	heat shield
difference	excitation	heavy water
dissection	exobiology	heliometer
distortion	exothermal	hemisphere
disulphate	exothermic	heptagonal
disulphide	experiment	hexahedral

hexahedron	latent heat	molybdenum
hexangular	lead-glance	monovalent
hexavalent	light valve	morphology
high-octane	linseed oil	mother cell
holohedral	logometric	multicurie
homochromy	Mach number	multiplier
homocyclic	macroprism	nanosecond
horse power	magnet pole	neutralize
hydraulics	mass defect	nitric acid
hydrolysis	mass energy	nitrometer
hydrolytic	mass number	noble metal
hyetograph	mathematic	nucleonics
hygrometer	maturation	nucleonium
hypotenuse	megaparsec	numeration
hypothesis	megascopic	oceanology
hypsometer	metabolism	octahedral
immiscible	metacentre	octahedron
incubation	metallurgy	octavalent
inductance	metamerism	odontogeny
involution	metastable	odorimetry
ion counter	microcurie	ombrometer
ionization	micrograph	organology
ionosphere	micrometer	ortho state
irrational	microphone	orthogonal
isonuclear	microscope	osteoblast
isothermal	microscopy	oxalic acid
katabolism	millicurie	pantograph
laboratory	mineralogy	pantometer
lactic acid	Mohr circle	parahelium

pasteurize	protoplasm	rutherford
path length	protractor	saccharate
pentagonal	pyknometer	saccharose
pentatomic	quadrangle	scientific
percentage	quadratrix	seismology
petri plate	quadrature	selenology
phlogiston	quadricone	semicircle
phosphorus	quadriform	sensitizer
photolysis	quaternary	sheet metal
photomeson	radio sonde	short waves
physiology	radiogenic	sodium lamp
picric acid	radiometer	solubility
piezometer	radiometry	somatology
planimeter	radiopaque	spacecraft
planimetry	radioscope	spallation
polycyclic	radioscopy	spirometer
polyhedral	radium dial	square root
polyhedron	rare earths	stabilizer
potamology	reactivity	statistics
power plant	reciprocal	step-rocket
precession	relativity	sterilizer
primordial	reluctance	subalgebra
projectile	resilience	subtrahend
promethium	resistance	sulphation
pronucleus	resolution	supersonic
propellant	rhomboidal	suspension
proportion	riboflavin	synchroton
propulsion	right angle	tachometer
protogenic	Rule of Coss	tachymetry

tagged atom	univalence	aeolotropic
taper gauge	versed sine	aeronautics
technetium	viscometer	aerophysics
technology	vital stain	afterburner
telegraphy	vivaparous	agglomerate
television	voltameter	agglutinate
tetragonal	volt-ampere	air leak tube
tetratomic	wash bottle	aliquot part
theodolite	watch glass	anticathode
thermistor	water gauge	antineutron
thermopile	water-level	approximate
thermostat	water-still	arsenic acid
thin target	wavelength	atmospheric
thorianite	white light	atom counter
three phase	Winchester	atomic clock
time switch	wind tunnel	atomic model
tintometer	X radiation	atomic table
tracer atom	xerography	atomiferous
transistor	yield point	atomologist
transition	zero-valent	atom-smasher
trapezioid	zoophysics	attenuation
triangular	zwitterion	Auger effect
trilateral	accelerator	autodiluter
triplicate	accumulator	auxanometer
trivalence	achromatism	baffle plate
trochotron	acidulation	barycentric
tryptophan	acrylic acid	bathyscaphe
turpentine	actinic rays	bathysphere
unilateral	actinometer	beaker flask

beam balance	carnot cycle	cubic system
benthoscope	cathode rays	cubical atom
benzene ring	cellulation	culture tube
benzoic acid	chemiatrist	cupro-nickel
bevel square	chloric acid	cytophysics
bicarbonate	chlorophyll	dehydration
binary digit	chloroplast	denominator
binary scale	chromic acid	deoxidation
biocoenosis	chromoplast	desiccation
bipartition	chronometry	dibasic acid
biquadratic	closed chain	diffraction
bombardment	coagulation	directrices
breeder pile	cobalt-bloom	dissolution
brittleness	cod liver oil	dodecagonal
burning test	coefficient	dynamometer
butyric acid	colorimeter	eccrinology
butyrometer	colour index	echo-sounder
cadmium lamp	combination	Einsteinium
calcination	complex atom	electricity
calcium lamp	composition	electrolyte
calculation	comptometer	electronics
calefaction	computation	elimination
calibration	conductance	endothermal
californium	constituent	energy level
calorimeter	contaminate	engineering
calorimetry	co-ordinates	enumeration
capillarity	correlation	environment
carbon cycle	cosmography	epidiascope
carbonation	crystalline	equidistant

equilateral	heat barrier	lactoflavin
equilibrium	heptahedron	landing beam
evaporation	heptavalent	lanthanides
excited atom	heterocycle	latus rectum
fast neutron	heterotopes	light shield
fast reactor	high-voltage	lipoprotein
fatigue test	holohedrism	lithosphere
fibre optics	homogenizer	litmus paper
filter paper	homonuclear	locus vector
filter press	hydrocarbon	logarithmic
fissionable	hydrogen ion	lyophilizer
fluorescent	hydrogenoid	macroscopic
fluorophone	hydrography	macrosmatic
fluoroscope	hydrosphere	manipulator
fluoroscopy	hygroscopic	mathematics
focal sphere	icosahedron	mendelevium
free radical	ignition laz	mensuration
fume cabinet	impermeable	mercury cell
gas analyser	insecticide	mercury lamp
gas detector	integration	mesothorium
generic name	interaction	metachemist
gradiometer	iridescence	metaphysics
graphometer	irradiation	metaprotein
gravitation	isochronism	meteorology
gravity cell	isodose line	micro beaker
great circle	jet blowpipe	microscopic
ground noise	katakinetic	milliameter
ground state	kinetic body	millimicron
haloid acids	lactalbumin	mirror image

mirror paint
mixed number
Mohr diagram
monomorphic
monovalence
Napier's rods
needle valve
nesslerizer
neucleonics
neutralizer
niacinamide
nuclear atom
nuclear rays
nuclear star
nucleoplasm
number field
observatory
obtuse angle
octet theory
opalescence
opeidoscope
open circuit
orthohelium
orthometric
overlap test
ovovitellin
oxidization
oxygen meter
passivation

pectization
pentahedral
pentahedron
pentavalent
peptization
permutation
persorption
phosphorous
photography
photoproton
photosource
photosphere
Pirani gauge
pitchblende
planetarium
planisphere
plasmolysis
polarimeter
polarimetry
polarograph
polymethane
polymorphic
polyvalence
porous plate
positive ray
positronium
primary cell
prime factor
prime number

progression
proposition
proteolysis
prussic acid
pure culture
quantometer
quantum jump
quicksilver
radiant heat
radioactive
radio-beacon
radiocarbon
radiocobalt
radiocopper
radiography
radioiodine
radiologist
radiolucent
radiopacity
radioparent
radiosodium
radium paint
radiumproof
rarefaction
reactor pile
rectangular
reflex angle
regenerator
retort stand

retro-rocket
rider weight
right-angled
right-angles
Röntgen rays
round number
rule of three
rule of thumb
sal ammoniac
sal volatile
salinometer
sand culture
seed crystal
seismograph
sensitivity
sesquialter
simple curve
slow neutron
soft landing
solar system
somatic cell
space rocket
space-charge
spelaeology
spirit-level
stellarator
stenothermy
stimulation
stirring rod

stroboscope
sub-critical
submultiple
subtraction
supercooled
synoecology
systematics
tablet press
technocracy
temperature
tensile test
tensiometer
test reactor
tetrahedron
tetravalent
thermionics
thermoduric
thermograph
thermolysis
thermolytic
thermometer
thick target
Thomson atom
transformer
transmitter
transparent
transuranic
trapezoidal
tripod stand

troposphere
tube counter
tube furnace
ultrasonics
ultra-violet
unicellular
univibrator
vacuum flask
vacuum gauge
vector ratio
volatile oil
waterlogged
wettability
whole number
xanthophyll
X-chromosome
x-generation
yarn balance
Y-chromosome
zero algebra
zero gravity
zoochemical
zooplankton
acceleration
acceptor atom
acid solution
actinic glass
aerodynamics
aero-embolism

afterburning
alpha carotin
Angström unit
anthropogeny
anthropology
anthropotomy
antineutrino
antiparticle
antithrombin
arithmograph
arithmometer
aspartic acid
assimilation
astrobiology
astronautics
astrophysics
atomechanics
atomic cannon
atomic energy
atomic engine
atomic number
atomic theory
atomic volume
atomic weight
atom-chipping
atom-smashing
Avogadro's law
bacteriology
barrier cream

Becquerel ray
beehive shelf
bicarbonates
biochemistry
biosatellite
biosynthesis
Blavier's test
boiling point
boost control
Bourden gauge
breathalyzer
brewer's flask
Buchner flask
bunsen burner
burette stand
burning glass
burning point
carat balance
carbohydrate
carbolic acid
carbonic acid
cathetometer
cell division
central force
chain of atoms
chain reactor
chemical bond
chemical pump
chiliahedron

chlorination
chlorous acid
cloud chamber
cobalt-glance
combinations
common factor
condensation
conic section
conical flask
constituents
counting tube
critical mass
critical path
cross-section
cryoplankton
crystallites
culture flask
deactivation
deceleration
decimal point
declinometer
deflagration
deionization
deliquescent
dialysis tube
dietotherapy
differential
direct sounds
discrete atom

disinfectant	fluorocarbon	impurity atom
displacement	fluorography	inactivation
dissociation	formaldehyde	inarticulate
distillation	fume cupboard	incident beam
dodecahedron	galvanometer	inclinometer
drying pistol	gamma carotin	infra-red lamp
ductilometer	gas generator	integral dose
duraluminium	geochemistry	interference
ebulliometer	geodesic line	ion exchanger
eccentricity	geomagnetism	isobaric spin
effervescent	geometrician	isodose curve
Einstein's law	glutamic acid	isotopic spin
electric cell	glycoprotein	katharometer
electric lamp	gram-molecule	keratogenous
electrometer	grinding mill	law of gravity
electron pair	guiding field	leak detector
electronvolt	heterocyclic	Leighton tube
electroplate	high-fidelity	lever balance
electroscope	Hirsch funnel	line geometry
essential oil	humidity oven	liquefaction
eurythermous	hydrocarbons	liquid oxygen
experimental	hydrogen atom	lone electron
extensometer	hydrostatics	long division
extranuclear	hyperalgebra	luminescence
fermentation	hyperphysics	lysurgic acid
ferrous oxide	iatrochemist	macrophysics
filter funnel	iatrophysics	magnetometer
flocculation	immune bodies	manesty still
fluorescence	impact tester	melting point

mesomorphous nuclear plate pressure suit
metageometry nuclear power psychrometer
metal fatigue nucleization purity tester
meteorograph oblique angle pyridoxamine
metric system oceanography pyroceramics
micro burette oil of vitriol quadrangular
microammeter optical laser quadrinomial
microbalance orthorhombic quadrivalent
microelement oscilloscope quantization
microohmeter oxycellulose radiobiology
microphysics oxychromatin radiochemist
microspecies pair creation radiocolloid
milleröntgen palaeobotany radio-compass
mine detector pangamic acid radioelement
minor element perambulator radioisotope
mirror nuclei permanganate radiolocation
mitotic index permeability radiolucency
mixed decimal photochemist radionuclide
monomorphous photofission radiotherapy
multiangular photoneutron radiothorium
multilateral photonuclear reactivation
multiplicand Platonic body reflex action
multivalence polarization refrigerator
muriatic acid polysulphide regeneration
Napier's bones positive rays respirometer
nicotinamide power-breeder rhombohedron
nitromethane power-reactor Roentgen rays
nomenclature power-station rose crucible
nuclear force praseodymium salient angle

sand-blasting	split the atom	tunnel effect
scintillator	spring balance	ullage rocket
selenium cell	static firing	ultramicrobe
serial number	stereophonic	unified field
serum albumin	stereopticon	valence shell
short circuit	straight line	Van Allen belt
simple tissue	stratosphere	vaporization
simplex group	substitution	vernier scale
smash the atom	tally counter	vibro-spatula
solar battery	tetrahedroid	virtual state
solar physics	thermal shock	vitaminology
space-station	thermocouple	water balance
spark chamber	thermoscopic	water culture
spark counter	trace element	wave-function
specific heat	transmission	X-ray spectrum
specific name	transuranian	zoochemistry
spectrometer	trigonometry	zoogeography

Natural History

This section includes all growing things—trees—
flowers and plants—fruit and vegetables—cereals
and grasses—gardens and pieces of land—garden
tools—genera—parts of plants—botanical terms—
some plant diseases.

ash	bay	ben	bud	cob	cow
awn	bed	box	bur	cos	dig

ear	soy	cork	kelp	plot
elm	tea	corm	kola	poke
fig	uva	corn	lawn	pome
fir	yam	crab	leaf	posy
fog	yew	crop	leek	rake
gum	akee	culm	lily	rape
haw	aloe	cyme	lime	reap
hay	arum	date	ling	reed
hip	axis	dhak	lint	rhea
hoe	balm	dill	loam	rice
hop	bark	dita	lush	rind
ivy	bass	dock	maze	ripe
lea	bast	fern	mint	root
lei	bean	flag	moly	rosa
log	beet	flax	moss	rose
mow	bent	fork	musk	rush
nut	bixa	gale	oats	rust
oak	bole	gall	okra	sage
oat	boll	gean	palm	seed
pea	bosk	hemp	park	sere
pip	bulb	herb	pear	silo
poa	burr	hose	peat	sium
pod	bush	hull	peel	sloe
rue	cane	husk	pepo	smut
rye	coca	ilex	piña	soil
sal	coco	irid	pine	soma
sap	cole	iris	pink	sorb
sod	cone	jute	pith	soya
sow	core	kale	plum	spur

star	algum	carob	flora	icaco
stem	almug	cedar	frith	ilama
tare	ament	chard	frond	jarul
taro	anise	chase	fucus	kokra
teak	apple	chive	fungi	kokum
till	arbor	cibol	furze	larch
tree	areca	clary	garth	lemna
tuft	aspen	clove	gemma	lemon
turf	aspic	clump	glade	liana
twig	aster	cocoa	glean	lilac
upas	balsa	copse	glume	lotus
vega	basil	couch	gorse	lupin
veld	beech	cress	gourd	maize
vine	berry	cubeb	graft	malva
weed	birch	cumin	grain	mango
whin	blade	cycad	grape	manna
wild	bloom	dagga	grass	maple
woad	bough	daisy	grove	melon
wood	bract	delve	guava	morel
wort	brake	drupe	gumbo	mould
zest	briar	dulse	halfa	mower
abaca	brier	durra	hardy	mulch
abele	broom	dwale	hazel	musci
abies	brush	ebony	heath	myrrh
abrus	cacao	elder	hedge	oasis
acorn	calyx	erica	henna	ocrea
agave	camas	field	holly	olive
alder	canna	firth	humus	onion
algae	caper	fitch	hurst	orpin

orris	sapan	thyme	arbute
osier	savoy	tilia	arolla
oxlip	scion	tract	azalea
paddy	scrub	trunk	balsam
palay	sedge	tuber	bamboo
pansy	senna	tulip	banana
papaw	sepal	umbel	banyan
patch	shell	veldt	baobab
peach	shoot	vetch	barley
pease	shrub	viola	ben nut
pecan	sisal	waste	bog-oak
peony	spade	wheat	borage
petal	spear	wrack	border
phlox	spike	yeast	bo-tree
piñon	spray	yucca	branch
pipal	sprig	yulan	bryony
plane	stalk	zamia	burnet
plant	starr	abroma	cacoon
poppy	stipe	acacia	cactus
prune	stock	achene	camass
pulse	stoma	acinus	carapa
radix	stone	agaric	carpel
ramie	straw	albino	carrot
ramus	style	almond	casaba
range	sumac	althea	cashew
roble	swale	ananas	cassia
roots	sward	annual	catkin
rowan	tansy	anther	catnip
salad	thorn	aralia	caudex

caulis	dog-hip	hyssop	mammee
celery	durian	indigo	manioc
cereal	endive	jarool	manuka
cherry	exotic	jarrah	maquis
cistus	fallow	jujube	marang
citron	fennel	jungle	marram
citrus	ferula	kalmia	marrow
clover	fescue	kernel	marrum
cobnut	floret	kiss-me	meadow
cockle	florid	kittul	mealie
coffee	flower	knawel	medick
common	forest	lalang	medlar
corkir	fucoid	lamina	mescal
cornel	fungus	laurel	millet
corona	garden	legume	mimosa
corymb	garlic	lentil	murphy
cosmos	garrya	lichen	muscat
cotton	ginger	lignum	myrica
cow pea	ginkgo	linden	myrtle
crocus	greens	litchi	nectar
crotal	groats	locust	needle
croton	growth	loquat	nettle
cummin	hanger	lovage	nostoc
dahlia	harrow	lupine	nutmeg
damson	hedera	lychee	orange
daphne	hen-bit	madder	orchid
deodar	hominy	maguey	orchis
desert	hotbed	mallee	orpine
dibble	hybrid	mallow	oxalis

pampas	rattan	sobole	tundra
papaya	red fir	sorgko	turnip
pappus	red-bud	sorrel	unripe
pawpaw	redtop	souari	vinery
peanut	rennet	spadix	violet
pepper	riddle	spathe	walnut
phylum	rocket	sprout	wattle
pignut	roller	spruce	willow
pinery	rosery	spurge	wreath
pistil	runner	spurry	yarrow
platan	russet	squash	zinnia
plough	sallow	squill	acantha
pollen	salvia	stamen	acerose
pomato	sapium	stigma	aconite
pomelo	sapota	stolon	ailanto
poplar	sappan	storax	alecost
potato	savory	sub rosa	alfalfa
privet	scilla	sucker	alkanet
prunus	scutch	sumach	all-heal
punica	scythe	sun-dew	althaea
queach	sea-fan	sundra	alyssum
quince	seamat	sylvan	amanita
raceme	sesame	tangle	ambatch
rachis	shadow	teasel	anemone
radish	shears	tedder	aniseed
raffia	sickle	thrift	apricot
raisin	silage	timber	aquatic
ramage	silene	tomato	arbutus
raphia	smilax	trowel	armilla

ash tree	cabbage	collard	duramen
auricle	cajuput	conifer	durmast
avocado	calamus	coppice	elm tree
babassu	caltrop	coquito	erodium
barrens	cambium	cork-oak	esparto
bay tree	campion	corncob	fan-palm
bebeeru	capsule	corolla	fertile
begonia	caraway	corsage	festoon
benthon	cardoon	cowbane	fig leaf
benthos	carline	cowslip	figwort
bistort	cassava	cow-tree	fir cone
blawort	catalpa	cow-weed	fir tree
blewits	catawba	creeper	firwood
blossom	catmint	crottle	foliage
blue-gum	cat's-ear	cumquat	foliole
bogbean	cattail	cup-moss	foliose
bog-moss	chamise	curcuma	foxtail
boscage	chamiso	currant	fuchsia
bouquet	champac	cutting	funicle
boxwood	chaplet	cypress	gall-nut
bracken	chervil	dagwood	garland
bramble	chicory	day lily	genipap
brinjal	clarkia	day's eye	genista
buckeye	clethra	deutzia	gentian
bugloss	climber	dika nut	ginseng
bulrush	clivers	dittany	goat-fig
burdock	clotbur	dogbane	godetia
burgeon	coconut	dog-rose	grapery
burweed	cola nut	dogwood	guaraná

guayule	lentisk	nutwood	plumcot
gum tree	lettuce	oak fern	pollard
haricot	lily pad	oak tree	prairie
harvest	linseed	oakling	primula
hassock	lip fern	oil-palm	produce
hawk-bit	live-oak	olitory	pruning
hayseed	lobelia	opuntia	pulasan
heather	logwood	orchard	pumpkin
hemlock	lucerne	osmunda	putamen
henbane	lycopod	palm nut	radical
herbage	madrona	palmyra	ragweed
hickory	malmsey	panacea	ragwort
hogweed	mammoth	panicle	rambler
holm-oak	maremma	papaver	rampick
honesty	margosa	papyrus	rampike
hop tree	may-lily	parsley	red bush
hornnut	mayweed	parsnip	red pine
jacinth	melilot	pasture	red rose
jaggery	milfoil	pedicel	red-root
jasmine	mimulus	penguin	redwood
jonquil	morello	petiole	rhizome
juniper	mudwort	petunia	rhubarb
kingcup	mullein	pigweed	rockery
kola nut	mustard	pimento	romaine
kumquat	nemesia	pine nut	rootage
labiate	new-mown	pinetum	rosebay
leaf bud	nigella	pinguin	rosebud
leafage	nosegay	pitanga	rose-hip
leaflet	nursery	platane	roselle

ruddock	spinach	verdant	ash-grove
ruellia	spindle	verdure	ash-plant
saffron	spinney	vervain	asphodel
saguaro	spiraea	vintage	auricula
salsify	spurrey	wall-rue	autocarp
sampire	statice	wax palm	baby fern
sandbur	succory	wax tree	banewort
sapling	sundari	weed out	barberry
sapwood	syringa	wig tree	basswood
savanna	tagetes	wild fig	bay berry
sea-kale	tangelo	wild oat	beam-tree
sea-moss	tanghin	woodlet	bear's-ear
sea-pink	taproot	wych-elm	beechnut
sea-reed	tarweed	Yule log	beefwood
sea-tang	tea rose	zedoary	beetroot
seaweed	tea tree	zenobia	bergamot
seed pod	tendril	zizania	betel nut
seedbox	thapsia	abutilon	biennial
sequoia	thicket	acanthus	bignonia
service	thistle	aesculus	bilberry
sesamum	thyrsus	ailantus	bindweed
setwall	tigella	alburnum	bird's-eye
shallot	timothy	allspice	bluebell
silk oak	tobacco	amaranth	blueweed
skirret	trefoil	angelica	bog grass
sorghum	truffle	anthesis	borecole
sorosis	tussock	apple pip	brassica
soursop	vanilla	arboreal	broccoli
soybean	verbena	arum lily	bromelia

buckbean
buddleia
caatinga
caducous
calamite
caltrops
camellia
camomile
canaigre
capparis
caprifig
capsicum
cardamom
cardamum
carnauba
catchfly
cat's-foot
cat's tail
caulicle
celeriac
centaury
charlock
chestnut
chick pea
chinampa
cinchona
cinnamon
citrange
clearing

cleavers
clematis
clubmoss
clubrush
cocculus
cocoanut
coco-palm
coco-tree
coco-wood
cole-wort
conferva
cork tree
corn-flag
costmary
cow-berry
cow-grass
cow-plant
cow-wheat
crab's-eye
crab-tree
crucifer
cucumber
cut grass
cyclamen
daffodil
date-palm
date-plum
date-tree
deadwood

death-cap
death-cup
dendroid
dewberry
dianthus
dicentra
divi-divi
dock leaf
dogberry
dog-daisy
dog-grass
dog-wheat
doom-palm
dropwort
duckweed
Dutch hoe
earthnut
edge tool
eelgrass
egg-plant
endocarp
ensilage
epicalyx
escarole
eucalypt
fern-ally
fernshaw
feverfew
fireweed

flaxseed	hardwood	laburnum
flourish	harebell	lady-fern
floweret	hawkweed	larkspur
follicle	hawthorn	lavender
force bed	hay-field	leucojum
forestry	hazelnut	licorice
foxglove	hedgehog	lily pond
fructose	hedgerow	lily pons
gardenia	hemp-palm	Lima bean
gas-plant	hemp-tree	locoweed
geranium	henequen	long moss
girasole	hepatica	mad-apple
gladioli	herb-weed	magnolia
glory-pea	hibiscus	mahogany
gloxinia	holly-oak	main crop
goat's-rue	honey-dew	mandarin
goatweed	honey-pot	mandrake
goutweed	hornbeam	mangrove
goutwort	hot-house	manna-ash
Greek fir	hyacinth	marigold
green pea	ice-plant	marjoram
greenery	iron-bark	May apple
grow lush	ironwood	maybloom
grow rank	jack-tree	medicago
guaiacum	japonica	meristem
gulfweed	kingwood	mesquite
hagberry	knapweed	milk tree
hag-taper	knotweed	milkweed
hair-tare	kohlrabi	milkwood

milkwort	peduncle	puffball
moonwort	perianth	purslane
moss rose	pericarp	quandong
mulberry	petalody	rain tree
muscatel	photinia	rambutan
mushroom	phyllome	ratsbane
musk-pear	piassava	red algae
musk-plum	pillwort	red cedar
musk-rose	pimiento	red maple
myosotis	pinaster	red poppy
navy bean	pine cone	reed-mace
Nikko fir	pine tree	ribgrass
ninebark	pin-grass	ripe corn
noble fir	pink ball	rock rose
nutshell	pinkroot	rockweed
oak-apple	plankton	root crop
offshoot	plantago	root-knot
oleander	plantain	rose bush
oleaster	plant-pot	rosemary
orangery	plantule	roseroot
origanum	plumbago	rosewood
osier-bed	pokeweed	royal oak
palm tree	pond lily	rutabaga
palmetto	pond scum	rye-grass
paradise	pondweed	sago-palm
peachery	poor crop	sainfoin
pear-tree	poor soil	saltwort
peasecod	primrose	samphire
peat moss	prunello	sapindus

sargasso	softwood	tuberose
scabiosa	soya bean	turmeric
scabious	spergula	turnsole
scallion	spigelia	valerian
scrub-oak	spikelet	vasculum
sea-acorn	stapelia	veronica
seaberry	starwort	viburnum
sea-blite	strobile	vine leaf
sea-grape	sun-drops	vineyard
sea-heath	sweet-bay	waybread
sea-holly	sweet-gum	white ash
sea-shrub	sweetpea	white fir
sea-wrack	sweetsap	white oak
seed leaf	sycamine	wild oats
seedcase	sycamore	wild rose
seedling	take root	wild sage
self-heal	tall tree	wistaria
seminary	tamarack	witch-elm
shadbush	tamarind	wolfbane
shaddock	tamarisk	wood fern
shamrock	tarragon	wood pulp
sloebush	tiger nut	woodbind
sloetree	toad-flax	woodbine
snap bean	tom thumb	woodland
snapweed	tree-fern	woodruff
snowball	tree-lily	wood-sage
snowdrop	tree-moss	xanthium
snuffbox	tremella	zucchini
soapwort	trillium	Aaron's rod

acrospire	baneberry	bulb field
adansonia	bearberry	bully tree
ailanthus	bear's-foot	bussu-palm
albespyne	bedded out	buttercup
alfilaria	beech fern	butternut
algarroba	beet sugar	calendula
alligator	bell-glass	campanula
allotment	bent grass	candle nut
aloes-wood	bifurcate	candytuft
alpine fir	bird's-foot	cane sugar
amarantus	bird's-nest	capitulum
amaryllis	birthwort	carnation
andromeda	black bent	carob bean
apple a day	blaeberry	carrageen
apple tree	bloodroot	cashew nut
aquilegia	blueberry	casuarina
arboretum	bluegrass	catchweed
arid waste	bluejoint	celandine
arrowhead	bog-myrtle	centaurea
arrowroot	bog-orchid	chain fern
artichoke	bonduc nut	chaparral
asparagus	bracteole	cherimoya
astrofell	Brazil nut	chickweed
astrophel	brier bush	China tree
aubergine	broomcorn	China-root
azedarach	broomrape	China-rose
baldmoney	brushwood	chincapin
balsa wood	buckthorn	chinkapin
balsam fir	buckwheat	cineraria

clove tree
clove-pink
cockscomb
cocoa-wood
coco-de-mer
colchicum
cold frame
cole-garth
colicroot
colocynth
coltsfoot
columbine
composite
coral-root
coreopsis
coriander
corn field
corn-salad
corozo nut
cotyledon
crab apple
crab grass
cranberry
crazyweed
crosswort
crowberry
crucifera
cryptogam
culver-key

cumara nut
cup-lichen
dandelion
day-nettle
deciduous
desert pea
digitalis
dittander
dock-cress
dog-violet
dry garden
duck's-foot
duck's-meat
dwarf tree
dyer's-weed
ear of corn
earth-star
edelweiss
eglantine
ephemeral
euphorbia
evergreen
fairy ring
fenugreek
feverroot
fire thorn
flagellum
flower bed
flower bud

flowerage
flowering
flower-pot
fly agaric
forsythia
fruit tree
full bloom
galanthus
galingale
gama-grass
garden pea
gelsemium
gemmation
germander
gladiolus
glasswort
golden rod
goosefoot
gramineae
grape fern
grape tree
grapevine
grassland
green bean
greengage
greenweed
greenwood
ground-ash
ground-ivy

groundnut	jenneting	mare's tail
ground-oak	jequirity	marijuana
groundsel	Judas tree	marsh fern
grugru nut	Juneberry	marshwort
guanabana	king-apple	mayflower
gynophore	knot-grass	meadow-rue
hair grass	labyrinth	melocoton
half-hardy	lady-smock	mesophyte
halophyte	lancewood	milk-vetch
heartwood	laserwort	mistletoe
hellebore	lawn-mower	monkey-nut
herb Paris	leaf mould	monk's-hood
herbarium	lemon peel	moon daisy
holly fern	lemon-weed	mugho pin
hollyhock	lilac time	muscadine
holy grass	lilac tree	musk-melon
home grown	lime grove	musk-plant
horehound	liquorice	naked lady
hornwrack	litchi nut	narcissus
horsetail	liverwort	navelwort
house-leek	long grass	nectarine
hydrangea	love-apple	nelumbium
in blossom	lovegrass	nuts in May
Indian fig	luxuriant	nux vomica
involucre	lychee nut	onion skin
Irish moss	lyme-grass	operculum
ivory palm	malcolmia	orange pip
ivory tree	manzanita	outer bark
jackfruit	maple leaf	overgrown

parnassia
paulownia
peach bell
peach-palm
pellitory
pennywort
perennial
perpetual
persimmon
petty whin
physic nut
pimpernel
pineapple
pinto bean
pistachio
pitch pine
pitchfork
plane tree
plant life
poison ivy
poison nut
poison oak
pollen-sac
pollinate
polygonum
pond apple
pony grass
poppy-head
portulaca

pyracanth
pyrethrum
quebracho
quillwort
raspberry
rattle-box
red pepper
reed-grass
remontant
rice paddy
richardia
rocambole
rock brake
rock plant
rockcress
root-house
root-prune
rootstock
root-tuber
rose-apple
rose-elder
rowan tree
royal fern
royal palm
sagebrush
salad herb
sand-grain
sand-grass
sapodilla

sargassum
sassafras
satinwood
saxifrage
scale moss
Scotch elm
Scotch fir
Scots pine
screw pine
scrubbard
seabottle
sea-girdle
sea-tentil
sea-tangle
secateurs
seed plant
shade tree
shrubbery
silk-grass
silver fir
sisal hemp
sloethorn
smartweed
snakeroot
snowberry
snowflake
snow-plant
soapberry
spearmint

speedwell	underwood	aftergrass
spikenard	vegetable	alexanders
star-arise	Veitch fir	almond tree
star-grass	vernation	amaranthus
stinkweed	wake-robin	androccium
stone pine	wasteland	annual ring
stonecrop	water-fern	*arbor vitae*
stonewort	water-flag	arrow-grass
succulent	water-leaf	aspidistra
sugar-beet	water-lily	banana skin
sugar-cane	water-vine	barley-corn
sugarplum	waterweed	basket fern
sunflower	wax flower	beach grass
sun-spurge	wax myrtle	beard-grass
swainsona	white moss	beauty bush
sweetcorn	white pine	bell pepper
sweet-flag	white teak	belladonna
sweetgale	white wood	bellflower
sword-bean	whitebeam	bird-cherry
symplocos	whitehorn	bird-pepper
tangerine	widow-wail	bitterroot
tear-grass	wild-grape	blackberry
thorn tree	wild-olive	blackbully
tiger lily	window-box	blackheart
toadstool	wire-grass	blackthorn
toothwort	wolf's-bane	bladder-nut
tree-onion	worm grass	blue spruce
triennial	wych hazel	bluebottle
tulip tree	adder's fern	bottle tree

brazilwood
breadfruit
brome-grass
brown algae
bullet tree
bumper crop
bunch grass
burnet-rose
bush squash
butter bean
butter tree
butter-dock
butterwort
button bush
buttonhole
buttonwood
calamander
Canada rice
cantaloupe
carpophore
champignon
China aster
China grass
chinaberry
chinquapin
chokeberry
cinquefoil
civet fruit
cliff brake

coffee bean
common kale
compositae
conference
coniferous
coral-berry
corncockle
cornflower
cos lettuce
cotton tree
cottonwood
couch-grass
cow-chervil
cow-parsley
cow-parsnip
cowrie pine
crabstones
crane's-bill
crown-graft
cruciferae
cuckoo-pint
cut flowers
daisy chain
damask rose
dead-finish
dead-nettle
delphinium
dendrology
Diana's tree

dog-parsley
dog's-fennel
Douglas fir
dragon tree
Duke cherry
Durmast oak
Dutch tulip
dyer's-broom
elderberry
elecampane
English elm
English ivy
English rye
eucalyptus
fiddlewood
field poppy
fleur-de-lis
floral leaf
floribunda
flote-grass
flower-head
flower-show
frangipani
French bean
French plum
fritillary
gaillardia
garden city
garden fork

garden herb	gypsophila	lady's-thumb
garden hose	hackmatack	laurustine
garden pest	heart's-ease	leaf cactus
garden spot	helianthus	lemon-grass
gelder rose	heliotrope	loganberry
German iris	hemp-nettle	lycopodium
glasshouse	herb garden	maiden pink
goat-sallow	herbaceous	maidenhair
goat's-beard	herd's grass	maidenweed
goat's-thorn	hickory nut	malaquetta
goat-willow	holly berry	mandragora
golden bell	hydrophite	mangosteen
golden seal	Idaean vine	Manila hemp
goldilocks	Indian corn	manna-grass
goose-grass	Indian hemp	manna-larch
gooseberry	Indian pink	manzanilla
grama grass	Indian pipe	marguerite
granauilla	Indian poke	marshlocks
grapefruit	Indian shot	mayblossom
grasswrack	indigenous	mignonette
greasewood	Italian rye	mock orange
green algae	jaboticaba	motherwort
green field	japati palm	mow the lawn
greenbrier	jardinière	musk-mallow
greenheart	Jimson weed	nasturtium
greenhouse	kaffir corn	new-mown hay
greensward	kidney bean	nicker seed
ground pine	king's-spear	nightshade
groundling	lady's-smock	nipplewort

nothofagus
olive grove
opium poppy
orange lily
orange peel
orangeroot
orange-wood
ox-eye daisy
paddy field
palm-branch
paper birch
passiflora
peach-bloom
penny-cress
pennyroyal
peppercorn
peppermint
pepperwort
periwinkle
pillar rose
pine-needle
plantation
plant-house
plume grass
poinsettia
poison-bean
poisonbush
poisonweed
poison-wood

polyanthus
potato peel
prayer-bead
prickly ash
Punic apple
purple-wood
quackgrass
queen-apple
quercitron
raffia palm
ragged-lady
rain forest
ranunculus
red cabbage
red currant
red jasmine
red-sanders
rest-harrow
rock-garden
rock-violet
roof-garden
root-rubber
root-sheath
rose-garden
rose-laurel
rose-mallow
rowan berry
runner bean
salad plant

sandalwood
sand-binder
sand-cherry
sand-myrtle
sarracenia
scarlet oak
Scotch kale
Scotch rose
sea-burdock
sea-cabbage
sea-campion
sea-lettuce
sea-whistle
second crop
seed vessel
semination
shield fern
silver tree
silver-bell
sisal grass
slime mould
snapdragon
snow wreath
sour cherry
Spanish fir
spear grass
spiderwort
spring-wood
spring-wort

stitchwort	water thyme	African teak
stork's bill	waterbloom	*agnus castus*
strawberry	watermelon	Algerian fir
strike root	Welsh onion	alpine plant
string bean	Welsh poppy	amboyna wood
sugar apple	wheat field	American elm
sugar maple	white cedar	an apple a day
swamp maple	white thorn	anchovy pear
sweet-briar	wild-carrot	anthrophore
sweet-brier	wild-cherry	antirrhinum
sweet-shrub	wild-cornel	avocado pear
sword grass	wilderness	baby's-breath
tallow tree	wild-flower	bald cypress
thale cress	wild-ginger	bastard balm
timberland	wild-indigo	bastard teak
transplant	willow-herb	bear's-breech
tree of life	willow-weed	beggar ticks
tree-mallow	witch hazel	beggar's lice
tree-tomato	wolf's-peach	bell-heather
tumbleweed	wood-sorrel	Bengal grass
turtlehead	yellow-pine	bittersweet
underbrush	yellow-root	black walnut
vegetation	yellow-weed	black willow
wallflower	yellow-wood	bladder fern
wall-pepper	yellow-wort	blue thistle
water avens	zebra-grass	boulder fern
water cress	Aaron's beard	*boutonnière*
water elder	acorn-squash	boysenberry
water lemon	Adam's needle	bramble bush

bur-marigold	cypress knee	goldenberry
burning-bush	dame's violet	graft-hybrid
cabbage-palm	death camass	great sallow
cabbage-rose	dog's-mercury	green pepper
cabbage-tree	dusty miller	green-dragon
cajuput tree	dwarf cornel	guelder rose
calceolaria	dyer's-rocket	guinea-grass
camel's-thorn	English rose	hair-cap moss
camphor tree	everlasting	hardy annual
canary grass	false acacia	hart's tongue
candleberry	farm produce	hesperidium
casaba melon	field-madder	honey-locust
cauliflower	finger grass	honeysuckle
chanterelle	Florida moss	horse-radish
chive garlic	flowery land	hound's berry
Cilician fir	forage-grass	huckleberry
citrus fruit	forget-me-not	Iceland moss
coconut-palm	fossil plant	Indian berry
convallaria	French berry	Indian cress
convolvulus	fuller's herb	Jaffa orange
copper beech	garden-glass	jaggery palm
corn in Egypt	garden-party	Japan laurel
cosmopolite	garden-spade	Japanese yew
cotoneaster	garden-stuff	juniper tree
cotton grass	germination	kidney-vetch
cotton plant	giant cactus	Korean spice
cruciferous	giant fennel	lady's-finger
cultivation	gillyflower	lady's-mantle
cut the grass	globe-flower	laurustinus

leatherleaf
leopardbane
lignum vitae
lingonberry
London pride
loosestrife
love-in-a-mist
luxuriation
Madonna lily
mammee apple
mammoth tree
manna-lichen
marram-grass
marrum-grass
marsh-mallow
meadow-grass
meadow-sweet
milk-thistle
mountain ash
musk-thistle
myrtle grass
Nancy pretty
navel-orange
Negro-pepper
night-flower
Nordmann fir
nutmeg melon
olive branch
orange grass

organ cactus
ostrich fern
oyster plant
palm-cabbage
palmyra palm
pampas-grass
Parma violet
pasture land
pepper shrub
peppergrass
phyllomania
pine barrens
plum-blossom
poison grass
poison sumac
poisonberry
pollen grain
pollination
pomegranate
pompelmoose
potting shed
prickly pear
propagation
pruning-bill
pruning-hook
pullulation
purple beech
purple medic
purpleheart

pussy willow
rabbit berry
ragged robin
rambler rose
red valerian
red-hot poker
ribbon grass
Roman nettle
root-climber
rose-campion
rubber plant
salad burnet
scarlet bean
scurvy grass
sea-colewort
sea-furbelow
sea-lavender
sea-milkwort
sea-purslane
service tree
sesame grass
shasta daisy
sheep laurel
shittah tree
silver birch
simple fruit
slippery elm
Spanish moss
spindle tree

spring onion	white spruce	bladderwrack
strawflower	white willow	blasted heath
St. John's wort	whitebottle	bog-pimpernel
stephanotis	wild cabbage	bougainvilia
summerhouse	wild flowers	bridal wreath
suwarrow nut	wild service	buffalo grass
swallow-wort	winter brake	cabbage patch
sweet cherry	wintergreen	calabash tree
sweet cicely	wintersweet	Canada balsam
sweet potato	witches'-meat	Carolina pink
sweet-willow	wood anemone	century-plant
switch grass	xanthoxylum	checkerberry
thistledown	Adam's flannel	cherry-laurel
tiger flower	alpine flower	chestnut tree
tree-creeper	American aloe	chilli pepper
trumpet vine	apple blossom	cholla cactus
tufted vetch	apple of Sodom	Christ's-thorn
turkeyberry	Austrian pine	climbing fern
undergrowth	autumn-crocus	Congo tobacco
varnish tree	baby-blue-eyes	conservatory
viper's-grass	balsam of Peru	corn in Israel
walking-fern	balsam of Tolu	corn on the cob
water garden	barrel cactus	corn-feverfew
water meadow	Bengal quince	corn-marigold
water pepper	Bermuda grass	Covent Garden
water violet	Bermuda onion	Coventry bell
watering-can	black currant	cuckoo-flower
wheel-barrow	black-eyed pea	cucumber tree
white poplar	bladder senna	custard apple

Dead Sea apple
Dead Sea fruit
decorticated
dragon's blood
English daisy
esparto-grass
feather-grass
fennel flower
flower border
flower garden
flower of Jove
flower-delice
flower-de-luce
flowering ash
flowers of tan
flyaway-grass
fool's parsley
forcing house
frankincense
fresh flowers
garden roller
garden shears
garden suburb
garden trowel
gastrolobium
golden wreath
green fingers
ground-cherry
hassock-grass

hedge trimmer
hortus siccus
hound's-tongue
Iceland poppy
Indian cactus
Indian turnip
Irish juniper
Jacob's ladder
Japanese rose
lady's-cushion
lady's-fingers
lady's-slipper
lady's-thistle
lamb's-lettuce
mangel-wurzel
market garden
marrow-squash
massaranduba
meadow-canopy
meadow-fescue
melon-thistle
monkey-flower
monkey-puzzle
morning glory
mulberry-bush
Norway spruce
old man's beard
orange-flower
orchard grass

parcel of land
pasque flower
passion fruit
peach-blossom
Persian berry
Persian melon
Philadelphus
piassava palm
pioneer plant
pistachio nut
plantain tree
poison laurel
primrose path
pruning-knife
quaking aspen
rambling rose
ramification
reindeer moss
rhododendron
rose of Sharon
rough chervil
salpiglossis
sassafras nut
sea-buckthorn
seaside-grape
service-berry
sheep's fescue
sheep's-sorrel
Shirley poppy

shooting star	stinking iris	waterflowers
skunk cabbage	striped grass	water-hemlock
snowdrop tree	summer squash	water-milfoil
snow-in-summer	sunken garden	water-parsnip
snuffbox-bean	sweet alyssum	wellingtonia
Solomon's seal	sweet William	white currant
Spanish broom	Timothy grass	white heather
Spanish cedar	tobacco plant	whortleberry
Spanish cress	tree of heaven	wild hyacinth
Spanish grass	umbelliferae	winter cherry
Spanish onion	umbrella-tree	winter greens
spur valerian	under the rose	witches'-broom
spurge-laurel	Venus' fly-trap	wood-hyacinth
St. John's bread	village green	yellow willow
St. Peter's wort	virgin forest	zantedeschia
staghorn moss	virgin's bower	zigzag clover

Machinery

This section includes machinery and plant—tools, machine tools, hand tools and implements—internal combustion engine—components and machine parts —accounting machines—locks—engines.

awl	bit	cog	gun	jaw	key
axe	cam	die	hod	jet	nut
bar	cap	fan	hoe	jib	ram
bed	car	gin	hub	jig	rig

saw	grid	rake	burin	inlet
tap	hasp	reel	cable	jemmy
vat	hi-fi	rule	chain	jenny
adze	horn	seal	chase	jimmy
bank	iron	shoe	choke	knife
bolt	jack	skip	clamp	ladle
bomb	kiln	slur	crane	lance
boom	knob	sump	crank	laser
bore	last	tank	crate	lathe
boss	lead	teep	clock	lever
buff	lens	till	davit	litho
burr	lift	tool	diode	meter
bush	link	tube	dolly	mixer
butt	lock	vane	dowel	motor
case	loom	vice	drain	mould
cell	luff	wire	drier	panel
cock	mast	yale	drill	pedal
coil	mike	yoke	earth	pivot
cowl	mill	adder	edges	plane
dial	mine	anode	Ernie	plant
drum	mole	anvil	fence	plate
duct	mule	Asdic	flare	press
file	nail	auger	forge	prong
flex	pick	baler	frame	punch
flue	pile	bevel	gauge	pylon
fork	pipe	block	gland	quill
fuse	plug	brace	gouge	quoin
gear	pump	brake	guide	radar
grab	rack	brush	hoist	radio

342

razor	valve	clutch	handle
relay	wedge	collar	harrow
rifle	wheel	con rod	heater
rivet	winch	cooker	hopper
robot	abacus	cooler	jigsaw
rotor	aerial	cutout	jumper
scoop	babbet	device	keyway
screw	baffle	diesel	klaxon
shaft	barrel	digger	leader
shank	barrow	dredge	magnet
shunt	beacon	dynamo	mallet
sieve	big end	engine	matrix
spade	binder	eolith	mincer
spool	blower	etcher	monkey
spray	bobbin	faggot	mortar
stick	bodkin	filter	muller
still	boiler	flange	muzzle
stove	bow saw	gadget	needle
strut	brayer	galley	nipple
thole	breech	gantry	nozzle
timer	broach	garnet	oil gun
tongs	buffer	gasket	oil rig
tooth	burton	G-clamp	outlet
torch	bus bar	gimlet	padder
tower	camera	grader	pharos
train	caster	grater	pickup
truck	castor	ground	pinion
TV set	chaser	gutter	pintle
usine	chisel	hammer	pistol

piston	spring	balance	decoder
platen	square	ballast	derrick
pliers	stator	bandsaw	dredger
plough	stroke	battery	dry cell
pulley	stylus	bearing	ejector
ram jet	switch	bindery	encoder
ramrod	tackle	blanket	exciter
reglet	Tannoy	blender	exhaust
riddle	tappet	booster	factory
rip-saw	ticker	bradawl	fanbelt
rocket	torque	buzz-saw	ferrule
roller	trepan	cadrans	flare-up
rounce	triode	caisson	foghorn
rudder	tripod	cannery	forceps
runner	trivet	capstan	foundry
saddle	trowel	cathode	fret-saw
scales	turret	chamber	frisket
scythe	turtle	charger	fulcrum
seeder	tympan	chassis	furnace
shaver	volery	chatter	fuse-box
shears	washer	chopper	gearbox
shovel	woofer	circlip	gripper
sickle	wrench	circuit	grommet
siphon	aerilon	cleaver	hacksaw
sleeve	airlock	cold-saw	handsaw
sluice	air-pump	combine	hatchet
smithy	antenna	compass	hayfork
socket	arc lamp	control	hayrake
spigot	arsenal	crowbar	hydrant

lighter	shuttle	wood-saw	cylinder
limiter	sleeper	wringer	Davy lamp
locknut	smelter	absorber	demister
magneto	spanner	actuator	detector
mattock	spatula	air brake	dip-stick
measure	speaker	air drill	dividers
monitor	spindle	air motor	dynamite
muffler	sprayer	armament	earphone
network	stapler	armature	elevator
overlay	starter	backlash	filament
padlock	stirrer	ballista	flash gun
palette	sweeper	bearings	flat iron
pattern	tannery	billhook	flypress
pentode	televox	bloomery	flywheel
pick-axe	terebra	blowpipe	fork-lift
pincers	toaster	bosshead	fuse wire
planter	tool-box	calipers	garrotte
pottery	tracker	camshaft	governor
push-rod	tractor	cant hook	gadgetry
ratchet	treadle	chain-saw	gaslight
reactor	trigger	clippers	gyrostat
riffler	trolley	cogwheel	hand tool
rotator	turbine	colliery	hardware
sawmill	tweeter	computer	haypitch
scalpel	utensil	controls	hemostat
scanner	welding	conveyor	hose-pipe
scraper	wet cell	coupling	ignition
shackle	winding	cross bit	impeller
shutter	wing nut	crucible	intercom

iron crow	resistor	vibrator
iron lung	rheostat	web press
isolator	saw-knife	wind pump
laser gun	scaffold	windlass
lift pump	scissors	windmill
linotype	selector	wireless
lock gate	servolab	X-ray tube
lock weir	shredder	Yale lock
logotype	silencer	zoom lens
manifold	slip ring	air-engine
monotype	smithery	air-hammer
neon tube	software	alarm bell
outboard	spray-gun	albertype
pendulum	sprocket	altimeter
penknife	spur-gear	amplifier
pinch bar	teetotum	apparatus
pinwheel	teletype	arc welder
pipeline	template	aspirator
polisher	terminal	automatic
pop rivet	thole-pin	automaton
power saw	thresher	autopilot
pulsejet	throttle	bar magnet
radiator	time bomb	belt punch
radio set	tommy bar	bevel gear
receiver	track rod	bilge pump
recorder	turbofan	blow-torch
refinery	turbojet	booby trap
register	tweezers	brake drum
repeater	underlay	brake shoe

bulldozer	flash bulb	harvester
burnisher	flash lamp	headlight
can-opener	floodgate	hydrofoil
capacitor	flour mill	implement
cement gun	flow valve	incubator
clockwork	flycutter	indicator
component	focus lamp	inlet port
condenser	food-mixer	insulator
contactor	foot-brake	interlock
converter	footstick	jack-knife
corkscrew	force pump	jackscrew
cotton gin	fumigator	jet engine
crankcase	fuse links	land rover
crosshead	fuseboard	lawnmower
diaphragm	gas engine	light bulb
die-sinker	gas-holder	limelight
disc brake	gasometer	liquefier
disc valve	gear lever	lithotype
disc wheel	gear train	loadstone
drop drill	gearwheel	mechanism
drop forge	generator	milk churn
drop press	grease gun	mill wheel
eidograph	gyroplane	milometer
electrode	gyroscope	monoscope
escalator	hair drier	neon light
excavator	half shaft	oiling can
explosive	hand-brake	overdrive
face lathe	hand-drill	page gauge
fire alarm	handspike	periscope

piston rod	spin-drier	zincotype
pitchfork	spotlight	aero engine
plug point	stamp mill	alarm clock
plumb line	star drill	alternator
pneumatic	steam iron	angle block
power line	steel mill	angle board
power pack	stink bomb	angle brace
preheater	stop light	angle plate
projector	strip mill	arc welding
propeller	sump guard	attachment
propshaft	tabulator	automation
prototype	tail-light	automobile
punch card	telephone	bench drill
punch tape	telescope	bowie knife
pyrometer	thyristor	box spanner
radiogram	tin-opener	calculator
rectifier	tool-chest	centrifuge
reflector	top burton	chain block
regulator	treadmill	chain drive
road drill	turbopump	check valve
rock drill	turntable	cine camera
rotary gap	type mould	claw hammer
sandpaper	tyre lever	coal shovel
separator	water cock	cobalt bomb
sidelight	watermill	coffee mill
skyrocket	wattmeter	cold chisel
small-bore	wood screw	commutator
solar cell	worm wheel	compass saw
sound unit	yardstick	compressor

controller
corking pip
cotton mill
crankshaft
crown wheel
crystal set
cultivator
depth gauge
dictaphone
dishwasher
diving bell
donkey pump
drop hammer
drum sander
dry battery
duplicator
earth mover
economiser
edging tool
emery board
emery wheel
escapement
explosives
filter pump
fire engine
flare light
flashlight
floodlight
gas turbine

grindstone
gudgeon pin
guillotine
hearing aid
heat engine
hectograph
hole cutter
hovercraft
humidifier
hydroplane
incendiary
inductance
keyhole saw
laundromat
lighthouse
lock washer
locomotive
luff tackle
Machine Age
magnet core
marker buoy
masonry pin
micrometer
microphone
mimeograph
miner's lamp
motorcycle
oil derrick
oscillator

osmium lamp
oxygen tent
pantograph
paramagnet
pari-mutuel
paper-knife
peen hammer
percolator
photoflash
photoflood
piledriver
pilot light
petrol pump
pipe wrench
piston pump
piston ring
powder mill
power brake
power drill
power press
prime mover
proof press
push button
quartz lamp
respirator
road roller
robot pilot
rose engine
rotary pump

sack barrow
safety fuse
safety lamp
serve valve
servomotor
shunt motor
silk screen
slide valve
sluice gate
snowplough
spring lock
stay tackle
stenograph
stereotype
strip light
sunray lamp
suppressor
suspension
switchgear
tachometer
television
thermistor
thermostat
ticker tape
time switch
timing-gear
transducer
transistor
twin triode

twist drill
typewriter
vacuum pump
vacuum tube
vapour lamp
ventilator
water-clock
water-gauge
water-tower
water-wheel
whirl drill
wind tunnel
yard tackle
zircon lamp
accelerator
accumulator
afterburner
aftercooler
anchor light
atomic power
autostarter
ball bearing
barrel scale
battery lamp
beam antenna
beam balance
bevel square
bicycle pump
brace and bit

brake lining
butcher's saw
cam-follower
carbon light
carburettor
caterpillar
choking coil
circular saw
cold welding
compensator
comptometer
cooling coil
dark lantern
depth charge
distributor
dolly camera
dovetail saw
drilling rig
dynamometer
echo sounder
electric arc
electric eye
electric saw
electron gun
electrotype
engine block
engine of war
exhaust pipe
exhaust port

feeler gauge
Ferris wheel
field magnet
filing block
glass cutter
hair trigger
interrupter
ironmongery
jumper-cable
junction box
letterpress
lie detector
limit switch
loud-speaker
machine shop
machine tool
machine work
machine-made
memory tubes
mercury lamp
microswitch
mortice lock
off-set litho
off-shore rig
oil refinery
on-off switch
pillar drill
platen press
ploughshare

pocketknife
pop-rivet gun
power shovel
preselector
pulley-block
radio beacon
range finder
relief valve
ring spanner
road-scraper
rocket motor
rolling mill
rotary drill
rotary press
safety razor
safety valve
sanding disc
scaffolding
screwdriver
searchlight
self-starter
series motor
signal light
slot machine
snatch block
solar engine
speedometer
spirit level
steam engine

steam hammer
steam roller
steam shovel
stirrup pump
stock ticker
storage cell
stuffing box
suction pump
surgeon's saw
switchboard
synchromesh
tackle block
tamping iron
teleprinter
totalisator
track rod end
transceiver
transformer
transmitter
tumble-drier
type foundry
weighbridge
wheelbarrow
X-ray machine
aerial camera
arithmometer
assembly line
balance wheel
barrel plater

battering ram
battery plate
binding screw
blast furnace
blinker light
burglar alarm
capstan-lathe
carving knife
cash register
control panel
control valve
conveyor belt
cooling tower
copying press
cylinder head
depth sounder
diesel engine
differential
donkey engine
driving force
electric cord
electric fire
electric iron
electric wire
filament lamp
flame-thrower
flashing lamp
forge foundry
fruit machine

grease nipple
grinding mill
hedge trimmer
high fidelity
hydraulic ram
landing light
lightning rod
machine ruler
magic lantern
magnetic tape
marine engine
marlinespike
masonry drill
micro circuit
mine detector
mobile camera
monkeywrench
national grid
nuclear power
pair of scales
palette knife
petrol engine
photocathode
piston engine
potter's wheel
power station
pressure mine
pulley tackle
radial engine

radio compass
ratchet drill
record player
refrigerator
resuscitator
rocket engine
rotary engine
rubber hammer
short circuit
signal beacon
signal rocket
single tackle
sledge-hammer
solar battery
soldering gun
sound limiter
sparking plug
spring washer
steam turbine
steering gear
supercharger
tantalum lamp
tape recorder
telecomputer
transmission
tungsten lamp
two-handed saw
walkie-talkie
wheel bearing

Medicine

This section includes list of diseases and afflictions—medical men and hospital staff—hospitals—remedies and cures—drugs—aids to health—phobias and psychiatric terms—medical instruments—medical sciences—anatomy—dentistry—first aid.

B.O.	E.N.T.	pus	band	daze
Dr.	eye	rib	bile	deaf
G.P.	fat	rub	body	diet
id	fit	sac	boil	dope
I.Q.	flu	spa	bone	dose
M.D.	gas	sty	bubo	drip
M.O.	gum	tea	burn	drug
os	gut	tic	burp	duct
T.B.	hip	toe	calf	dumb
ail	ill	vet	case	face
arm	jaw	wan	cast	fade
bed	L.D.S.	wen	cell	fall
cup	lab	abed	chin	flux
cut	leg	ache	clot	foot
D.T.s	lip	acne	cold	gall
doc	L.S.D.	ague	coma	game
ear	mad	amok	corn	gash
E.C.G.	oil	back	cure	germ
E.E.G.	pep	bald	cusp	gout
ego	pox	balm	cyst	grip

guts	lung	scab	yawn	break
hair	maim	scar	yaws	build
halt	malt	shin	acute	bulla
hand	mask	shot	agony	bursa
harm	mole	sick	algid	canal
head	mute	skin	alive	catch
heal	nail	slim	ament	chafe
heel	nape	sole	amuck	cheek
hemp	neck	sore	ancon	chest
hips	noma	spot	ankle	clava
home	nose	stab	anvil	colic
hurt	numb	stye	aorta	colon
hypo	oral	swab	atomy	conch
ilia	otic	tent	aural	cough
iris	pain	turn	bathe	cramp
iron	pale	ulna	baths	crazy
itch	palm	umbo	belch	crick
junk	pang	vein	birth	croup
kibe	pest	vena	blain	dagga
kink	pill	wale	bleed	dandy
knee	plug	wall	blind	death
lame	pock	ward	blood	decay
lens	pons	wart	bolus	digit
limb	pore	weal	borax	dizzy
limp	rash	welt	botch	donor
lint	rest	wilt	bowel	drain
lips	ribs	wits	brace	dream
lisp	roof	womb	brain	drill
lobe	root	X-ray	brash	drops

dying	hives	nasal	scalp	throe
edema	hyoid	navel	seedy	thumb
elbow	ictus	nerve	senna	tibia
ether	ileum	nevus	serum	tired
faint	ilium	nurse	shell	tonic
femur	incus	opium	shock	tooth
fever	inion	organ	sight	torso
fibre	inlay	ovary	sinew	trace
flesh	jerks	palsy	sinus	tract
flush	joint	panel	skull	treat
fossa	jowls	pinna	sleep	trunk
frame	lance	plate	sling	tummy
fugue	lazar	polio	smart	ulcer
Galen	leech	polyp	sopor	ulnar
gauze	leper	probe	sound	uncus
gland	liver	psora	spasm	unfit
go mad	local	pulse	spine	urine
gonad	locum	pupil	stall	uvula
gored	lungs	purge	sting	vagus
gouty	lymph	quack	stupe	valve
graft	lysis	qualm	sweat	villi
graze	mamma	quick	swoon	virus
gripe	mania	rabid	tabes	vomer
gumma	manic	ramus	tabid	vomit
gyrus	medic	raphe	taint	waist
heart	miasm	renal	talus	wheal
helix	molar	rheum	teeth	whelk
herbs	mouth	salts	thigh	wince
hilum	mumps	salve	throb	wound

wreck	benign	codein	eczema
wrist	biceps	coelom	elixir
abulia	binder	comedo	embryo
aching	biopsy	concha	emetic
addict	blanch	corium	engram
ailing	bowels	cornea	eschar
albino	bracer	corpse	eyelid
alexia	breast	cortex	fascia
amytal	breath	coryza	fester
anemia	bruise	costal	fibula
anemic	bulimy	cow-pox	figure
angina	bunion	crisis	fillip
anoint	caecum	crusta	finger
apathy	caligo	crutch	foetus
apnoea	callus	cuboid	fornix
areola	cancer	cuneus	frenzy
armpit	canker	damage	fundus
artery	caries	dartre	fungus
asthma	carpus	deadly	gargle
asylum	cavity	defect	goitre
ataxia	cervix	demise	gripes
atocia	chafed	dengue	grippe
attack	chiasm	dental	growth
aurist	choler	dermis	gullet
autist	chorea	doctor	hallux
axilla	clavus	dorsum	hammer
balsam	clinic	dosage	healer
bedlam	clonus	dossil	health
bedpan	coccyx	dropsy	hearty

hernia	lotion	nasion	queasy
heroin	lumber	nausea	quinsy
herpes	lunacy	needle	rabies
humour	lunula	neuron	rachis
immune	madman	nipple	radial
in pain	maimed	oculus	ranula
infirm	malady	opiate	raving
injury	maniac	osteal	reflex
insane	marrow	palate	relief
instep	matron	pallor	remedy
insula	measly	papule	retina
intern	meatus	pelvis	rhesus
iodine	medico	peptic	rictus
IQ test	medius	phlegm	robust
junkie	megrim	phobia	roller
kidney	member	physic	sacrum
labial	memory	pimple	sadist
labour	meninx	plague	saliva
laid up	mental	plasma	scrape
lambda	mentum	pleura	scurvy
lancet	miasma	plexus	seeing
lappet	midrib	poison	senses
larynx	mongol	poorly	sepsis
lavage	morbid	potion	septic
lesion	mucous	psyche	serous
libido	muscle	psycho	sicken
lichen	mutism	ptisan	sickly
lipoma	myopic	puncta	simple
lobule	naevus	pyemia	sister

slough	thorax	voyeur	aphonia
sneeze	throat	weaken	apraxia
spinal	throes	weakly	arcanum
spleen	thrush	wrench	aspirin
splint	thymus	writhe	assuage
spotty	ticker	xyster	atebrin
sprain	tingle	zygoma	atrophy
sputum	tisane	abdomen	auricle
squint	tissue	abscess	autopsy
stapes	tongue	acidity	bacilli
stasis	tragus	aconite	bandage
stigma	trance	adrenal	bedfast
stitch	trauma	ailment	bedsore
strain	tremor	airsick	berserk
stress	trepan	alcohol	bilious
strium	trocar	allergy	bismuth
stroke	troche	allheal	bladder
struma	tumour	amentia	blister
stupor	twinge	amnesia	booster
stylet	unwell	ampulla	bow legs
suffer	ureter	anaemic	bromide
suture	vector	anaemic	bubonic
tablet	vesica	analyst	bulimia
tampon	vessel	anatomy	cadaver
tarsus	villus	anodyne	calcium
temple	viscus	antacid	calomel
tender	vision	antigen	camphor
tendon	vitals	anxiety	cannula
tetter	vomica	aphasia	capsule

carcass	cupping	femoral	humerus
cardiac	cure-all	fibroid	hygiene
carious	cuticle	fidgets	icterus
carrier	deathly	filling	illness
carsick	decease	fimbria	incisor
cascara	decline	fistula	innards
catarrh	deltoid	flushed	insides
cautery	dentist	foramen	insulin
chalone	derange	forceps	invalid
chancre	disease	forearm	ischium
chemist	draught	frailty	jawbone
chiasma	ear lobe	freckle	jejunum
cholera	earache	frontal	jugular
chorion	eardrum	game leg	kneecap
choroid	earshot	gastric	kneepan
chronic	emotion	*Gestalt*	laid low
ciliary	empathy	glasses	lanolin
cocaine	epithem	gumboil	lazaret
cochlea	erosion	haggard	lentigo
colicky	ethmoid	hashish	leprosy
colitis	eyeball	heal-all	leprous
complex	eyebrow	healing	linctus
condyle	eyewash	healthy	lockjaw
cordial	failing	hearing	lozenge
coroner	fantasy	hipbone	lumbago
crack-up	fatigue	history	lunatic
cranium	febrile	hormone	madness
cricoid	feel ill	hospice	malaise
cripple	feeling	hot bath	malaria

malleus	ovaries	quassia	soother
massage	panacea	quinine	spastic
masseur	papilla	ranting	spitoon
mastoid	paresis	regimen	springs
maxilla	parotid	relapse	stammer
measles	pass out	removal	sterile
medical	passage	reviver	sternum
medulla	patella	ribcage	stirrup
menthol	patient	rickets	stomach
microbe	persona	rubella	stutter
midwife	pessary	rubeola	sublime
milk leg	phalanx	run-down	sulphur
mixture	pharynx	rupture	sun bath
myringa	pigment	saccule	sun lamp
nail bed	pill-box	sarcoma	surgeon
nervous	pinkeye	scabies	surgery
nostril	placebo	scalpel	symptom
nostrum	plaster	scapula	syncope
obesity	pledget	scratch	syntone
occiput	podagra	seasick	syntony
oculist	pterion	seconal	syringe
omentum	punctum	section	tactile
operate	pustule	seizure	taenial
orbital	putamen	seltzer	take ill
orderly	pyaemia	sensory	talipes
organic	pylorus	sick bay	tampion
osseous	pyramid	sickbed	tapetum
ossicle	pyretic	sinking	tear-bag
otology	pyrexia	skin man	tetanus

theatre	abnormal	assuager	catheter
theriac	abortion	asthenia	cathexis
thermae	abrasion	atropine	cephalic
thyroid	accident	autacoid	cerebral
toenail	acidosis	bacillus	cervical
tonsils	acromion	backache	choleric
tormina	adenoids	backbone	cicatrix
toxemia	adhesion	bacteria	clavicle
trachea	agar-agar	baldness	clinical
travail	agraphia	barbital	club-foot
triceps	albinism	beriberi	cockeyed
trional	alienism	bicuspid	cold sore
typhoid	alienist	bifocals	collapse
unction	allergic	bile duct	comatose
unguent	allopath	bistoury	compress
unsound	alopecia	black eye	confined
urethra	amputate	black-out	contract
utricle	analysis	bleeding	coronary
vaccine	anatomic	blind eye	critical
vapours	antibody	blockage	crutches
variola	antidote	brachial	curative
veronal	aperient	break out	cyanosis
verruca	apoplexy	bulletin	cynanche
vertigo	aposteme	caffeine	dandruff
viscera	appendix	cannabis	deathbed
vitamin	appetite	carditis	debility
whitlow	arteries	casualty	decrepit
witless	Asian flu	cataract	delicate
zymotic	asphyxia	catching	delirium

delivery	emulsion	furuncle
delusion	*enceinte*	gallipot
demented	engramma	ganglion
dementia	entrails	gangrene
dentures	epidemic	glaucoma
deranged	epilepsy	glycerin
détraqué	epiploon	*grand mal*
diabetes	eruption	hair-ball
diagnose	erythema	handicap
digestif	escapism	hard drug
diplegia	etiology	hay fever
disabled	euphoria	headache
diseased	excision	heat lamp
disgorge	exit dose	heat-spot
disorder	exposure	heel bone
dispense	eye drops	hemostat
diuretic	eye patch	hip-joint
dog-tired	eyesalve	holotony
dosology	eyesight	home-sick
dressing	eye-tooth	hospital
drop dead	face lift	hot flush
druggist	first aid	houseman
drumhead	fixation	hypnosis
ductless	flat feet	hypnotic
duodenum	follicle	hysteria
ecraseur	forehead	*idée fixe*
edgebone	fracture	immunity
ego-ideal	frenulum	impetigo
embolism	fumigant	impotent

incision	marasmus	otoscope
infected	masseter	overdose
inflamed	masseuse	pancreas
inhalant	maturant	pandemia
inner ear	medicate	papillae
insanity	medicine	paranoia
insomnia	membrane	paranoid
instinct	midbrain	parasite
internal	migraine	parietal
iron lung	mind cure	paroxysm
irritant	morphine	pectoral
jaundice	muscular	peduncle
languish	mycology	pellagra
laudanum	naked eye	perspire
lavement	narcosis	*petit mal*
laxative	narcotic	phalange
lenitive	necrosis	pharmacy
lethargy	nembutal	philtrum
leukemia	neoplasm	phthisis
ligament	neuritis	physical
ligature	neurosis	physique
lincture	neurotic	pia mater
liniment	nosogeny	pick-me-up
lip-salve	nosology	pisiform
lobotomy	novocain	placenta
love-drug	numbness	pleurisy
mal de mer	ointment	podagric
malarial	olive oil	podiatry
mandible	operator	posology

poultice	sedation	stitches
practice	sedative	striatum
pregnant	senility	subacute
premolar	serology	sudarium
prenatal	shinbone	sufferer
procaine	shingles	superego
prostate	shoulder	surgical
psychist	sick abed	swelling
pulmonic	sickling	take sick
pump room	sickness	tear drop
purblind	sickroom	tear duct
pus basin	sinapism	teething
pyorrhea	skeletal	temporal
reaction	skeleton	teratoma
receptor	skin dose	thalamus
Red Cross	skin-deep	the bends
remedial	smallpox	thin skin
resident	smarting	thoracic
rest cure	soft drug	thyroxin
ringworm	somatist	tingling
roborant	soothing	tocogony
run amuck	sore spot	tocology
salivary	soreness	toponymy
sanatory	specimen	trachoma
scaphoid	speculum	trephine
scarring	sphenoid	true skin
sciatica	sphygmus	tubercle
scrofula	splenium	tumorous
secretin	stinging	tympanum

ulcerous	ambulance	blue-blood
unciform	analeptic	body odour
unhinged	analgesia	boric acid
unstable	analgesic	bow-legged
uroscopy	anamnesis	brain cell
vaccinia	anklebone	breakdown
valerian	ankylosis	broken arm
variolar	antenatal	broken leg
vascular	antihelix	Caesarean
vaseline	antiserum	calenture
vena cava	antitoxin	callipers
venotomy	arthritis	callosity
vertebra	aspirator	calmative
vesicant	assuasive	calvities
vitality	audiology	cankerous
vomiting	auriscopy	carbuncle
wall-eyed	bacterium	carcinoma
wandered	bandaging	cartilage
weakling	barbitone	caruncula
wet nurse	bath chair	case-sheet
addiction	bedridden	castor oil
admission	behaviour	catalepsy
adrenalin	bellyache	cataplasm
aitchbone	birth-mark	cataplexy
alcoholic	blackhead	catatonia
alkalizer	blind spot	catatonic
alleviate	blindness	catch cold
allopathy	blood bank	catharsis
amaurosis	blood test	cathartic

cauterize	depth dose	endolymph
cheekbone	diagnosis	energumen
chilblain	diaphragm	ephedrine
chincough	diarrhoea	epidermis
chiropody	diathermy	epileptic
cicatrice	dichotomy	epiphyses
cirrhosis	diet sheet	esotropia
claustrum	digitalis	exotropia
cleansing	discharge	extremity
collyrium	dispenser	extrovert
complaint	distemper	eye doctor
condition	dizzy turn	eyelashes
conscious	dosimeter	faith cure
contagion	dosimetry	fallopian
contusion	drain tube	fallotomy
corpuscle	dropsical	false ribs
cortisone	dura mater	febrifuge
cough drop	dysentery	febrility
crash diet	dyspepsia	festering
cretinism	dyspeptic	fetishism
cross-eyed	dystrophy	fever heat
cuneiform	echolalia	fever ward
curvature	electuary	fixed idea
dead faint	emaciated	flatulent
dead tired	embrocate	fore-brain
defective	emergency	frostbite
delirious	emollient	fumigator
demulcent	emotional	fungosity
dentistry	endocrine	funny bone

gastritis	ingestion	medicated
gathering	inhalator	medicinal
geriatric	injection	memory gap
germicide	inoculate	mesentery
give birth	impatient	mesocolon
gladiolus	introvert	middle ear
glandular	invalided	midwifery
glycerine	iron pills	milk teeth
go berserk	iron tonic	mongolism
halitosis	isolation	morbidity
hammer toe	jail fever	mortified
hamstring	king's evil	mouthwash
heartbeat	knee-joint	nappy rash
heartburn	labyrinth	narcotics
histamine	lachrymal	nasal duct
homeopath	lazaretto	nauseated
horehound	leucocyte	near-sight
hunchback	life force	nebulizer
hypnotism	lymphatic	neophobia
hysterics	long sight	nephritis
idiopathy	malar bone	nerve cell
ill-health	malignant	neuralgia
in plaster	malleolus	neurology
incubator	manubrium	neuropath
incurable	marihuana	nightmare
infection	marijuana	noncompos
infirmary	masochist	nutrition
infirmity	maternity	nux vomica
influenza	maxillary	nystagmus

obsession
occipital
off-colour
officinal
olfactory
on the mend
operation
optic disc
optometry
osteology
osteopath
otologist
pacemaker
paralogia
paralysis
paranoiac
paranomia
parapathy
paregoric
parotitis
pathology
perilymph
pertussis
pesthouse
phagocyte
phalanges
phlebitis
phrenetic
physician

pin and web
pituitary
pneumeter
pneumonia
poisoning
pollution
possessed
precuneus
premature
prescribe
prognosis
prophasis
prostate
psoriasis
psychosis
psychotic
pulmonary
purgative
purifying
quadratus
rachidial
radiogram
radiology
raving mad
resection
sartorius
sassafras
sauna bath
sclerosis

sclerotic
sebaceous
secretion
seediness
semi-lunar
sensorium
sinusitis
skingraft
sociopath
soporific
spare-part
splay feet
squeamish
squinting
sterilize
stiff dose
stiff neck
stillborn
stimulant
stretcher
subsultus
sudorific
suffering
sunstroke
suppurant
sweat bath
syntectic
taste buds
tear-gland

tegmentum	washed-out	antitragus
thanatoid	waste away	apoplectic
therapist	water cure	apothecary
thighbone	wax glands	applicator
thyrotomy	well-being	astragalus
toothache	wristbone	barium meal
tooth-pick	X-ray plate	batophobia
trapezium	zoophobia	belladonna
trapezius	zooplasty	bestiality
traumatic	aberration	Black Death
treatment	abirritant	blood count
tricuspid	abreaction	blood donor
tummy-ache	acetabulum	blood group
umbilical	acrophobia	bloodstain
umbilicus	Adam's apple	bloody flux
unguentum	aerophobia	bonesetter
unhealthy	affliction	brain fever
urticaria	afterbirth	brainstorm
vaccinate	algophobia	breastbone
varicella	alienation	breathless
varicosis	alimentary	broken bone
venectomy	amputation	broken dose
ventricle	anesthesia	broken nose
vermifuge	ankle-joint	bronchitis
vertebrae	antibiotic	buccinator
vestibule	antipoison	canker rash
voyeurism	antisepsis	castration
vulnerary	antiseptic	catalepsis
wandering	antisocial	catholicon

cerebellum
chickenpox
chloroform
chromosome
cibophobia
collarbone
commissure
common cold
compulsion
concussion
conscience
consultant
contagious
convalesce
convulsion
corn doctor
corrective
cotton wool
cough syrup
crackbrain
cracked wit
cyclothyme
cynophobia
cystectomy
cystoscope
dandy fever
danger list
deathwatch
dentifrice

depressant
depression
dermatitis
dim-sighted
diphtheria
dipsomania
dirty nurse
disability
discomfort
disfigured
dispensary
distracted
dizzy spell
doraphobia
draw breath
dream state
drop serene
drug addict
dypsomania
ear trumpet
ectodermal
elbow-joint
emaciation
embonpoint
embryology
emplastrum
enclampsia
entodermal
epispastic

epithelium
Epsom salts
ergophobia
erotomania
eructation
euthanasia
extraction
faith curer
false teeth
farsighted
feebleness
fever pitch
fibrositis
fine fettle
fingernail
five senses
flatulence
fonticulus
foot doctor
gallstones
gamophobia
gastrotomy
geriatrics
grey matter
gripewater
haunch bone
healing art
health farm
hearing aid

heatstroke	laboratory	nerve fibre
hemaglobin	laceration	nettle rash
hematology	laparotomy	neuropathy
hemiplegia	laryngitis	night float
hemisphere	last breath	night nurse
hemophilia	lazar house	nosophobia
hemophobia	leechcraft	obstetrics
homeopathy	lethal dose	oesophagus
hot springs	loss of life	odontogeny
hypodermic	lymph gland	optic nerve
hypodermis	main stream	optic tract
idiopathic	medical man	orthopraxy
immunology	medicament	orthoscope
Indian hemp	medicaster	ossiferous
indisposed	medication	osteoblast
infectious	meningitis	osteoclast
inhibition	mental test	osteopathy
insolation	mesogaster	out of sorts
inspirator	metabolism	outpatient
instrument	metacarpus	overweight
internship	metatarsus	oxygen mask
intestines	microscope	oxygen tank
invalidate	mind-healer	oxygen tent
invalidism	monomaniac	padded cell
invalidity	monophobia	paediatric
irritation	mutilation	painkiller
kill or cure	nail matrix	palliative
kiss of life	narcissist	paramnesia
knock-knees	nauseation	parapathia

paraphasia	prevention	saucer eyes
paraphilia	preventive	scarlatina
paraplegia	prognostic	scrofulous
paronychia	protective	semeiology
pathognomy	psychiater	semeiotics
pathomania	psychiatry	sense organ
pediatrics	psychology	septicemia
pediatrist	psychopath	serologist
pedophilia	public ward	shellshock
penicillin	pyretology	short sight
periosteum	pyrophobia	sick as a dog
peritoneal	radiograph	sickliness
peritoneum	radiometer	sitophobia
perversion	radioscopy	sixth sense
pestilence	radium bath	soft palate
pharmacist	ray therapy	somatology
phenacetin	recuperate	sore throat
phlebotomy	regression	specialist
physiology	repression	spectacles
pigeon-toed	resistance	sphacelate
pineal body	respirator	spinal cord
plague spot	rheumatics	spirograph
podiatrist	rheumatism	spirometer
polychrest	root-sheath	splanchnic
polyclinic	rude health	squint eyes
poor health	salivation	staff nurse
post-mortem	salt-cellar	sterilizer
premaxilla	sanatorium	strabismus
presbyopia	sanitarian	strict diet

strychnine	wheel chair	basket cells
subliminal	withdrawal	betatherapy
sublingual	wonder drug	blood stream
suprarenal	xenophobia	blood stroke
sweat gland	yellow jack	blood-vessel
teratology	yellow spot	booster dose
theophobia	witch hazel	brain damage
thrombosis	abnormality	breaking out
tonic spasm	abortionist	caesarotomy
toothpaste	agoraphobia	canine tooth
toponymics	airsickness	cardiograph
topophobia	ambiversion	carminative
tourniquet	amphetamine	car-sickness
toxicology	an apple a day	case history
transplant	anaesthesia	cephalalgia
traumatism	anaesthetic	chiroplasty
trochanter	androphobia	chiropodist
truth serum	Anglophobia	chiropraxis
tumescence	antifebrile	choroid coat
ulceration	antipyretic	circulation
unbalanced	aphrodisiac	cleft palate
urinalysis	application	coconscious
varicotomy	arteriotomy	cod liver oil
vesicotomy	astigmatism	cold therapy
veterinary	astraphobia	colour blind
Vichy water	auscultator	confinement
vital force	aussage test	conjunctiva
vital spark	bactericide	consumption
vocal cords	barbiturate	consumptive

convolution	famine fever	Hippocratic
convulsions	fatty tissue	hormonology
coprophilia	fibre optics	hospitalize
corn plaster	fingerstall	hydrophobia
decrepitude	floating rib	hypnophobia
deep therapy	fluoroscope	hypsophobia
deobstruent	fomentation	indigestion
derangement	frustration	ink-blot test
dermaplasty	gall-bladder	inoculation
dermatology	Gallophobia	internal ear
diagnostics	gastrectomy	intravenous
diaphoretic	gerontology	ipecacuanha
dipsomaniac	gild the pill	irradiation
dislocation	gnawing pain	horse doctor
drive insane	gold therapy	hospital bed
dromophobia	granule cell	isodose line
dull-sighted	growing pain	jugular vein
eccrinology	gynaecology	kidney basin
Elastoplast	haemorrhage	kleptomania
elixir vitae	hagiophobia	laughing gas
embrocation	handicapped	locum tenens
endocardium	health salts	long-sighted
ethical self	healthiness	lycanthropy
examination	heart attack	maladjusted
exoskeleton	heat therapy	malfunction
expectorant	hebephrenia	malpractice
extremities	hectic fever	median nerve
face lifting	hectic flush	mediastinum
facial nerve	heteropathy	medicine man

megalomania

melancholia

mental block

mental shock

miracle drug

miscarriage

mitral valve

mortal wound

motive force

musculature

nasopharynx

naturopathy

nearsighted

necrophilia

necrophobia

negrophobia

nerve ending

nerve supply

neurologist

neuroplasty

neuroticism

neutralizer

nursing home

nyctophobia

nymphomania

observation

obstruction

ochlophobia

optometrist

orthodontia

orthopaedic

orthopedics

orthopedist

palpitation

Pandora's box

pantophobia

paraphrenia

parathyroid

parturition

pathologist

pelvic colon

peptic ulcer

pericardium

peristaltic

peritonitis

personality

pharyngitis

phobophobia

phonophobia

photophobia

physiognomy

plaster cast

play therapy

prickly heat

private ward

probationer

prognostics

prophylaxis

prostration

psychognosy

psycholepsy

psychologue

psychometer

psychometry

psychomotor

psychotaxia

quack remedy

quacksalver

rabbit fever

radiography

radiologist

radiopraxis

radiothermy

respiration

restorative

rheumaticky

rhinoplasty

rigor mortis

roentgen ray

running nose

Russophobia

sal volatile

sal-ammoniac

schizoidism

schizothyme

Scotophobia

seasickness

self-control	venesection	breath of life
senile decay	war neurosis	brontophobia
skin disease	warm springs	canal of Petit
slipped disc	water canker	cardiophobia
solar plexus	wisdom tooth	cardioplasty
stasiphobia	X-ray machine	central canal
stethoscope	X-ray therapy	chemotherapy
stirrup bone	yellow fever	chiropractic
stomach-ache	aelurophobia	chiropractor
stomach-pump	aeroneurosis	cold compress
stomatology	alexipharmic	collywobbles
sudden death	anaesthetist	come down with
suppression	anthropotomy	complication
suppuration	antiantibody	*compos mentis*
surgeon's saw	appendectomy	conditioning
teleophobia	appendicitis	constipation
temperature	aptitude test	consultation
the sniffles	aquapuncture	contact lens
therapeutic	at death's door	convalescent
thermometer	athlete's foot	coronary vein
tonsillitis	auscultation	cough mixture
tooth powder	bacteriology	countervenom
transfusion	balm of Gilead	court plaster
trench fever	behaviourism	cremnophobia
trench mouth	bibliophobia	critical list
tumefaction	bill of health	curietherapy
Turkish bath	bismuth salts	debilitation
unconscious	black-and-blue	demonophobia
vaccination	bloodletting	dietotherapy

disinfectant	hallucinosis	malnutrition
dissociation	harquebusade	mammary gland
electrolysis	head shrinker	mass-hysteria
elixir of life	health resort	megalomaniac
emergency bed	heart disease	minor surgery
emotionalism	heart failure	morbid growth
encephalitis	heresyphobia	muscle fibres
endoskeleton	hydropathist	natural death
extroversion	hydrotherapy	nervous wreck
faith healing	hypertension	neurasthenia
fallen arches	hypochondria	obstetrician
family doctor	hysterectomy	optic chiasma
felinophobia	immunization	orthodiagram
feminophobia	immunologist	orthodontics
fever blister	inflammation	orthodontist
feverishness	insane asylum	orthopaedics
formaldehyde	integral dose	orthopaedist
Francophobia	intoxication	ossification
friar's balsam	introversion	palpitations
gammatherapy	island of Reil	parasitology
gastric juice	kleptomaniac	parietal bone
gastroplasty	knock-out drop	parotid gland
geriatrician	light therapy	pediatrician
glands of Moll	lock hospital	pelvic girdle
grinding pain	lose one's head	perspiration
group therapy	lose strength	pestilential
gynecologist	loss of memory	pharmaceutic
hair follicle	mad as a hatter	pharmacology
hair restorer	major surgery	pharmacopeia

phlebotomist	rubber gloves	streptomycin
phototherapy	scarlet fever	student nurse
pigmentation	schizophrene	subconscious
post-hypnotic	schizothymia	subcutaneous
preconscious	serum therapy	surgical boot
prescription	sesamoid bone	suture needle
preventative	shaking palsy	therapeutics
prophylactic	shock therapy	therapeutist
psychiatrics	shooting pain	thyroid gland
psychiatrist	shortsighted	tonsillotomy
psychognosis	simple reflex	toxicophobia
psychologist	sleep-inducer	trained nurse
psychopathic	sleeping pill	tranquillize
psychophobia	sleepwalking	transference
psychrometer	slimming diet	traumatology
purblindness	solar therapy	tuberculosis
radiosurgery	somnambulism	turn a deaf ear
radiotherapy	sphygmograph	varicose vein
reflex action	sphygmometer	violent death
rehabilitate	spinal column	vitreous body
resectoscope	spotted fever	water blister
respirometer	St. Vitus' dance	word deafness
resuscitator	stabbing pain	zinc ointment
robust health	strait-jacket	

Warfare

This section includes list of fighting men—formations of soldiers—weapons, historical and present-day—types of warfare—armour and ammunition—spies, deserters and enemies—victory and defeat—attack—military architecture, defence and fortification.

G.I.	R.A.F.	A.W.O.L.	D-day	helm
M.P.	ram	ball	dike	hero
pa	rat	band	dirk	hilt
R.A.	rod	barb	dove	hold
R.E.	row	bard	duck	host
R.N.	sap	bill	duel	H-war
arm	spy	bird	dump	I.C.B.M.
axe	sub	bola	duty	impi
bat	Tyr	bolt	épée	jack
bow	T.N.T.	bomb	feud	jamb
cap	van	bone	file	jeep
cut	vet	bout	fire	Jock
dud	W.A.F.	butt	fish	keep
egg	war	camp	flak	kill
foe	ally	club	foil	kris
gat	ammo	cock	fort	levy
gun	Ares	coif	fray	load
Hun	arms	Colt	guns	lock
N.C.O.	army	cosh	hate	mace
P.O.W.	A-war	dart	hawk	mail

Mars	wage	brave	harry	recco
mere	wall	broch	H-bomb	recon
mine	ward	Buffs	H-hour	redan
moat	W.A.V.E.	burst	jerid	repel
mole	wing	cadre	Jerry	rifle
navy	W.R.N.S.	chute	jihad	rowel
Odin	Y-gun	clash	jingo	ruade
park	zone	corps	knife	sally
peel	Zulu	cover	kukri	salvo
peon	AA gun	Croat	lager	scarp
pike	A-bomb	ditch	lance	scene
post	aegis	draft	leave	scout
rack	arena	drive	Luger	sepoy
rank	armed	enemy	mêlée	serve
rath	armet	feint	mound	shaft
riot	array	fence	nitre	shako
rock	arrow	field	onset	shell
rout	at bay	fight	orgue	shoot
rush	at war	flail	parry	siege
shot	baton	flank	pavis	skean
slug	beset	fleet	plate	sling
spit	bilbo	foray	poilu	snake
spur	billy	fosse	posse	sowar
stab	blade	front	power	spahi
tace	blank	fusee	rally	spear
tank	blast	fusil	range	spike
tuck	blitz	Gerry	ranks	spray
unit	Boche	grape	rebel	spurs
W.A.C.S.	bolas	guard	recce	squad

staff	air gun	cannon	escort
steel	alpeen	casque	fewter
stick	Amazon	castle	flight
stone	ambush	casual	foeman
storm	animus	charge	forage
sword	Anzacs	cleche	forces
targe	archer	cohort	gabion
tasse	Archie	column	galoot
tommy	argosy	combat	glacis
train	armada	convoy	glaive
troop	armour	cordon	gorget
truce	ash-can	corium	greave
U-boat	askari	creese	*guerre*
uhlan	assail	cudgel	gunner
visor	attack	cuisse	gun-shy
W.A.A.C.S.	barbel	curfew	Gurkha
W.A.A.F.S.	barrel	dagger	gusset
waddy	batman	defeat	hagbut
W.A.S.P.S.	battle	defend	hammer
W.A.V.E.S.	beaver	detail	hanger
Woden	bellum	digger	hanjar
wound	big gun	donjon	harass
W.R.A.C.S.	billet	dry run	heaume
W.R.A.F.S.	bomber	duello	helmet
Wrens	breech	dugout	hot war
abatis	bugler	dumdum	hussar
Ack-Ack	bullet	enlist	impact
action	bunker	ensign	impale
air arm	camail	escarp	in arms

inroad	picket	sentry	war-dog
jereed	pierce	set gun	war-god
jingal	pistol	shield	weapon
laager	pogrom	slogan	womera
labrys	pompom	sniper	yeoman
lancer	powder	sortie	Zouave
legion	pow-pow	sparth	abattis
lorica	quiver	spying	advance
mailed	rafale	strafe	aerogun
maquis	Rajput	strike	air raid
marine	ramrod	swivel	amnesty
Mauser	rapier	talion	archery
merlon	rappel	target	armoury
minnie	ray gun	tenail	arsenal
morion	razzia	thrust	assagai
mortar	rebuff	to arms	assault
musket	reduit	tocsin	atom gun
muster	report	Toledo	atom war
muzzle	revolt	tom-tom	balista
oilcan	rioter	trench	bar shot
outfit	rocket	troops	barrack
panzer	rookie	tulwar	barrage
parade	salade	turret	barrier
parole	sallet	vallum	basinet
patrol	salute	valour	bastion
pavise	sangar	Vandal	bat bomb
pellet	sapper	victor	battery
pepper	sconce	volley	bayonet
petard	scutum	war-cry	bazooka

beat off	charger	dudgeon	gun-park
Bellona	chauvin	dueller	gunplay
big guns	chicken	dungeon	gun-port
big shot	citadel	echelon	gunroom
blowgun	cold war	enomoty	gunshot
Boer War	command	escopet	hackbut
bombard	company	fall-out	halberd
bombing	conchie	fend off	halbert
booster	conquer	fighter	handjar
bravado	cordite	firearm	harness
bren gun	corslet	fortify	hatchet
bricole	cossack	fortlet	hauberk
brigade	coupure	foxhole	heroism
buckler	courage	gallant	Hessian
bulldog	courser	gallery	heyduck
bulwark	crusade	gas bomb	hold off
burp gun	cudgels	gas mask	holster
caisson	cuirass	germ war	holy war
caitiff	curtain	gisarme	hostage
calibre	curtana	go to war	invader
caliver	curtape	grapnel	jackman
caltrop	cutlass	grenade	jambeau
cap-a-pie	dastard	gunboat	jankers
carbine	defence	gundeck	javelin
carcass	disband	gunfire	jollies
carrier	distaff	gunlock	knifing
cashier	dragoon	gunnage	kremlin
cavalry	draught	gunnery	lambast
chamber	dry fire	gunning	lamboys

Long Tom	pédieux	section	ward off
longbow	pedrero	self bow	war-drum
lookout	petrary	service	warfare
lunette	phalanx	shoot at	war-head
lyddite	pikeman	shooter	warlike
machete	pillbox	shotgun	warlock
make war	platoon	soldier	warlord
maniple	poleaxe	Spartan	warpath
mantlet	polygon	sparthe	warring
marines	poniard	spinner	warrior
martial	private	sten gun	warship
matross	quarrel	tactics	war-wolf
megaton	rampage	tear-gas	weapons
militia	rampart	tenable	wind gun
missile	ravelin	the fray	woomera
mission	recruit	theatre	wounded
morrion	red army	torpedo	yatagan
neutral	redcoat	traitor	aceldama
offence	redoubt	trigger	activate
on guard	regular	trooper	air force
open war	repulse	tumbril	air rifle
outpost	retreat	uniform	air-to-air
outwork	riposte	vanfoss	akeldama
paladin	Sabaoth	veteran	all-clear
panoply	sabaton	victory	alliance
parados	salient	wage war	ammo dump
paragon	samurai	war club	anabasis
parapet	sandbag	war game	anti-mine
patriot	Seabees	war song	apostate

arbalest	brattice	defender
armament	brickbat	demilune
armature	broadaxe	deserter
armoured	Browning	destrier
arms race	buckshot	dirt bomb
arquebus	buttress	division
art of war	buzzbomb	doughboy
atom-bomb	cabasset	drum call
attacker	campaign	drumfire
aventail	cannonry	drumhead
ballista	cartouch	duellist
banderol	casemate	dynamite
bang! bang!	catapult	embattle
bannerol	cavalier	enfilade
barbette	chaffron	enlistee
barbican	chamfron	entrench
barracks	champion	envelope
bartisan	chasseur	errantry
baselard	chivalry	escalade
battalia	civil war	exercise
battling	claymore	falchion
bear arms	cold feet	falconet
besieger	commando	fasthold
betrayer	conflict	fastness
blockade	corselet	fencible
blowpipe	crossbow	field gun
bludgeon	cry havoc	fighting
bomb rack	culverin	file fire
bomb site	cylinder	fire bomb

fire upon	infantry	Maxim gun
fireball	informer	melinite
firelock	invading	militant
flotilla	invasion	military
fortress	invasive	mobilize
fugleman	ironclad	muniment
furlough	janizary	munition
fusilier	jazerant	mushroom
gambeson	jingoism	musketry
garrison	jump area	nerve gas
gauntlet	killadar	open fire
Great War	knuckles	ordnance
guerilla	lancegay	orillion
gunflint	land-army	outguard
gunmetal	land-mine	pacifist
gunpoint	*Landwehr*	palisade
gunsmith	langrage	palstaff
gunstick	last post	palstave
gunstock	launcher	parallel
hang fire	Leon mine	partisan
heavy gun	Lewis gun	password
hedgehog	loophole	pauldron
hell bomb	magazine	petronel
herisson	mailclad	pikehead
hill-fort	man-of-war	poltroon
hireling	mantelet	puncheon
hornwork	marksman	quisling
howitzer	martello	quo vadis
inductee	massacre	recreant

regiment

renegade

repulsor

reserves

reveille

revolver

ricochet

rifleman

risaldar

runagate

safehold

scabbard

scimitar

sentinel

shrapnel

side arms

siege cap

siege gun

skean dhu

skip-bomb

skirmish

soldiery

solleret

space gun

spadroon

spearman

spontoon

squadron

stabbing

stalwart

stave off

stiletto

stockade

strafing

strategy

struggle

surprise

surround

swan shot

tac-au-tac

take arms

tenaille

the front

the sword

time bomb

time fire

tomahawk

Tommy gun

total war

transfix

trenches

turnback

turncoat

turntail

up in arms

uprising

vambrace

vamplate

vanguard

vanquish

vendetta

war cloud

war dance

war horse

war hound

war paint

war whoop

warcraft

warfarer

Waterloo

wayfarer

weaponry

world war

yeomanry

zero hour

accoutred

acropolis

aggressor

air-to-ship

ambuscade

archenemy

army corps

army issue

army lists

arrowhead

artillery

assailant

atomic gun	bombsight	cross fire
atomic war	booby trap	cubitière
attacking	boomerang	defensive
attrition	broadside	derringer
automatic	Brown Bess	desert rat
auto-rifle	brown bill	deterrent
backplate	camouflet	detonator
ballistic	cannonade	discharge
banderole	cannoneer	doodlebug
bandolier	caparison	double sap
banquette	carronade	drop a bomb
barricade	carry arms	earthwork
bastinado	cartouche	embattled
battalion	cartridge	encompass
battle-axe	casemated	enemy camp
battle-cry	casquetel	enemy fire
beachhead	castellan	escopette
beat up for	cease fire	espionage
beefeater	chain mail	explosive
beleaguer	chain shot	face guard
bellicism	challenge	fence wall
bellicose	chamfrain	field army
Big Bertha	chassepot	fieldwork
black bill	cold steel	fire a shot
blackjack	combatant	firepower
bloodshed	combative	fireworks
bomb-happy	conqueror	first line
bombs away	conscript	flintlock
bombshell	crackshot	flying sap

fortalice	in defence	minefield
fortified	incursion	Minnehaha
forty-five	incursive	minutemen
fourth arm	ironbound	monomachy
free-lance	irregular	mousetrap
front line	irruption	munitions
fulgurite	janissary	musketeer
fusillade	jesserant	musketoon
gas attack	katabasis	needle gun
gelignite	keep guard	nose guard
gladiator	keep vigil	nosepiece
glide-bomb	lance-jack	offensive
grapeshot	*Landsturm*	onslaught
grenadier	langridge	open enemy
guardsman	last ditch	open order
guerrilla	legionary	operation
guet-apens	levy war on	other side
gun battle	lie in wait	overthrow
gun turret	lionheart	panoplied
guncotton	logistics	parachute
gunpowder	long-range	peel-house
habergeon	*Luftwaffe*	peel-tower
harquebus	make war on	pikestaff
headpiece	man-at-arms	prick-spur
heavy fire	manoeuvre	projector
heroic act	march-past	protector
Home Guard	matchlock	proton gun
hostility	mercenary	pugnacity
hydrobomb	militancy	pyroxylin

ram rocket
razon bomb
rearguard
rebel call
rebellion
rerebrace
ressaldar
rifle ball
rocket gun
rocket man
round shot
roundhead
rowel spur
Royal Navy
sally port
saltpetre
sea battle
seat of war
self arrow
sentry box
shellfire
signalman
single sap
ski troops
sky troops
skyrocket
slaughter
slingshot
slung shot

small arms
small bore
small-shot
smoke bomb
soldier on
soldierly
son of a gun
sonic mine
spearhead
spring gun
stand fire
stink bomb
strategic
subaltern
submarine
super bomb
surprisal
surrender
swivel gun
sword-play
take sides
tank corps
target day
task force
tit for tat
torpedoed
torpedoer
trainband
trebuchet

trench gun
troopship
truncheon
under arms
under fire
vallation
vigilante
volunteer
War Office
war rocket
warmonger
watchword
white flag
woomerang
zumbooruk
activation
active army
active duty
active list
adventurer
aerial bomb
aerial mine
aggression
aggressive
Air Command
air service
ambushment
ammunition
antagonism

Armageddon
armed force
armed guard
armed truce
armigerous
armipotent
arm's length
atomic bomb
atomic pile
atom-rocket
ballistics
barbed-wire
battle flag
battle hymn
battle line
battlement
battleship
blitzkrieg
blockhouse
bold stroke
bombardier
bowie knife
box barrage
breastwork
bridgehead
brigandine
broadsword
bugle corps
call to arms

camel corps
camouflage
campaigner
cannon ball
cannon shot
cantonment
carabineer
carry on war
cavalryman
chauvinism
coast-guard
coat of mail
combat area
combat team
commandant
contingent
cross-staff
cuirassier
declare war
defendable
defensible
demobilize
detachment
direct fire
dragonnade
dragoonade
drawbridge
drummer boy
embankment

encampment
engarrison
éprouvette
escadrille
escalation
expedition
faint heart
field train
fieldpiece
fiery cross
fire trench
firing area
flying bomb
flying tank
Foot Guards
foot rifles
fusion bomb
Gatling gun
ground fire
ground mine
ground-zero
halberdier
heavy-armed
heroic deed
impalement
incendiary
investment
jingoistic
knighthood

knobkerrie	other ranks	skysweeper
kriegspiel	over the top	slit trench
lambrequin	oyster mine	smallsword
lay siege to	paratroops	smooth bore
Life Guards	percussion	spill blood
light-armed	picket-duty	stand guard
line of fire	point blank	state of war
loaded cane	portcullis	strategist
long knives	private war	stronghold
lookout man	projectile	submachine
machine gun	raking fire	sure as a gun
martiality	rally round	sword-fight
militarize	raw recruit	swordstick
militarism	Resistance	sworn enemy
militiaman	revolution	take to arms
missile man	rifle-range	take up arms
mob tactics	robot blitz	tenderfoot
mount guard	rocket bomb	ten-pounder
mural crown	rocket fire	test rocket
musket-shot	run-through	touch paper
mustard gas	second line	trajectile
napalm bomb	sentry duty	trajectory
no man's land	serviceman	under siege
nuclear war	shell-shock	vanquisher
obsidional	shillelagh	volunteers
occupation	short-range	war-goddess
old soldier	siege train	Winchester
on the march	siegecraft	air-to-ground
operations	six-shooter	antenna mine

antimissile
antitank gun
area bombing
armed combat
armed forces
armoured car
auxiliaries
balistraria
barnstormer
battle array
battle order
battle royal
battledress
battlefield
battle-plane
beach-master
bersaglieri
besiegement
bitter enemy
blockbuster
bloody shirt
blunderbuss
bombardment
bomber pilot
bomb-release
bow and arrow
breastplate
British Army
British Navy

buck private
bullet-proof
buoyant mine
bushwhacker
camaraderie
carriage bow
castellated
castle-guard
caterpillar
change sides
combat train
contentious
Cossack post
countermine
coup de poign
crack troops
declaration
demibastion
depth charge
dive-bombing
Dreyse rifle
emplacement
enemy action
engine of war
enlisted man
envelopment
faussebraie
faussebraye
fighting men

fire a volley
fire tactics
firing party
firing squad
firing table
fission bomb
flare rocket
flying corps
foot soldier
footed arrow
footslogger
force of arms
forced march
friend or foe
full harness
full of fight
gang warfare
Garand rifle
generalship
germ warfare
giant powder
ground-to-air
guerrillero
gun-carriage
hair trigger
hand grenade
heavy armour
heavy bomber
high dudgeon

hill station
Horse Guards
horse pistol
hostilities
inactive war
infantryman
Irish Guards
iron rations
Juno Curitis
land warfare
langrel shot
light bomber
lionhearted
Lochaber axe
loggerheads
look daggers
magazine gun
Maginot line
Marine Corps
might of arms
military man
mine thrower
moral defeat
morgenstern
morning-star
mountain gun
naval bomber
naval forces
nitre powder

nitrocotton
nuclear bomb
open warfare
pattern bomb
peace treaty
Pickelhaube
picket-guard
plate armour
platoon fire
postern gate
powder grain
put to flight
pyroballogy
rallying cry
rank and file
rebel action
reconnoitre
recruitment
regular army
retro-rocket
rolling fire
rules of war
safe-conduct
safety catch
Scots Guards
service call
ship-to-shore
shock troops
shoot to kill

shooting war
shuttle raid
Signal Corps
skip-bombing
smell powder
smoke rocket
smoke screen
sneak attack
soldatesque
soldierlike
soldiership
spar torpedo
spent bullet
spring a mine
stand at ease
stand of arms
step rockets
stormtroops
stray bullet
subdivision
Swiss Guards
sword-in-hand
take by storm
thin red line
thunder tube
Tommy Atkins
torpedo boat
trench knife
trigger talk

true colours	breakthrough	floating mine
trusty sword	breechloader	flying column
twilight war	buccaneering	forward march
under attack	bushfighting	fowling piece
Underground	canister shot	gladiatorial
up and at them	cannon fodder	glide-bombing
war of nerves	cannon's mouth	go over the top
war to end war	chauvinistic	grand tactics
warlikeness	chested arrow	ground forces
warriorlike	civil defence	guerrilla war
water-cannon	combat rocket	guided weapon
wooden horse	council of war	heavy dragoon
wooden walls	counter march	home reserves
acoustic mine	counterscarp	homing rocket
advanced work	court martial	horse and foot
anti-aircraft	cut-and-thrust	horse marines
appeal to arms	daggers drawn	hydrogen bomb
armour-plated	deadly weapon	Juno Quiritis
army reserves	demi-culverin	lady from hell
artilleryman	dumdum bullet	langrage shot
atomic cannon	Dutch courage	launching pad
awkward squad	electron bomb	leathernecks
banzai attack	encirclement	Light Brigade
banzai charge	engines of war	light dragoon
battering ram	entrenchment	line of action
battleground	escaramouche	line of battle
beat a retreat	false colours	machicolated
belligerence	field of blood	magnetic mine
bolt position	flame-thrower	march against

marching song	pyrotechnics	sudden attack
Medical Corps	quarterstaff	superbazooka
medium bomber	reactivation	supply troops
military zone	religious war	sword bayonet
mine detector	ricochet fire	tactical unit
mobilization	rifled cannon	take the field
moral courage	rifle-grenade	theatre of war
moral support	rocket attack	throwing iron
moral victory	sharpshooter	tooth and nail
muzzle-loader	shock tactics	trench mortar
naval militia	shooting iron	trigger happy
naval reserve	shoulder a gun	under the flag
naval warfare	shoulder arms	vertical fire
on the warpath	siege warfare	virus warfare
Parthian shot	signal rocket	warmongering
Pearl Harbour	single combat	white feather
picked troops	sliderule war	who goes there
pioneer corps	splint armour	window rocket
plunging fire	standing army	winged rocket
powder charge	stormtrooper	yellow streak
pressure mine	stouthearted	

Geography

This section includes geographical features—land formations—natural phenomena—maps—seasons and tides—climate, weather and meteorology—geological terms—elements and minerals—rocks and gem-stones—astronomy—stars, planets and constellations.

air	gas	ria	beck	city
ait	gem	rip	belt	clay
alp	G.M.T.	sea	berg	coal
Ara	har	sky	bill	cold
bay	ice	sod	*bise*	coma
bed	icy	sun	blow	cove
ben	I.G.Y.	tin	bolt	crag
bog	jet	wad	bomb	dale
cay	jut	wax	Bora	damp
col	Leo	wet	bore	dawn
cwm	low	adit	brae	deep
dam	map	Afer	buhr	dell
dew	mud	apex	burn	dirt
dip	nip	Apus	burr	down
ebb	oil	arch	bush	duct
eye	orb	area	calf	dune
fen	ore	Argo	calm	dusk
fog	pap	arid	cape	dust
gap	pit	bank	cave	dyke

397

4

east	Hebe	Lynx	ores	sial
eddy	high	Lyra	park	sill
eyot	hill	main	pass	silt
fall	hoar	marl	Pavo	sima
fell	holm	Mars	peak	site
firn	home	mere	peat	slag
floe	hook	mesa	plat	smog
flow	Iris	mica	pole	snow
flux	iron	*midi*	pond	soil
foam	isle	mild	pool	spar
Föhn	jade	mire	purl	spit
fold	Juno	mist	race	spot
fork	kame	mode	rack	spur
foss	kelp	moon	rain	star
gale	khor	moor	reef	surf
gang	kyle	moss	Rhea	talc
gill	lake	mull	rias	tarn
glen	land	naze	rift	thaw
gold	lava	neap	rill	tide
grit	lead	neck	rime	till
gulf	lias	ness	ring	tilt
gust	lieu	névé	rock	town
haar	limb	node	ruby	trap
hade	lime	noon	salt	tufa
hail	linn	nova	sand	tuff
halo	loam	olam	scar	vale
haze	loch	onyx	scud	vane
head	lock	ooze	seam	Vega
heat	lode	opal	seat	vein

398

4–5

Vela	atlas	Cetus	dross	gelid
veld	atoll	chain	druse	geode
void	azure	chalk	dunes	geoid
wadi	basin	chart	dwarf	ghyll
wane	bayou	chase	eagre	glare
ward	beach	chasm	earth	globe
warm	bedew	chill	emery	gorge
wash	beryl	chine	erode	grail
wave	bight	cliff	esker	grove
weir	blast	clime	ether	gully
well	bleak	close	Eurus	gusty
west	blowy	cloud	falls	heath
wind	bluff	coast	fault	hoary
wold	boggy	comet	fauna	humid
zinc	borax	coomb	fiord	humus
zoic	boron	coral	firth	Hydra
zone	bourn	crack	fjord	Indus
abysm	brash	craig	flats	ingot
abyss	briny	creek	flint	inlet
adobe	broad	crust	flood	islet
agate	broch	cycle	flora	Janus
Algol	brogh	deeps	fluor	joint
alpha	brook	delta	focus	jokul
amber	brush	Dione	foggy	karoo
ambit	burgh	ditch	frith	knoll
apsis	butte	downs	front	kopje
argil	campo	Draco	frost	kraal
Ariel	canal	drift	froth	lapse
Aries	cañon	drink	gault	layer

399

Lepus	Norma	saros	spume
leste	north	sault	stack
levee	Notus	scale	stars
level	oasis	scarp	state
Libra	ocean	scaur	stone
llano	orbit	scree	storm
loamy	Orion	serac	stria
local	ox-bow	shade	sunny
locus	ozone	shaft	sunup
loess	phase	shale	surge
lough	place	sheer	swale
lunar	plain	shelf	swamp
Lupus	plash	shire	swell
magma	*playa*	shoal	swirl
Malus	plaza	shore	table
marge	Pluto	situs	talus
marly	point	slack	Titan
marsh	polar	slate	topaz
Mensa	rains	sleet	tract
metal	rainy	slope	umbra
Mimas	range	slush	urban
misty	rapid	smoke	vault
mould	reach	solar	veldt
mount	realm	solum	Venus
mouth	ridge	sough	*ville*
muggy	Rigel	sound	Virgo
Musca	river	south	wacke
nadir	rural	spate	waste
nodes	salse	Spica	weald

wilds	branch	common	eddies
windy	breeze	copper	efflux
world	breezy	corona	empire
Aeolus	broads	corral	Eocene
afflux	brough	corrie	eothen
albedo	brumal	Corvus	erbium
alpine	burrow	cosmic	ethnic
Antlia	Caelum	cosmos	Europa
aplite	Cancer	coulée	facies
apogee	canopy	county	faluca
Aquila	canton	course	famine
arctic	canyon	crater	feeder
astral	carbon	cuprum	flatus
Auriga	Carina	Cygnus	flinty
aurora	Castor	Davida	flurry
autumn	Caurus	defile	Flysch
barite	cavern	degree	fogbow
barium	cerium	Deimos	Fornax
barrow	chilly	deluge	fossil
basalt	chrome	depths	freeze
billow	circle	desert	gabbro
binary	cirque	dew-bow	galaxy
bolide	cirrus	dingle	galena
Boötes	clayey	Dipper	gangue
border	cloudy	dolmen	garnet
boreal	clunch	domain	Gemini
Boreas	cobalt	Dorado	geodes
bosses	colony	dry air	geyser
bottom	colure	dry ice	gneiss

gnomon	isobar	nation	polder
gravel	isohel	native	Pollux
groove	jargon	nebula	Psyche
grotto	jasper	nekton	puddle
ground	jungle	Nereid	pumice
gulley	kaolin	nickel	Puppis
gypsum	karroo	nimbus	pyrite
haboob	lagoon	nuclei	quaggy
hamlet	laguna	Oberon	quarry
heaven	layers	Octans	quartz
helium	levant	Orient	quasar
Hermes	locale	osmium	radium
hiatus	lochan	outlet	rapids
hiemal	lunate	oxygen	ravine
hollow	Lyrids	pampas	Recent
hot air	maltha	parish	red sky
hot day	map out	parsec	reflux
Hyades	marble	pebble	region
Hydrus	margin	period	riding
Hygeia	marine	petrol	rillet
Icarus	marshy	Phobos	ripple
Ice Age	massif	Phoene	roller
icecap	matrix	Pictor	rubble
icicle	menhir	Pisces	runlet
indium	meteor	placer	runnel
influx	mirage	plains	rustic
inland	molten	planet	rutile
iolite	morass	plasma	saddle
island	morion	plenum	salina

samiel	source	tremor	almanac
sarsen	sphere	trench	antapex
Saturn	spinel	Triton	Antares
schist	splash	tropic	antisun
scoria	spring	trough	apatite
Scutum	squall	Tucana	appulse
sea air	starry	tundra	apsides
sea fog	steppe	tunnel	asphalt
seabed	stormy	upland	aureola
season	strait	Uranus	azimuth
seaway	strand	valley	azurite
sebkha	strata	verano	backing
sector	strath	vernal	barrens
Selene	stream	vortex	bauxite
serdab	strial	Vulcan	bedding
serein	stuffy	wallow	bedrock
shadow	suburb	welkin	benthos
shower	sultry	wester	Bielids
sierra	summer	window	big wind
silica	summit	winter	biotite
silver	sun dog	zenith	bismuth
simoom	sunset	zephyr	Blighty
sinter	swampy	zircon	blue sky
Sirius	syzygy	zodiac	bluster
skerry	talcum	adamant	bone bed
slough	Taurus	aeolian	Boötids
slurry	Tethys	air mass	bornite
sodium	torgul	Aleyone	bottoms
solano	trades	alluvia	boulder

breaker	commune	draught	freshen
breccia	compass	drought	freshet
cadmium	conduit	drizzle	full sun
calcite	conflux	drumlin	gallium
calcium	contour	dry land	geodesy
caldera	corcass	earthly	geogony
Canopus	*couloir*	East end	geology
capture	country	ebb tide	gibbous
cascade	crannog	eclipse	girasol
casting	crevice	element	glacial
cat's-eye	crystal	emerald	glacier
catspaw	culvert	enclave	göthite
Cepheus	cumulus	endemic	granite
channel	current	epidote	gregale
chimney	cyclone	epigene	grey sky
chinook	Cygnids	equator	habitat
chuckie	daystar	equinox	hachure
citrine	daytime	Eridani	hafnium
clachan	Dead Sea	erosion	harbour
clement	debacle	estival	heavens
climate	deep sea	estuary	high fog
cluster	demesne	euripus	high sea
coal-bed	diabase	expanse	hillock
coastal	diamond	faculae	hilltop
cold air	diorite	Far East	holmium
cold day	diurnal	felspar	horizon
Columba	dog days	fenland	hot wind
colures	dog star	fissure	hummock
comites	doldrum	folding	hyaline

hyalite	Lacerta	new town	Polaris
ice cave	lakelet	Niagara	pot hole
ice floe	land-ice	niobium	prairie
ice pack	lapilli	noonday	Procyon
ice raft	Leonids	norther	profile
iceberg	lignite	nunatak	pyrites
ice-cold	lithium	Oceania	quarter
icefall	lithoid	oceanic	quietus
icy wind	long sea	oil-well	radiant
igneous	low tide	olivine	rainbow
ill wind	lowland	oppidum	raining
incline	machair	outcrop	rare gas
insular	meander	outlook	raw wind
iridium	mercury	outpost	realgar
Iron Age	mill run	overlap	red spot
iron ore	mineral	pack-ice	Regulus
iron-pan	Miocene	paludal	rhenium
isobase	mistral	passage	riptide
isohyet	mock sun	pea soup	rivulet
isthmus	mofette	peat bog	road map
jacinth	monsoon	Pegasus	roaster
Japetus	moon-bow	pelagic	rock oil
jargoon	moraine	peridot	Sagitta
Jupiter	mundane	perigee	salband
kerogen	narrows	perlite	salt pan
khamsin	nebulae	Permian	sandbar
kingdom	Neogene	Perseus	savanna
kunzite	Neptune	Phoenix	Scorpio
kyanite	new moon	plateau	sea line

sea loch	sunrise	Umbriel	apse line
sea-mist	sunspot	uplands	Aquarids
section	surface	uranium	Aquarius
Serpens	sweltry	veering	Arcturus
settled	tectite	village	Argestes
sextile	tempest	volcano	argonite
shingle	terbium	warm air	Arietids
showery	terrain	washout	asbestos
sirocco	*thalweg*	wavelet	asteroid
sizzler	the blue	weather	Aurigids
sky line	the line	West end	autumnal
snow bed	thermal	worldly	basanite
snow ice	thorium	yttrium	Bassalia
snowcap	thulium	zeolite	beam wind
souther	thunder	zincite	bearings
squally	tideway	Achernar	Beaufort
station	tin-mine	Achilles	becalmed
stellar	Titania	aerolite	black ice
straits	topical	affluent	blizzard
stratum	topsoil	alluvial	blow over
stratus	tornado	alluvion	bone-cave
stretch	torrent	alluvium	boom town
subsoil	transit	Almagest	boondock
suburbs	trickle	altitude	borehole
subzero	tripoli	amethyst	boundary
sulphur	Trojans	amygdule	brookite
sun dial	tropics	anabatic	brooklet
sunbeam	turgite	antimony	calciole
sundown	typhoon	aphelion	Cambrian

Canicula	Cynosure	Eolithic
Cassiope	darkling	epifocal
catacomb	darkness	epsomite
cataract	date line	Eridanus
causeway	daylight	eruption
Cepheids	dead wind	europium
cerulean	dendrite	evection
chlorite	detritus	exposure
chromite	dew-point	fall wind
chromium	dibstone	favonian
cinnabar	diggings	Favonius
Circinus	diluvium	feldspar
clear day	dirty sky	fenestra
clear sky	district	fine snow
cleavage	doldrums	fire opal
climatic	dolerite	fireball
cloud cap	dolomite	firebolt
coal mine	dominion	flocculi
cold cell	downpour	fluorite
cold snap	downtown	föhn wind
cold wave	drainage	fold-axis
cold wind	draughty	forecast
confines	dustbowl	foreland
corundum	east wind	fountain
corridor	easterly	fracture
corundum	ecliptic	freezing
crevasse	effluent	fresh air
cryolite	elements	frontier
cyclonic	empyrean	full moon

8

full tide
fumarole
galactic
Ganymede
gemstone
girasole
gold dust
gold mine
gold rush
granules
graphite
gritrock
half moon
haziness
head wind
headland
headrace
heat haze
heatwave
heavenly
heavy sea
heavy sky
hematite
Hercules
hibernal
hick town
high seas
high tide
high wind

highland
hillside
homeland
humidity
Huronian
hyacinth
hydrogen
Hyperion
hypogene
hypogeum
ice field
ice sheet
ice storm
iceblink
icequake
idocrase
ilmenite
indented
indigent
infra-red
inkstone
interior
iron-clay
irrigate
isobront
isochasm
isocheim
isocryme
isostasy

isothere
isotherm
Jurassic
Laetitia
lakeland
land form
land mass
landslip
latitude
lava-flow
lazurite
leap year
left bank
lenticle
levanter
Lewisian
libeccio
limonite
liparite
littoral
location
lodestar
low cloud
low water
lowlands
luminary
lunar bow
lutecium
magnesia

408

mainland	noontide	polar ray
maritime	nutation	pole star
mean tide	obsidian	polonium
mean time	Occident	porphyry
Menevian	occluded	position
meridian	ocean air	precinct
Mesozoic	ocean bed	pressure
metallic	offshore	prospect
midnight	Old World	province
Milky Way	on the map	pumicite
millpond	ordnance	purlieus
millpool	Orionids	pyroxene
millrace	overcast	quagmire
mock moon	overfold	rain belt
moderate	overhang	rain drop
monazite	parallax	rainfall
monolith	Pegasids	rainy day
monticle	penumbra	red dwarf
moonbeam	Perseids	red giant
moorland	photomap	red shift
mountain	pinnacle	rhyolite
mudstone	plankton	ring-dyke
mylonite	plateaux	riparian
neap tide	platinum	river bed
Near East	Pleiades	riverine
Nearctic	Pliocene	rock salt
nephrite	plumbago	rotation
New World	Pointers	rough sea
night sky	polar cap	rubidium

sabulose
salt lake
samarium
sand dune
sand reef
sandbank
sandhill
sandspit
sapphire
sardonyx
scandium
scorcher
Sculptor
sea floor
sea level
seaboard
seascape
seashore
sediment
seedtime
selenite
shallows
sharp air
short sea
sidereal
siderite
Silurian
skerries
snowball

snowbank
snowberg
snowfall
snowland
snow-line
soft hail
soft rock
solar day
Solstice
sounding
spectrum
spillway
spithead
stagnant
steatite
stibnite
Stone Age
streamer
suburban
sun spark
sunburst
sunlight
sunshine
sunspots
sunstone
syncline
tailrace
tantalum
telluric

Tertiary
thallium
tidal rip
tide gate
tide race
time zone
tinstone
titanium
township
trachyte
traprock
Triassic
tungsten
twilight
Uncle Sam
undertow
undulate
universe
upheaval
upper air
vanadium
vicinity
volcanic
warm cell
warm wave
water gap
westerly
west wind
Wild West

wind belt	aragonite	carbuncle
wind cock	argentite	carnelian
wind cone	Armorican	carnotite
wind eddy	astrolabe	catchment
wind vane	astrology	celestial
workings	astronomy	celestite
xenolith	avalanche	Centaurus
zastruga	backwater	champaign
adumbrate	backwoods	china clay
aerolites	barometer	choppy sea
affluence	baroscope	cisalpine
Afric heat	below zero	city-state
alabaster	beryllium	cliff-face
Aldebaran	billabong	cloud bank
aluminium	black drop	cloud over
ambergris	black opal	cloudland
americium	blacklead	coalfield
amphibole	blue skies	coastland
anabranch	bourasque	coastline
anchor ice	brilliant	cockscomb
Andromeda	brimstone	coelostat
anemology	Britannia	cold front
anemostat	Bronze Age	cold spell
anglesite	brushland	colt's-tail
antarctic	burrstone	concourse
anthelion	bysmalith	continent
anticline	cairngorm	coral reef
antipodes	canicular	cornbrash
apoastron	Capricorn	corposant

9

cosmogony
cosmology
cosmorama
curl cloud
curvature
dead water
Delphinus
demantoid
detrition
diatomite
down under
Draconids
dripstone
dust devil
dust storm
dwarf star
earth-wave
elaterite
Enceladus
ephemeris
epicentre
esplanade
estuaries
estuarine
everglade
evolution
exosphere
fall-cloud
fenestral

firmament
fixed star
flagstone
flocculus
flood tide
floodgate
fluorspar
fogginess
foliation
fool's gold
foothills
foreshore
fossil oil
freestone
fresh wind
frostbite
gale force
gemmology
germanium
ghost town
giant star
glacieret
gnomonics
goat's-hair
gold fever
goldstone
Gould Belt
granulite
Great Bear

green belt
gritstone
ground ice
gumbo soil
haematite
hailstone
hailstorm
hairstone
hard frost
harmattan
heavy rain
heliostat
Herculids
high cloud
high water
highlands
hoar-frost
Holarctic
homotaxis
hour angle
hurricane
hypogaeum
ice action
ice needle
icy blasts
idioblast
inclement
intrusion
ironstone

412

isoclinal
Jack Frost
jackstone
jadestone
Julian day
Kainozoic
kaolinite
Lacertids
laccolite
laccolith
lake basin
landscape
landslide
lanthanum
lapideous
lapse rate
leaf mould
levin bolt
light wind
light year
lightning
limestone
lithology
lit-par-lit
loadstone
localized
lodestone
lodestuff
lofty peak

London fog
longitude
low ground
lunar halo
lunar rays
macrocosm
maelstrom
magnesite
magnesium
magnetite
magnitude
malachite
manganese
manometer
marcasite
mare's-tail
marigraph
marlstone
marshland
mattamore
mesopause
metalloid
meteorite
meteoroid
microlite
midday sun
midstream
midsummer
midwinter

mild spell
milkstone
mispickel
mistiness
Monoceros
moonlight
moonshine
moonstone
morganite
neodymium
Neolithic
nephology
night time
nimbosity
nor'easter
north east
north pole
North star
north west
north wind
northerly
nor'wester
obsequent
occlusion
off the map
Oligocene
Ophiuchus
orography
overcloud

ozocerite
palladium
parallels
paramorph
parhelion
Patrocles
pegmatite
peneplain
peninsula
periclase
petroleum
petrology
phacolith
phenomena
phonolite
planetary
planetoid
plutonium
polar axis
polar star
potassium
pozzolana
precipice
quartzite
quicklime
quicksand
radio star
rain cloud
rain gauge

rainspout
rainstorm
rainwater
rare earth
rare gases
refluence
refractor
relief map
reservoir
rhodonite
right bank
rime frost
riverhead
riverside
rock basis
ruthenium
salt marsh
salt water
sand devil
sand dunes
sand-blast
sandspout
sandstone
sandstorm
satellite
scheelite
Scorpiids
sea breeze
sea margin

Secondary
semimetal
seven seas
sharp wind
sheer drop
shoreline
siderites
situation
slabstone
snow field
snow under
snowdrift
snowfield
snowflake
snowscape
snowstorm
soapstone
solar apex
solar halo
solar wind
solfatara
solstices
sou'easter
south east
south land
south pole
south west
south wind
southerly

sou'wester	turbulent	wind gauge
spodumene	turquoise	wind scale
starlight	underfoot	wind shear
starstone	unsettled	wind speed
statehood	upcountry	wind-blown
streamlet	uraninite	windiness
streamway	Ursa Major	windstorm
strontium	Ursa Minor	windswept
subregion	veinstone	wulfenite
summer day	veranillo	ytterbium
supernova	volcanoes	zirconium
survey map	vulcanism	achondrite
surveying	vulcanite	adamantine
swelterer	Vulpecula	adder stone
tableland	warm front	aerography
tectonics	wasteland	aerosphere
telescope	water flow	air current
tellurium	water hole	alkali flat
temperate	water opal	almacantar
territory	waterfall	almucantar
tidal bore	watershed	anemometer
tidal flow	waterside	antitrades
tidal flux	weak front	anvil cloud
tidal wave	whirlpool	aquamarine
tide guage	whirlwind	arable land
tidewater	white spot	arid desert
tornadoes	wide world	astrograph
trade wind	williwaws	atmosphere
tributary	wind field	aventurine

barysphere
bathometer
Bengal heat
binary star
biting wind
black frost
bloodstone
body of land
Boreal zone
borderland
borderline
bottom land
bradyseism
breakwater
brownstone
Caledonian
campestral
Canis major
Canis minor
Cape doctor
Cassiopeia
chalcedony
chalcocite
chalk downs
chalkstone
Chamaeleon
chersonese
chessylite
choppiness

chrysolite
cirro-velum
cismontane
clear skies
clinkstone
cloud atlas
cloudburst
cloudiness
coastal fog
colatitude
collimator
common salt
confluence
consequent
contortion
cool breeze
copper mine
cordillera
cosmic dust
countersun
Crab nebula
demography
denudation
deposition
depression
direct tide
double star
drakestone
dreikanter

driven snow
drosometer
druid stone
drying wind
dysprosium
eaglestone
earthlight
earthquake
earthshine
ebb and flow
embankment
ephemerist
equatorial
escarpment
Euroclydon
excavation
fatherland
fieldstone
floatstone
fore-shocks
fossilized
foundation
freshwater
frontal low
frost smoke
gadolinium
gather brew
gentle wind
geographer

geophysics	ice erosion	midchannel
glaciation	Indian heat	Middle East
glauconite	insolation	millstream
globulites	insularity	mineral oil
graptolite	inundation	mineralogy
gravel spit	ionosphere	molten lava
green flash	irrigation	molybdenum
greenstone	jet streams	morphology
ground mass	lacuscular	motherland
hailstones	lacustrian	narrow seas
hard winter	lacustrine	native land
headstream	landlocked	native soil
headwaters	large scale	natural gas
heavy swell	latent heat	nebulosity
heliotrope	lead-glance	no man's land
hemisphere	Lesser Bear	noble metal
high ground	light-curve	nubilation
hinterland	lithomarge	old country
homosphere	low stratus	ombrometer
hornblende	luminosity	oppressive
Horologium	mappemonde	Ordovician
hot springs	map-reading	ore deposit
hot weather	market town	Orion's Belt
hour circle	meerschaum	orogenesis
hyetograph	metallurgy	orthoclase
hyetometer	meteor dust	outer space
hygrometer	metropolis	outline map
hypocentre	mica-schist	overshadow
ice crystal	micrometer	overthrust

Oxford clay	rock desert	stalactite
Palaeogene	rock pillar	stalagmite
Palaeozoic	rock series	star stream
paraselene	rose quartz	starry host
peacock ore	rupestrian	steep slope
periastron	saddle-reef	still water
perihelion	sand column	stinkstone
phenomenon	sea breezes	storm cloud
phosphorus	seismic map	storm track
photometry	seismology	stormblast
picture ore	serpentine	stratiform
pitchstone	settlement	strong wind
plot of land	sharp frost	subsequent
polar frost	silver mine	subsidence
population	slingstone	substratum
potamology	small scale	subterrene
powder snow	smokestone	subtropics
promethium	snail cloud	summer heat
promontory	snakestone	summertide
quadrature	snow flurry	summertime
radio stars	snow squall	technetium
radiosonde	snow wreath	terminator
rain forest	solar cycle	terra firma
rare metals	solar flare	terrestrial
raw weather	solar tower	theodolite
rice grains	spinel ruby	topography
rift valley	spring tide	torrid zone
river basin	springtime	touchstone
rock bottom	squall line	tourmaline

trade route	wintry wind	cartography
tramontana	wolframite	cassiterite
tramontane	abyssal zone	cataclastic
Triangulum	aeolian clay	cats and dogs
tropopause	after-shocks	chinook wind
turbulence	alexandrite	chorography
undercliff	alto-cumulus	chrysoberyl
undulation	alto-stratus	chrysoprase
vegetation	Andromedids	circumbinar
visibility	anticyclone	circumpolar
waning moon	archipelago	cirro-fillum
water front	arctic front	cirro-macula
water gauge	arm of the sea	cirro-nebula
waterflood	aurora glory	cirrus cloud
waterspout	Austral zone	climate zone
water-table	back country	climatology
waxing moon	Baily's beads	clinochlore
weather eye	barrier lake	cold weather
weather map	bathyal zone	colorimetry
weathering	bathysphere	Continental
weatherman	beetlestone	contour map
wet weather	*bergschrund*	convergence
white dwarf	Biela's comet	coral island
white frost	bottom glade	coronagraph
wilderness	boulder clay	cosmic space
willy-nilly	broiling sun	cosmography
wind sleeve	buffer state	cosmosphere
wintertide	capital city	counterflux
wintertime	*Carte du Ciel*	counter-glow

country rock
country town
countryside
crag and tail
dark nebulae
deep blue sea
doldrum belt
driving rain
drusy cavity
dust counter
earth metals
earth pillar
earth's crust
earth-tremor
echo sounder
environment
equinoctial
evening mist
evening star
exploration
falling star
fata Morgana
fingerstone
flaming June
flash floods
fresh breeze
frigid zones
frontal zone
frozen north

frozen stiff
frozen water
frontal wave
fulmination
gale warning
Gegenschein
Giacobinids
Giant Hunter
grain of sand
gravelstone
gravity wind
ground frost
ground swell
harvest moon
harvest time
hatchettite
head of comet
hunter's moon
Hunting Dogs
hydrometeor
hydrosphere
hyperborean
Iceland spar
ice-movement
ichnography
igneous rock
ignis-fatuus
impermeable
indentation

iron pyrites
isogeotherm
katabothron
Kelvin scale
Kepler's laws
lake dweller
land feature
land measure
land surface
lapis lazuli
layer of rock
light breeze
lithosphere
lone prairie
low pressure
lowering sky
lunar crater
Lydian stone
mackerel sky
major planet
mercury pool
meteor swarm
hetereology
midnight sun
mineral coal
mineral salt
mineral vein
minor planet
molybdenite

monsoon wind
monticolous
morning star
mountaintop
mural circle
nationality
native heath
native lands
native stone
neritic zone
noble metals
northeaster
northwester
observatory
occultation
ocean depths
open country
Orion's Hound
Orion's Sword
Palaearctic
passage beds
pebblestone
pelagic zone
peristalith
petrography
photosphere
pile dweller
pissasphalt
pitchblende

planetarium
pluviometer
polar aurora
polar circle
polar lights
polar region
potter's clay
pouring rain
Pre-Cambrian
precipitate
prominences
Quadrantids
quarrystone
quicksilver
radio-source
rainy season
raised beach
raw material
reclamation
rising coast
river course
river system
river valley
rock crystal
rottenstone
Sagittarius
sarsen stone
schistosity
seismic zone

seismograph
shadow bands
sheet of rain
sidereal day
slant of wind
snow blanket
snow crystal
solar corona
solar energy
solar plasma
solar system
southeaster
southwester
spell of rain
spill-stream
star cluster
stella maris
stone circle
stony ground
storm centre
stratopause
submergence
subtropical
swallow-hole
synodic year
tail of comet
Telescopium
temperature
tempestuous

terrestrial	watercourse	chromosphere
thermal cell	wave erosion	cirro-cumulus
thermograph	weathercock	cirro-stratus
thermometer	weathervane	cirrus stripe
thrust-plane	whereabouts	clastic rocks
thunderball	white cliffs	coal measures
thunderbolt	white horses	commonwealth
thunderclap	wind erosion	compass point
thunderpeal	zero weather	conglomerate
torridonian	alkali metals	crescent moon
transalpine	alluvial flat	cross-bedding
transandine	anthraconite	cumulo-cirrus
translunary	arctic circle	cumulo-nimbus
transmarine	argillaceous	cumulus cloud
Trojan group	arsenopyrite	cyclogenesis
troposphere	artesian well	cyclonic cell
true horizon	astronomical	cyclonic spin
ultra-violet	astrophysics	drift current
under the sun	barren ground	elevated area
underground	biogeography	Elgin marbles
universally	bitterly cold	etesian winds
verd-antique	Black country	evaporimeter
vermiculite	black diamond	false bedding
vesuvianite	blow up a storm	false horizon
volcanic ash	Camelopardus	field of force
vulcanicity	Canis majoris	fountainhead
vulcanology	cartographer	freezing cold
warm springs	chalcopyrite	frozen tundra
water pocket	Charles's wain	fuller's earth

geanticlinal	main sequence	Palaeolithic
geochemistry	man in the moon	parcel of land
geographical	marginal land	peculiar star
geomagnetism	mean sea level	petrification
geosynclinal	metamorphism	piercing wind
geotectonics	metasomatism	pilot balloon
giant's-kettle	meteor crater	Piscis Volons
glacial drift	meteorograph	plutonic plug
glacial epoch	microclimate	polarization
glaciologist	Microscopium	praesodymium
gradient wind	midcontinent	pressure belt
granular snow	migratory low	pressure wave
Halley's comet	mineral pitch	principality
heavenly body	moderate wind	protactinium
heterosphere	mother of coal	quasistellar
high pressure	mountain pass	rainy weather
Indian summer	mountain peak	red sandstone
isobaric line	municipality	residual clay
jack o' lantern	mushroom rock	rising ground
keraunograph	native metals	running water
Lake district	nebulous star	selenography
lake dwelling	neighbouring	semi-diameter
law of gravity	nephelometer	shooting star
Little Dipper	offshore wind	sidereal time
Local Cluster	one horse town	sinking coast
lowroll cloud	opposite tide	snow blizzard
macroclimate	oriental opal	solution lake
magnetic axis	otherworldly	space station
magnetic pole	palaeobotany	spectral type

spectrograph	thundercloud	Variable zone
spectroscope	thunderplump	vertical rays
spectroscopy	thunderstorm	volcanic cone
spiral galaxy	tidal current	volcanic rock
star sapphire	transleithan	volcanic wind
star-spangled	transmundane	weather chart
stratigraphy	transoceanic	weather gauge
stratosphere	tropical heat	weatherglass
subcontinent	tropical year	will o' the wisp
subterranean	tropical zone	wind velocity
synodic month	unconformity	wollastonite
telluric line	undercurrent	yawning abyss
the seven seas	variable star	zoogeography

COMMUNICATIONS AND TRADE

This general heading includes sections for Transport, and Trade and Commerce.

Transport

This section includes all forms of transport and modes of travel—travellers and luggage—road traffic, road and road signs—internal combustion engine and vehicle parts—trains and track—ships, seaways and shipping terms—boats and small boats —anchors, rigging, ropes and knots—communications and signals—lighthouses.

A.A.	bag	cox	hoy	lug	rut
A.B.	bay	cub	hub	M.O.T.	sea
A1	bob	fan	jet	m.p.h.	ski
go	bow	fin	jib	map	sos
G.T.	bus	fly	jog	oar	sub
M1	cab	gad	key	oil	tar
ABC	cam	gas	lag	ply	ton
ace	car	gig	lap	ram	top
aft	cat	guy	lee	rev	tow
air	cog	H.M.S.	leg	rig	tub
ark	con	hop	log	run	tug

U.F.O.	cart	grip	lock	push
van	case	gyro	loop	quay
via	code	hack	lost	raft
way	cork	haul	luff	rail
yaw	crew	head	Mach	reef
ahoy!	curb	heap	mail	ride
A-one	dash	heel	mast	ring
auto	deck	helm	mini	road
axle	dhow	hike	moke	roam
back	dial	hold	mole	roll
bail	dive	hood	moor	rove
bank	dock	horn	navy	saic
bark	dory	hove	nest	sail
beak	drag	hulk	nose	salt
beam	draw	hull	oars	scow
bend	dray	idle	pace	ship
biga	duck	jack	park	sink
bike	fare	jeep	pass	skid
bitt	fast	junk	path	skip
boat	flap	keel	pier	skis
body	flee	kerb	poke	sled
boom	flit	kite	poop	span
boot	flow	kiwi	port	spar
brig	ford	knot	post	spin
bunk	fore	land	pram	stay
buoy	fork	lane	prop	stem
busk	gaff	lift	prow	step
buss	gait	line	pull	tack
buzz	gear	list	punt	tail

tank	alley	cleat	fluke	loran
taxi	aloft	climb	foist	lorry
tide	amble	coach	forth	march
toll	apron	coast	found	morse
tour	araba	coble	funny	motor
tram	*avion*	coupé	glide	mount
trap	awash	craft	going	naval
trek	balsa	crank	G.T. car	nomad
trim	barge	crash	guard	on tow
trip	beach	crate	guide	orbit
trot	below	cycle	haste	pedal
tube	berth	dandy	hatch	phone
tyre	bilge	davit	hawse	pilot
vang	blimp	ditch	hiker	pitch
veer	board	dodge	hobby	plane
vent	bosun	dolly	hoist	praam
visa	brail	drift	horse	prang
wain	brake	drive	hurry	pylon
wake	buggy	drome	jaunt	Q-boat
walk	bungo	E-boat	jetty	racer
warp	byway	embus	jolly	radar
wash	cabby	facia	kayak	radio
wire	cabin	fanal	kedge	rally
yard	cable	ferry	ketch	range
yawl	canal	flare	lay-by	reach
zoom	canoe	fleet	leech	relay
abaft	cargo	flier	lie to	rev up
afoot	choke	float	light	rider
afoul	chute	flota	liner	ropes

rotor	stern	access	bonnet
route	stray	adrift	braces
royal	strip	afloat	bridge
sally	strut	air log	bucket
screw	stunt	air ram	bumper
scull	sweep	airing	busman
sedan	thole	airman	by-lane
shaft	ton up	airway	by-pass
sheer	track	alight	bypath
sheet	trail	anchor	byroad
shell	train	argosy	caïque
shift	tramp	armada	calash
shunt	tread	arrive	call up
sidle	trike	artery	camber
skiff	truck	ascent	canard
skirt	trunk	astern	canter
slips	U-boat	avenue	canvas
sloop	umiak	aweigh	careen
smack	U-turn	back up	career
smash	valve	bargee	carfax
spars	visit	barque	carina
speed	way in	barrow	chaise
spill	wharf	basket	clutch
sprit	wheel	bateau	coaler
stage	xebec	beacon	cobble
stall	yacht	berlin	cockle
stamp	Z bend	big end	con rod
start	aboard	bireme	conner
steam	abroad	bomber	convoy

copter	galiot	jet set	mutiny
course	galley	jetsam	nip off
cruise	gallop	jib guy	nose up
cut out	garage	jigger	octane
cutter	gas jet	jostle	on deck
decked	gasket	junket	on foot
de-icer	gay-you	kit bag	one-way
depart	glider	klaxon	onward
detour	gocart	landau	outing
dinghy	gunnel	lascar	outset
divert	hangar	lateen	oxcart
diving	hansom	launch	packet
dogger	hatbox	leeway	paddle
driver	haul to	lerret	petrol
dry run	hawser	letter	pharos
dugout	hearse	litter	pickup
earing	hooker	lock-up	pile up
egress	hot rod	lorcha	piston
elevon	hove to	lugger	porter
embark	hubcap	mahout	propel
engine	hurtle	Manche	pursue
escape	hustle	marina	ram jet
exodus	Icarus	marine	ramble
fender	idling	marker	randem
fiacre	impact	mayday	raster
flight	in trim	mirror	rating
flying	intake	mizzen	ratlin
fo'c'sle	island	mobile	reefer
funnel	jalopy	motion	return

rigged	spiral	troika	**airlift**
rigger	splice	trudge	airline
ring up	spring	tunnel	airpark
rocket	stocks	turret	airport
rudder	stoker	unmoor	airship
runner	strake	valise	airsick
runway	street	vessel	almadia
sailor	stride	volant	ambages
saloon	stroll	voyage	arrival
sampan	subway	waggon	autobus
sculls	surrey	wander	autocar
seaman	swerve	way out	autovac
seaway	tackle	whaler	aviator
sender	tandem	wherry	aviette
set out	tanker	whisky	baby-jib
sheets	tannoy	address	baggage
shoran	tartan	aerobus	baggala
shroud	tender	aground	bail out
siding	ticker	aileron	ballast
signal	ticket	air base	balloon
skates	tiller	air crew	banking
skerry	timber	air flow	barge in
skyway	tin can	air jump	battery
slaver	toddle	air lane	bay-line
sledge	toggle	air legs	beeline
sleigh	torque	air line	bicycle
smoker	totter	airboat	biplane
sortie	towbar	airdrop	birdman
sparks	travel	airfoil	blister

boating	carport	cruiser	flattop
boatman	carrack	cyclist	flivver
bobstay	carrier	day trip	flotsam
bollard	catboat	descent	fluking
bomb bay	cat-head	detrain	fly past
booking	cat's-eye	dodgems	flyboat
booster	catwalk	dogcart	flyover
bow fast	channel	draught	foretop
bowline	chariot	drayman	formula
boxhaul	charter	dredger	founder
box-kite	chassis	drifter	four-oar
boxseat	chopper	drive-in	freeway
britzka	chutist	driving	frigate
bulwark	circuit	droshky	frogman
bunting	clipper	dry dock	futtock
bus stop	coaster	dry land	galleon
busline	cockpit	ejector	galleys
buzz off	collide	emplane	gangway
buzzing	collier	*en route*	gearbox
caboose	commute	engaged	get lost
call box	compass	entrain	getaway
capsize	contact	*essence*	gliding
capstan	co-pilot	exhaust	go ahead
capsule	coracle	explore	go below
captain	corsair	express	go by air
caravan	courier	fairing	go-devil
caravel	crack-up	fairway	gondola
cariole	crewman	felucca	gosport
carpark	crock-up	fetch up	grapnel

growler	jaw rope	make for	outride
guichet	jet pipe	make off	painter
gun deck	jib boom	man-o'-war	pair-oar
gunboat	jibstay	mariner	parking
guy-rope	journey	marline	parting
gyro-car	joy ride	Martian	passage
hackney	keelson	matelot	pathway
halyard	keep off	meander	payload
hammock	killick	migrant	pelorus
handbag	killock	milk run	phaeton
harbour	L driver	minibus	pig boat
hardtop	L plates	minicab	pillion
harness	landing	minicar	pinnace
haywain	lanyard	minisub	piragua
head for	learner	mission	pirogue
head off	lee helm	monitor	polacca
headset	lee tack	mooring	polacre
headway	leewide	mud hook	pontoon
heave to	leeward	nacelle	postage
helibus	lift-off	no entry	postman
highway	lighter	oarsman	precede
holdall	logbook	odyssey	proceed
hot line	luggage	offside	pull out
hurry up	lugsail	old salt	Pullman
iceboat	lymphad	omnibus	push car
impetus	Mae West	on board	railway
impulse	magneto	on the go	ratline
ingress	mail van	ongoing	rebound
Jack Tar	maintop	opening	re-entry

7

resojet	seaward	tartane	travels
retrace	send-off	taxicab	trawler
retreat	set sail	taxiing	tripper
reverse	shallop	taxiway	trireme
ride out	shipway	teleran	trolley
rigging	shuttle	telpher	trundle
ring off	side-car	Telstar	trysail
ripcord	skid-fin	termini	tugboat
road-hog	skid-pan	test hop	tumbrel
road-map	skipper	tilbury	tumbril
road-tax	skysail	to horse	turning
rolling	sleeper	tonneau	twin-jet
rope-tow	slipway	top deck	vagrant
ropeway	smash-up	topmast	vehicle
rowboat	spanker	topsail	viaduct
rowlock	sputnik	topside	vis-à-vis
run away	start up	torsion	visitor
run into	starter	tourist	*voiture*
runners	station	towards	volante
sailing	steamer	towboat	voyager
satchel	steward	towpath	wanigan
saunter	stopway	towrope	warship
scamper	surface	tractor	waybill
scooter	sweeper	traffic	wayfare
scupper	swifter	trailer	wayworn
scuttle	tackler	traipse	welcome
sea lane	tail end	tramcar	winging
sea legs	tail fin	tramway	wingtip
seasick	take-off	transit	wrecker

433

yardarm	autobahn	bulwarks
zooming	autogyro	buntline
aerodyne	aviation	cabin boy
aerofoil	aviatrix	cable car
aerogram	back seat	cableway
aeronaut	backfire	camshaft
aerostat	backstay	caracole
air brake	backwash	carriage
air coach	ballonet	cast away
air force	bargeman	castaway
air route	barnacle	catapult
air scoop	barouche	cat's-eyes
air scout	beakhead	causeway
air speed	beam ends	clarence
air-borne	bearings	clearway
aircraft	becalmed	coach-box
airfield	bilander	coachman
airframe	binnacle	coachway
airliner	boat deck	coasting
airscrew	boat hook	cockboat
airspace	boat line	commuter
airstrip	bodywork	converge
airwoman	bolt-rope	corridor
all at sea	bowsprit	corvette
alleyway	Bradshaw	coxswain
altitude	brancard	crabbing
approach	broach to	crescent
arterial	brougham	crossing
at anchor	bulkhead	cruising

cul-de-sac	fall back	forkroad
curricle	farewell	fuel ship
cylinder	fast lane	full load
dahabeah	fastback	fuselage
dearborn	ferryman	gad about
deck hand	fine ship	galleass
derelict	fireboat	garboard
dipstick	flagging	gasoline
dismount	flagship	get ahead
ditty bag	flat spin	glissade
downhaul	flat tyre	go aboard
drag wire	flatboat	go ashore
dragoman	floating	go astray
dragster	flotilla	go before
driftway	flywheel	go by rail
drive off	fogbound	Godspeed
driveway	footfall	gradient
dust cart	footpath	grounded
eight-oar	footslog	half deck
elevator	footstep	handcart
emigrant	fore jack	hang back
emigrate	fore lift	hatchway
entrance	forefoot	hawse bag
envelope	foremast	head fast
equipage	foresail	head into
evacuate	foreship	hedgehog
even keel	forestay	heel over
exchange	foretack	heliport
excursus	foreyard	helmsman

hepteris	kickback	mainsail
high seas	knapsack	mainstay
highroad	land ahoy!	manifold
homeward	landfall	man-of-war
horse-box	larboard	maritime
horseman	lateener	Mars ship
ice canoe	launcher	masthead
ice yacht	lee sheet	mine ship
icebound	leeboard	momentum
ignition	level off	monorail
in flight	life belt	moon base
in motion	life buoy	moon ship
inner jib	life line	moonsail
intercom	life raft	moonshot
ironclad	lifeboat	moorings
jackstay	lift wire	motorbus
jerrican	log canoe	motorcar
jet pilot	long haul	motoring
jet plane	longbeat	motorist
jet power	longeron	motorway
jettison	loose-box	muleteer
journeys	Mach cone	multi-jet
joy-rider	mail boat	navarchy
joystick	main deck	nearside
junction	main lift	newsreel
jury sail	main road	nose down
jurymast	main yard	nose into
kamikaze	mainline	nose-cone
keel over	mainmast	nosedive

oil gauge	post boat	sail fine
old crock	postcard	sail free
oleo gear	progress	sail loft
on the run	prowl car	sailboat
on-coming	pulsejet	schedule
one-horse	puncture	schooner
open road	pushcart	scout car
operator	put to sea	sea route
ordinary	quadriga	seafarer
outboard	radiator	seagoing
outer jib	railroad	seaplane
overhaul	receiver	set forth
overland	red light	shanghai
overpass	reef band	sheer off
overseas	reef knot	sheer-leg
overtake	repulsor	ship ahoy
overturn	rickshaw	ship oars
passer-by	rigadoon	shipmate
passover	ring road	shipping
passport	road sign	short hop
pavement	roadster	shoulder
periplus	rockaway	show a leg
pilotage	roof rack	showboat
platform	ropeband	side road
Plimsoll	ropework	side step
poop deck	rucksack	sideslip
port tack	run ahead	sidewalk
porthole	runabout	silencer
portside	rush hour	skidding

skidmark	tail spin	warplane
slip road	tailpipe	water bus
slow down	taxi rank	waterway
slow lane	telegram	wayfarer
snap roll	teletype	way-train
sociable	terminal	wear ship
spaceman	terminus	wind cone
spar deck	thole-pin	wind sock
speeding	throttle	windward
squad car	toboggan	wing drag
staff car	tollgate	wing over
stanhope	tramline	wireless
start off	traverse	withdraw
start out	tricycle	yachting
staysail	trim sail	yawmeter
steerage	trim ship	Zeppelin
steering	trimaran	zero hour
sternway	turbojet	about-ship
stock car	turn away	addressee
stopover	turn over	aerodrome
stowaway	turnpike	aeromotor
straggle	under way	aeroplane
straying	unicycle	after deck
stunt man	velocity	air pocket
suitcase	victoria	air-bridge
tackling	volatile	air-sleeve
tag along	volplane	airworthy
tail boom	wagon-lit	all aboard
tail skid	wardroom	**altimeter**

ambulance	break bulk	countdown
amidships	broadside	crankcase
amphibian	brolly-hop	crash boat
anchorage	bubble car	crash-land
applecart	bulldozer	crocodile
astrodome	bus driver	crossjack
astronaut	cab driver	cross-road
atom-liner	cablegram	crosstree
autopilot	cabriolet	crowd sail
avigation	canalboat	crow's nest
back water	cargo boat	curbstone
backropes	carpetbag	cut and run
bandwagon	cartwheel	dashboard
bargepole	catamaran	Davy Jones
basic load	chandelle	day letter
Bath chair	charabanc	day return
below deck	charrette	deceleron
bilge keel	chauffeur	departure
black gang	chief mate	depot ship
blockship	clearance	destroyer
blue peter	clew lines	diesel oil
boathouse	coach road	diligence
boatswain	coachwork	dining car
boat-train	collision	dip switch
bob-sleigh	combat car	direction
bon voyage	concourse	dirigible
boulevard	conductor	dirt-track
bowl along	cosmonaut	disembark
box waggon	couchette	diversion

dodgem car
drag force
drift wire
drive away
drop a line
duffel bag
eagle boat
Early Bird
earphones
empennage
escalator
esplanade
estate car
excursion
extension
false keel
family car
fare stage
ferryboat
first mate
first-rate
flying jib
footropes
forebrace
foreroyal
foresheet
free wheel
freeboard
freighter

French lug
front seat
fuel gauge
funicular
gain speed
gallivant
gangplank
gather way
gear lever
ghost ship
give a ring
globe-trot
go aground
gondolier
goose step
grand tour
grape-vine
gross lift
groundhog
guard ship
guard's van
guess-warp
guest-rope
gyropilot
gyroplane
handbrake
hansom cab
haversack
hawse hook

hawsepipe
headphone
helidrome
hit-and-run
hitch-hike
hoist sail
hook a ride
horseback
houseboat
hump speed
hydrofoil
ice skates
immigrant
immigrate
inch along
indicator
ironsides
itinerant
itinerary
jaunty car
jaywalker
jet bomber
jollyboat
kerb drill
kerbstone
kick-start
lag behind
land rover
landaulet

landplane	morse code	phone book
launch pad	motorbike	phone call
launching	motorboat	pillar box
leave home	motorcade	pilot boat
letter box	mule-train	point duty
leviathan	multi-prop	police car
lightship	navigable	police van
limousine	navigator	portfolio
lose speed	newsflash	post-haste
lower boom	nosewheel	postilion
lower deck	ocean lane	power dive
lunar base	ocean trip	powerboat
Mach meter	on the move	press-gang
mail coach	on the wing	privateer
mainbrace	orientate	prize-crew
mainroyal	orlop deck	promenade
mainsheet	orthopter	propeller
major road	outrigger	racing car
make haste	overboard	radar nose
manoeuvre	overdrive	radio beam
mass media	overshoot	radiogram
milestone	pack-horse	radius rod
milkfloat	palanquin	ram rocket
milometer	pancaking	reach land
mine layer	parachute	reef point
miss stays	party line	river-boat
mizzentop	passenger	road block
monoplane	patrol car	road sense
moonraker	periscope	road works

roadstead	ship's crew	spritsail
rocket car	shipshape	stage boat
rocket man	shipwreck	stanchion
rotor ship	sidelight	starboard
round trip	sidetrack	stateroom
royal mast	sight land	steal away
royal road	sightseer	steam line
royal sail	signal box	steamboat
rudder bar	signalman	steamship
sac de nuit	single jet	steersman
saddlebag	skyriding	step aside
sailplane	slow train	stern fast
sally port	slowcoach	sternpost
saloon car	smack boat	stevedore
sand yacht	small boat	stratojet
satellite	snowshoes	streetcar
saucerman	sonic boom	stretcher
sea anchor	sonic wall	strike out
sea gasket	space crew	stringers
seafaring	space suit	stokehold
seaworthy	spacedock	storeship
semaphore	spaceport	storm boat
set on foot	spaceship	sub-chaser
sharp bend	spacewalk	submarine
sheer-hulk	spare part	surfacing
ship of war	speedboat	surfboard
ship route	speedster	switch off
shipboard	spinnaker	tail rotor
ship-plane	sports car	tail shaft

tailboard	turn aside	air control
tail-light	turn round	air cruiser
tailplane	turnmeter	air hostess
take leave	turret top	air service
taximeter	twin-screw	air steward
taxiplane	two-seater	air support
tea waggon	under sail	amber light
telegraph	underpass	ambulation
telemotor	upper deck	ambulatory
telepathy	veer short	anchor deck
telephone	vehicular	antifreeze
telephony	war galley	automobile
telephoto	water line	ball turret
test pilot	whaleback	ballooning
third mate	whaleboat	balloonist
timenoguy	wheel base	barkentine
timetable	wheel spin	barrel-roll
touch down	white line	batten down
traipsing	wirephoto	battleship
tramlines	yachtsman	bear down on
transport	A1 at Lloyd's	Bermuda rig
traveller	a head start	bilge pump
triptyque	able seaman	Black Maria
troopship	aboard ship	blind alley
trunk call	access road	bomb vessel
trunk line	adventurer	boneshaker
trunk road	aerobatics	branch line
turboprop	aeronautic	breakwater
turbopump	aerophobia	breast fast

bridge deck	crankshaft	first class
bridle-path	crossroads	flight deck
brigantine	dandy horse	flight path
bubble hood	dawn rocket	flight plan
bucket seat	day tripper	flight time
bus service	decampment	floatplane
bus station	delta wings	fly-by-night
cabin plane	dickey seat	flying boat
camouflage	dipping lug	flying disc
cantilever	disemplane	flying wing
cargo plane	dive bomber	footbridge
cast anchor	diving-bell	fore and aft
catch a crab	double bend	forecastle
catch a ride	double-prop	forerunner
chapel cart	double-reef	foresheets
clear house	downstream	forge ahead
clew-garnet	drift along	four-in-hand
coach-horse	drift angle	four-master
cockleboat	driftmeter	gain ground
column gear	drop anchor	gather head
command car	dusk rocket	gear change
congestion	emigration	glass coach
connection	evacuation	go in the van
control rod	expedition	goods train
conveyance	expressway	green light
cosmodrome	fall aboard	ground crew
country bus	fall behind	ground loop
covered way	feed system	hackney cab
cow-catcher	fire engine	half galley

hawsepiece	lateen sail	normal loop
headlights	lead the way	normal spin
heat shield	lettergram	nose turret
heave round	lever pilot	ocean liner
heave short	lie athwart	ocean-going
helicopter	life jacket	on a bowline
helivector	lighthouse	on the march
High street	limber hole	on the rocks
hit the deck	locomotion	open waggon
hitch-hiker	luggage van	outer space
home and dry	main artery	overbridge
homecoming	make tracks	packet boat
hovercraft	manipulate	packet line
hurrah boat	manoeuvres	packet ship
hydroplane	marker buoy	paddle boat
icebreaker	martingale	parcel post
inter-urban	middle deck	pathfinder
invalid car	midshipman	patrol boat
jaywalking	mizzen sail	pedestrian
jet fighter	mizzen stay	Penny Black
jigger mast	mizzenmast	petrol pump
Jolly Roger	monkey deck	petrol tank
Joyce stick	monkey rail	picketboat
jury-rigged	motor truck	pilgrimage
jury-rudder	motorcoach	pilot plane
knockabout	motorcycle	pilothouse
landing run	naval cadet	pipe aboard
land-lubber	navigation	porpoising

port anchor
port of call
post chaise
Post Office
propellant
propulsion
public walk
quadrireme
quadruplex
radial tyre
rear mirror
reduce sail
rendezvous
repair ship
rescue boat
rev counter
ride a storm
ride and tie
right of way
road safety
roadworthy
robot plane
rocket boat
rocket ship
rope bridge
roundabout
round-house
roustabout
rowing boat

rudderpost
rumble seat
run afoul of
safety belt
safety wire
sail teaser
sally forth
seamanship
second mate
sedan chair
sens unique
servo-pilot
set the pace
sheave hole
sheepshank
shipentine
shipmaster
side street
sidesaddle
single-prop
sky writing
skyscraper
slipstream
sloop of war
smoking car
solo flight
spacecraft
spare wheel
speed limit

spiral loop
square away
square sail
stagecoach
stand first
state barge
static tube
step-rocket
stewardess
streamline
submariner
sun compass
supercargo
supersonic
supply ship
suspension
switchback
tachometer
tanker ship
target boat
tea-clipper
telegraphy
telepathic
television
telewriter
telpherage
test flight
test rocket
thumb a lift

ticker tape	wanderlust	balloon sail
tip-up lorry	water plane	battleplane
toll bridge	watercraft	beaten track
topgallant	watertight	belaying pin
touring car	way-station	bid farewell
tracklayer	way-traffic	blind corner
traffic jam	wheel chair	blind flying
train-ferry	wheel-horse	break ground
trajectory	wheel-house	built-up area
travel sick	whirlybird	bullock cart
travelling	windjammer	camel-litter
travel-worn	windscreen	carburetter
triaconter	wing mirror	card compass
triphibian	abandon ship	carriageway
trolley bus	accelerator	carrick-bend
true course	aeronautics	catch a train
turret ship	after shroud	caterpillar
two-wheeler	afterburner	cat's-whisker
under steam	aileron roll	ceiling zero
undershoot	air controls	cell gondola
useful lift	air terminal	centreboard
vanity case	air umbrella	*chaise-marée*
velocipede	airsickness	close-hauled
veteran car	anchor fluke	club topsail
V-formation	anchor light	coach driver
vintage car	armoured car	cockleshell
volitation	articulated	combat plane
volplaning	assault boat	come forward
wanderings	attack plane	compartment

contraprops
convertible
country road
cover ground
crash helmet
crash waggon
crowd of sail
delivery van
destination
distributor
double march
dreadnought
driving test
ejector-seat
electropult
engaged line
engine gauge
entrainment
escape hatch
escape-route
exhaust pipe
fares please
ferry rocket
find one's way
fire balloon
fishing boat
fishing dory
fishtailing
fleet of foot

flight strip
flying kites
flying speed
flying visit
forced march
fore-skysail
fore-topsail
forward deck
free balloon
galley foist
galley slave
gather speed
get under way
go alongside
go overboard
goods waggon
gosport tube
ground speed
gyro horizon
gyrocompass
hawse timber
head for home
highway code
hit the trail
horse-litter
hug the shore
hydroglider
ignition key
immigration

interceptor
in the saddle
in the wake of
ironclad ram
jaunting car
jolly jumper
journeyings
journey's end
kedge anchor
keep station
kite balloon
kite sausage
laminar flow
landing deck
landing skis
lazy painter
leading edge
leave-taking
limber board
line engaged
loop the loop
lorry driver
lose one's way
luggage rack
magic carpet
mail catcher
mail phaeton
main skysail
main topsail

make headway	parachutist	road licence
make sea room	paratrooper	road traffic
make strides	penteconter	rocket motor
man from Mars	peregrinate	rocket plane
merchantman	peripatetic	rocket power
mess steward	petrol gauge	rotorblades
mine-sweeper	phone number	rudderstock
mizzen-royal	pick up speed	run out a warp
montgolfier	pillion seat	running knot
moon landing	planicopter	sailing boat
moon station	pony and trap	sailing ship
mooring buoy	portmanteau	scuttlebutt
mooring mast	private line	search plane
morse signal	push bicycle	seasickness
Moses basket	pusher-plane	second class
motor launch	put into port	self starter
motor vessel	quarterdeck	send packing
mystery tour	quarterjack	sesquiplane
naval rating	quinquereme	set in motion
naval vessel	racing shell	Shanks's mare
near the wind	radio beacon	Shanks's pony
night letter	radio mirror	sheet anchor
orientation	request stop	shelter deck
ornithopter	rescue plane	ship the oars
out-of-the-way	reservation	shroud lines
outside loop	retroaction	shuttle trip
outside roll	retro-rocket	sightseeing
package tour	reverse turn	sinking ship
paddle wheel	road haulage	skysail mast

skysail yard	switchboard	weather helm
sleeping bag	synchromesh	weather side
sleeping car	tailless jet	weigh anchor
soft landing	take the lead	wheelbarrow
solar rocket	tandem plane	whisker boom
space centre	telecontrol	wind flapper
space flight	teleprinter	wing loading
space island	telpher line	wrong number
space patrol	testing area	aircraftsman
space rocket	three-in-hand	airfreighter
space travel	three-master	air-sea rescue
spanker boom	throughroad	all systems go
spanker gaff	ticking over	antidrag wire
spanker vang	torpedo boat	approach road
speedometer	trafficator	arrester hook
stagger wire	transmitter	arterial road
standing lug	transporter	autorotation
steal a march	travel agent	baby carriage
steam engine	true heading	Bailey bridge
steam launch	trysail gaff	beaching gear
step rockets	tube station	beacon lights
stern anchor	under canvas	bearing plate
stern sheets	underground	belly landing
strap-hanger	vapour trail	between-decks
string along	waggon train	blind landing
stunt flying	waggon wheel	cabin cruiser
submersible	waiting-room	cable railway
subsonic jet	walking tour	caulking iron
sunshine roof	weather deck	centre anchor

change course | fighter pilot | hospital ship
channel patch | fishing fleet | in the train of
chart a course | fishing smack | inclinometer
clear the land | Flemish horse | inverted spin
coach-and-four | flight tester | Jacob's ladder
coach-and-pair | flipper turns | jet propelled
coach-builder | flying banana | king's highway
companionway | flying circus | landing craft
conning tower | flying jib guy | landing field
control stick | flying saucer | landing light
control tower | flying tanker | landing speed
countermarch | forestaysail | landing stage
crash landing | forward march | landing strip
cylinder head | free-wheeling | lateen-rigged
désobligeant | freight train | launch window
dialling code | fuel injector | launching pad
dialling tone | Gladstone bag | launching way
dispatch boat | glide landing | level landing
diving rudder | globe-trotter | light cruiser
double-bubble | go by the board | long distance
double-decker | *Graf Zeppelin* | longshoreman
draught horse | ground tester | lost and found
dual controls | hackney coach | luggage label
East Indiaman | happy landing | luggage train
ejection seat | harbour light | magic carpet
end of the line | heavy cruiser | maiden flight
entrance lock | hedgehopping | maiden voyage
escape rocket | hempen bridle | main staysail
express train | here and there | make a beeline

make good time   puddle jumper   shoot ballast
make progress   pursuit plane   single-decker
man overboard   quarterlight   sinking speed
manned rocket   radar scanner   slacken speed
merchant ship   radar station   snub the chain
monkey-rigged   radio compass   sonic barrier
mosquito boat   radio monitor   sound barrier
motor scooter   radio station   space capsule
motor vehicle   raise the dead   space station
night fighter   return ticket   spanker sheet
nose radiator   ride at anchor   sparking plug
off like a shot   ride bareback   speed of sound
overnight bag   road junction   splinter deck
pantechnicon   rocket assist   square-rigged
parking light   rocket engine   square-rigger
parking meter   rocket glider   stall landing
parking orbit   roller skates   steer clear of
passing place   rolling stock   steering gear
perambulator   rolling stone   stream anchor
petty officer   rough passage   streamlining
pilot balloon   running board   studding sail
plain sailing   running light   Sunday driver
platform deck   sacred anchor   survival suit
pleasure boat   sailing barge   take bearings
pleasure trip   sailing canoe   take-off strip
Plimsoll line   sailing yacht   tallyho coach
Plimsoll mark   season ticket   tearing hurry
postage stamp   shape a course   tender rocket
pressure suit   shipping line   the bitter end

thoroughfare	train service	walk the plank
three-wheeler	transmission	Wandering Jew
through train	travel agency	weather sheet
ticket office	trolley track	weatherboard
touch the wind	tubeless tyre	windward side
tourist class	upset the boat	
tractor plane	utility plane	
traffic light	VIP transport	

Trade and Commerce

This section includes general terms of business, trading and commerce—money, especially slang terms—markets—the stock exchange—taxes—banking—buying and selling—employment, unemployment and places of work—shifts and strikes.

C.A.	dot	owe	tax	bulk
co.	due	par	tin	bull
HP	dun	pay	tip	bury
r.d.	E.E.C.	pit	wad	call
bag	fee	pro	agio	cant
bar	I.O.U.	put	back	cash
bid	job	rig	bank	cess
B.O.T.	lot	sag	bear	char
buy	Ltd.	S.E.T.	bond	chip
cap	net	sum	boom	coin
C.O.D.	oof	tag	buck	co-op

453

corn	gild	note	swap	bonus
cost	gilt	paid	tare	boost
crop	giro	pawn	task	booth
curb	glut	PAYE	tick	brand
deal	gold	peag	till	brass
dear	good	perk	toll	broke
debt	hawk	pool	tout	bucks
desk	hire	post	vend	bulls
dibs	hive	rags	wage	bunce
dole	hold	raid	ware	buy up
drug	idle	rate	work	buyer
dues	IOUS	reap	agent	by-bid
dump	item	rent	amass	cadge
dust	jack	risk	angel	cargo
duty	kale	roll	assay	cheap
earn	kite	roup	asset	check
E.F.T.A.	lend	ruin	at par	chink
fair	levy	sack	audit	chips
fees	line	safe	baron	chore
file	loan	sale	batch	clear
fine	long	salt	bazar	clerk
fire	loss	save	beans	costs
firm	make	scab	bears	craft
fisc	mart	sell	bid up	crash
free	meed	shop	block	cycle
fund	milk	sink	blunt	Danae
gain	mill	slug	board	debit
game	mint	sold	bogus	depot
gift	nail	stag	bones	Dives

454

dough	offer	shark	*usine*
dowry	order	shift	usury
draft	owing	short	utter
entry	panic	skill	value
Ernie	paper	slash	venal
exact	piece	slump	wages
files	pitch	smash	wares
float	plant	smith	welsh
forge	pound	snide	works
funds	price	spend	worth
gilts	prize	spiel	yield
gnome	purse	spots	abacus
goods	queer	stake	accept
gross	quota	stall	accrue
guild	quote	stand	afford
hoard	rails	stint	agency
house	rally	stock	agenda
index	rebuy	store	amount
ingot	remit	strop	appeal
issue	repay	tally	arrear
lease	rhino	taxes	assets
lucre	rocks	terms	at cost
maker	salve	tithe	avails
means	scalp	token	backer
Midas	scoop	trade	banker
miser	score	treat	barker
money	scrip	trend	barter
mopus	set up	truck	bazaar
ochre	share	trust	bearer

boodle	cowrie	growth	merger
borrow	credit	guinea	*métier*
bought	crisis	haggle	minute
bounce	custom	hammer	moneys
bounty	deal in	hard up	monger
bourse	dealer	hawker	monies
branch	debtee	import	notice
broker	debtor	impose	nugget
budget	defray	impost	octroi
bureau	demand	in bulk	odd job
bursar	dicker	in cash	odd lot
button	drawer	in debt	*oeuvre*
buy out	dunner	income	office
buying	enrich	in-tray	on call
cambio	equity	job lot	on tick
career	errand	jobber	oncost
cartel	excise	labour	option
cash in	expend	leader	outbid
change	export	ledger	outcry
charge	figure	lender	outlay
cheque	fiscal	liable	outlet
client	fold up	living	output
coffer	freeze	luxury	packet
consol	future	*maison*	parity
copper	garage	mammon	patron
corner	godown	margin	pauper
corpus	go-slow	market	pay for
costly	gratis	mature	pay out
coupon	grease	mazuma	pay-day

paying	resale	sundry	allonge
pay-off	resell	supply	annuity
payola	resign	surtax	arrears
peddle	retail	swings	article
pedlar	retire	tariff	atelier
picket	return	taxman	auction
pirate	reward	teller	auditor
pit man	rialto	tender	automat
pledge	riches	tenths	average
plunge	ruined	ticker	backing
Plutus	salary	ticket	bad debt
pocket	save up	towage	balance
policy	saving	trader	ballast
profit	sell up	treaty	banking
public	settle	tycoon	bargain
purvey	shares	unload	berries
racket	shiner	unpaid	bidding
raffle	shorts	usurer	bonanza
rating	silver	valuta	bondage
ration	simony	vendor	boycott
realty	smithy	vendue	bullets
rebate	specie	wallet	bullion
recoup	spiral	wampum	bursary
redeem	sponge	wealth	buy back
refund	spread	worker	cabbage
reject	stable	wright	calling
remedy	staker	abscond	cambist
render	stocks	account	capital
rental	strike	actuary	cash box

7

cashier	deposit	full lot	limited
ceiling	deviser	futures	lockout
chaffer	dockage	gabelle	Lombard
chapman	draw out	gift box	long-run
charity	due bill	go broke	lottery
chinker	dumping	go under	lump sum
clinker	economy	good buy	*magasin*
coinage	effects	good sum	manager
coining	embargo	guerdon	man-made
company	emption	half-day	mintage
concern	endorse	harvest	mission
consols	engross	haulage	moneyed
contact	entrust	head tax	nest-egg
convert	expense	holding	net gain
coppers	exploit	imports	notions
corn pit	exports	in funds	nummary
cottons	face par	inflate	oddment
counter	factory	intrust	on offer
Croesus	failure	invoice	on terms
cumshaw	fall due	iron men	on trust
customs	finance	jingler	opening
cut-rate	flutter	jobbers	opulent
damages	foot lot	jobbing	out-tray
daybook	for sale	jobless	package
dealing	foreman	journal	parlour
declare	forgery	killing	parvenu
default	fortune	leading	pay cash
deficit	foundry	lending	payable
deflate	freight	lettuce	payment

458

pay-rise	reissue	solvent	welfare
payroll	release	sponger	well off
payslip	requite	sponsor	welsher
peddler	reserve	squeeze	wildcat
pending	retiral	stipend	workday
pension	returns	storage	above par
pet bank	revenue	striker	accredit
plunger	rich man	subsidy	affluent
poll tax	rigging	surplus	after tax
poor man	roanoke	swindle	agiotage
portage	rollers	takings	agronomy
pre-empt	room man	taxable	amortize
premium	rouleau	tax-free	appraise
prepaid	royalty	terrier	at a price
pricing	sacking	the city	auditing
produce	salable	tidy sum	automate
product	salt tax	trade in	baby bond
profits	salvage	trading	bad money
promote	savings	traffic	badly off
pro-rata	scalper	trustee	ballyhoo
prosper	seconds	utility	bank loan
provide	sell out	vacancy	bank note
pursuit	selling	vending	bank rate
pyramid	service	venture	bankbook
realize	shekels	voucher	bank-roll
realtor	shopman	walkout	bankrupt
receipt	shopper	war bond	base coin
refusal	skilled	warrant	basic pay
regrate	smelter	wealthy	bear pool

459

bear raid	commerce	exchange
beat down	consumer	expended
below par	contango	expenses
billfold	contract	exporter
blackleg	converts	face ruin
blue chip	counting	finances
board lot	credit to	fire sale
boardman	creditor	flat rate
bondager	currency	floorman
boom town	customer	for a song
borrower	cut-price	free gift
boutique	day shift	free port
breakage	dealings	function
brochure	defrayal	gasworks
bull pool	director	gazetted
bull raid	disburse	gift shop
business	discount	gilt-edge
buying in	disposal	giveaway
campaign	dividend	gold mine
carriage	dockyard	gold rush
cash down	dry goods	good will
cash sale	earnings	gratuity
cashbook	embezzle	grow rich
circular	employee	hallmark
clientry	employer	hard cash
clinkers	emporium	hard sell
close out	entrepôt	hardware
cold cash	estimate	hoarding
commands	evaluate	homework

hot money	make a bid	overseer
huckster	make good	overtime
importer	man power	Pactolus
in arrear	manifest	par value
in pocket	mark down	passbook
in the red	material	pawn shop
increase	maturity	pay-talks
indebted	merchant	pin money
industry	mint drop	pipeline
interest	monetary	pittance
investor	moneybag	position
issuance	moneybox	post paid
issue par	monopoly	poundage
jeweller	mortgage	practice
junkshop	net price	premises
keep shop	net worth	price cut
knitwork	no charge	price war
labourer	notation	proceeds
lame duck	notecase	producer
large sum	oddments	property
largesse	off price	prospect
legation	on credit	purchase
levanter	on demand	put price
lifework	on strike	quit rent
live high	operator	rack rent
live well	opulence	rag trade
long side	ordinary	rainy day
low price	overhaul	receipts
low water	overhead	reckoner

recorder	sideline	trade off
recovery	sinecure	treasure
refinery	small sum	Treasury
register	smithery	turnover
regrater	soft sell	underbid
requital	solatium	undercut
reserves	solidity	valorize
retailer	solvency	valuable
retainer	spending	venality
richesse	spot cash	vendible
richling	spot sale	vocation
round lot	square up	wash sale
round sum	sterling	watch-dog
rush hour	sundries	well-to-do
salaried	supertax	wharfage
saleroom	supplies	wheat pit
salesman	swapping	work late
salt down	take-over	workaday
scalping	tallyman	workroom
scarcity	tax dodge	workshop
schedule	taxation	write off
security	taxpayer	absconder
self-made	the hares	*ad valorem*
shipment	time bill	affiliate
shipyard	tolbooth	affluence
shopping	tool shop	aggregate
short-run	toolwork	allowance
showcase	top price	amount due
showroom	trade gap	appraisal

arbitrage	call price	dishonour
arrearage	cash grain	dismissal
avocation	catalogue	dollar gap
back shift	cellarage	draw wages
bad cheque	cheap-Jack	drug store
bank clerk	cheap-John	easy money
bank stock	check rate	easy terms
barrow boy	clearance	economics
bartering	clientage	economies
bear panic	clientele	economize
blind pool	closing bid	emolument
board room	co-emption	establish
bon marché	coin money	exchequer
bond crowd	commodity	excise tax
bond issue	cost price	exciseman
bonus bond	costerman	executive
borrowing	craftsman	expansion
box office	cut a melon	expensive
brand-name	death duty	exploiter
bread-line	debenture	export tax
brokerage	deduction	extortion
bucketing	defaulter	face value
bull panic	deflation	fair price
buy in bulk	depositor	fair trade
by auction	dime store	fat profit
by-bidding	direct tax	fiat money
by-product	directors	financial
cable code	dirt-cheap	financier
cable rate	discharge	firm offer

firm price
flash note
flat broke
flotation
free trade
full purse
gilt-edged
going rate
gold piece
good price
greenback
grubstake
guarantee
guarantor
half-price
handiwork
hard goods
hard money
head buyer
heavy cost
high price
high value
holy stone
hot market
hush money
import tax
in arrears
in deficit
in the city

incentive
income tax
indemnity
inflation
insolvent
insurance
invention
inventory
ironworks
job of work
joint bank
keep books
knock-down
late shift
legal bond
liability
life's work
liquidate
list price
long purse
low-priced
luxury tax
mail order
make a sale
market day
marketing
middleman
money belt
moneybags

mortgagee
neat price
negotiate
net income
night safe
off market
officiate
on account
on the nail
operative
order book
out of debt
out of work
outgoings
outworker
overdraft
overdrawn
overheads
overspend
patronage
patronize
pay dearly
pay in kind
paymaster
pecuniary
pecunious
penniless
penny wise
petty cash

piece-work	refinance	statement
piggy bank	reflation	stock list
plutocrat	registrar	stock rate
poorly off	reimburse	stockpile
portfolio	repayment	strike pay
possibles	resources	strongbox
pound note	restraint	subsidize
pourboire	sacrifice	substance
practical	sale block	sumptuary
price ring	sales talk	surcharge
price rise	salesgirl	sweatshop
priceless	saltworks	sweet shop
price-list	secretary	syndicate
prime cost	sell short	synthetic
principal	shift work	take stock
profiteer	shop floor	tax return
promotion	short sale	technical
purchaser	short side	the actual
qualified	sight bill	the market
quittance	single tax	the street
quotation	situation	tie-in sale
ratepayer	soft goods	timocracy
ready cash	sole agent	tollbooth
real wages	soundness	trade fair
recession	speculate	trade name
reckoning	spending3	trademark
reduction	spot grain	trade-sale
redundant	spot price	tradesman
reference	stability	traffic in

treadmill	accumulate	buy futures
treasurer	adjustment	calculator
undersell	advertiser	capitalize
union card	appreciate	capitalism
unit trust	apprentice	capitalist
unsalable	assessment	cats and dogs
unskilled	assignment	chain banks
up for sale	at a bargain	chain store
utilities	at a premium	chancellor
utterance	at the spear	chargeable
valuation	auction off	chargehand
vendition	auctioneer	cheapening
wage claim	automation	cheapskate
wage scale	average out	chequebook
warehouse	bank credit	chrematist
wash sales	bankruptcy	chrysology
wealth tax	bear market	closed shop
well-lined	bearer bond	collateral
whitewash	best seller	colporteur
wholesale	bill broker	commercial
work force	bill of sale	commission
work study	blood money	compensate
workhouse	bonus stock	conference
workplace	bondholder	consortium
World Bank	bookkeeper	contraband
yellow boy	brassworks	cost centre
acceptance	bucket shop	coupon bond
accountant	bulk buying	credit card
accounting	buy and sell	credit slip

curb broker	exposition	hard market
curb market	false money	have in hand
daily bread	fancy goods	head office
defrayment	fancy price	heavy purse
defalcator	fancy stock	high-priced
deep in debt	filthy rich	hold office
dead market	first offer	honorarium
del credere	fiscal year	import duty
demand bill	fixed price	imposition
department	fixed trust	in business
depository	flat market	in the black
depreciate	forced sale	in the money
depression	free gratis	income bond
dirty money	free market	incumbered
dividend on	free sample	incur a debt
dollar bill	free trader	industrial
dummy share	freightage	insolvency
Dutch treat	floor price	instalment
easy market	full stocks	investment
economizer	funded debt	job-hunting
efficiency	give credit	joint bonds
employment	glassworks	joint-stock
encumbered	go on strike	jumble sale
end product	go shopping	laboratory
enterprise	gold nugget	lighterage
estate duty	governments	liquidator
evaluation	grindstone	livelihood
ex-dividend	half stocks	living wage
exorbitant	handicraft	loan market

long market
long seller
loss leader
man of means
management
marked down
market hall
marketable
mass market
meal ticket
member bank
mercantile
merchantry
Midas touch
mint leaves
money order
moneyed man
monopolize
monopolist
moratorium
negotiable
nightshift
nominal fee
nominal par
nonpayment
no-par stock
no-par value
    hand
    atic

obligation
occupation
off licence
oil of palms
on the block
on the cheap
on the rocks
on the shelf
open market
opening bid
out of funds
overcharge
paper money
pawnbroker
percentage
peppercorn
picket duty
pig in a poke
pilot plant
plutocracy
pocketbook
power plant
pre-emption
preference
prepayment
price index
price level
printworks
Prix unique

production
profession
profitable
prospector
prospectus
prosperity
provide for
public roup
purchasing
pure profit
put and call
ration book
ready money
real estate
recompense
recoupment
redeemable
redundancy
remittance
remunerate
repair shop
reparation
repository
repurchase
retail shop
retirement
rigid trust
rock bottom
round trade

run up a bill
salability
sales force
saving bank
saving game
scrapworks
scrip issue
second-hand
securities
serial bond
settle with
settlement
share index
shoestring
shop window
shopkeeper
short bonds
sick market
skilled man
slave trade
slow market
smart money
soft market
sole agency
speciality
speculator
split shift
spondulies
statistics

steelworks
steep price
stock issue
stockpiles
stony broke
straitened
stronghold
strongroom
sum of money
swap horses
take a flier
taskmaster
tax evasion
technician
technocrat
the needful
thin margin
ticker tape
tour of duty
trade board
trade cycle
trade guild
trade price
trade route
trade union
treaty port
typewriter
typing pool
underwrite

unemployed
upset price
wad of notes
wage policy
wage-freeze
walk of life
Wall Street
waterworks
wealthy man
well afford
well-heeled
wholesaler
window-shop
work to rule
working day
written off
account book
accountancy
acquittance
advertising
agriculture
antique shop
appointment
asking price
association
at face value
auction ring
bank account
bank balance

bank manager
bank holiday
bank of issue
bargain sale
bear account
bear the cost
betting shop
big business
bill of costs
billionaire
black market
blank cheque
bobtail pool
boilerworks
bonus scheme
book-keeping
bottom price
bread winner
brisk market
budget price
bull account
businessman
capital gain
carbon paper
cash account
catallactic
caught short
᠁ ᠁ank
᠁e

chamberlain
chancellery
chemist shop
chrysocracy
circulation
closing down
come to terms
company rule
competition
compte rendu
comptometer
cool million
commodities
common stock
competitive
consumption
co-operative
copperworks
corn in Egypt
corporation
counterfeit
cover charge
co-operative
cum dividend
custom house
customs duty
danger money
defence bond
delinquence

demarcation
demand curve
deposit slip
devaluation
direct cost
display case
distributor
dividend off
double entry
down payment
drive a trade
earn a living
economic law
economic man
economy size
embarrassed
endorsement
established
estate agent
expenditure
fabrication
famine price
fetch a price
filthy lucre
fixed assets
fixed income
floor broker
floor trader
fluctuation

foot the bill	long account	on easy terms
foreclosure	long service	on good terms
free harbour	loose change	on the market
future grain	machine shop	open account
future price	machine-made	open-end bond
gingerbread	made of money	out of pocket
gross income	make a bargain	outstanding
hard bargain	manufactory	overpayment
high finance	manufacture	package deal
horse market	market overt	paper credit
impecunious	market place	partnership
indirect tax	market price	pay cash down
industrials	mass-produce	pay on demand
inexpensive	merchandise	pay spot cash
institution	millionaire	pay the piper
insular bond	minimum wage	Physiocrats
intercourse	mint of money	piece of work
ironmongery	money broker	pilot scheme
joint return	money dealer	place of work
key industry	money to burn	pocket money
king's ransom	moneylender	polytechnic
lap of luxury	money's-worth	possessions
legal tender	negotiation	postal order
liberty bond	nest factory	pots of money
life savings	net interest	poverty line
line of goods	net receipts	premium bond
liquidation	nuisance tax	pretty penny
local branch	numismatics	price-fixing
local office	occupy a post	price-freeze

price-spiral
price-ticket
property tax
proposition
provided for
purchase tax
put-up market
Queer Street
quoted price
raw material
reserve bank
resignation
restriction
retiring age
risk capital
rummage sale
run into debt
safe deposit
sales ledger
sales person
savings bank
self-service
sell at a loss
sell forward
sell futures
share ledger
sharebroker
shareholder
shopping bag

short change
short seller
single entry
sinking fund
slot machine
small change
small trader
sole emption
speculation
sponsorship
stock dealer
stock ledger
stock market
stockbroker
stockholder
stockjobber
stockpiling
stocktaking
storekeeper
strong market
subsistence
supermarket
take-home pay
take-over bid
tare and tret
Tattersall's
tax-assessor
tax-gatherer
technocracy

the have-nots
tight budget
tight market
time-bargain
tired market
to the tune of
trade school
trading post
transaction
travel agent
truck system
undercharge
underwriter
vendibility
wherewithal
working life
workmanlike
workmanship
works outing
world market
accepted bill
active market
ad valorem tax
amalgamation
amortization
amortizement
arithmometer
assembly line
auction stand

balance sheet	circular note	exhaust price
bank examiner	clearing bank	extend credit
bargain offer	closing price	extravagance
bargain price	common market	fair exchange
barter system	compensation	fill an office
be in business	consumer good	first refusal
bill of lading	cook the books	fiscal policy
blind bargain	cost of living	fiscal reform
board meeting	costermonger	fixed capital
Board of Trade	counting-room	floating debt
bond to bearer	credit rating	folding money
bottom dollar	currency note	foreign trade
bottomry bond	current price	gate receipts
branch office	customs union	general store
broker's agent	denomination	get rich quick
brokers' board	depreciation	going concern
business deal	direct labour	gold standard
business life	disbursement	goods for sale
businesslike	discount rate	great expense
buyer's market	distribution	haberdashery
buying public	dollar crisis	hard currency
callable bond	durable goods	high-pressure
capital gains	Dutch auction	hire purchase
capital goods	early closing	hungry market
capital stock	earned income	in conference
cash and carry	econometrics	in the gazette
cash register	economy drive	indebtedness
casual labour	entrepreneur	interest rate
catallactics	exchange rate	internal bond

joint account
keep accounts
labour of love
laissez-faire
leather goods
line of credit
live in clover
lively market
long interest
make a fortune
make delivery
make one's pile
manipulation
manufacturer
marginal cost
mass-produced
mercantilism
monetization
money changer
money matters
mortgage bond
national bank
nearest offer
nine till five
nominal price
nominal value
nouveau riche
odd-lot dealer
offer for sale

offered price
office junior
open-end trust
opening price
organization
packing house
pay as you earn
pay in advance
peg the market
pegged market
ply one's trade
porte-monnaie
pressure belt
price ceiling
price control
price current
price of money
price rigging
productivity
professional
profiteering
profit margin
profit motive
purse strings
rags to riches
rate of growth
redeployment
regional bank
remuneration

remunerative
reserve price
retaining fee
retrenchment
rig the market
rigged market
rising prices
robot factory
rolling stock
rubber cheque
sale by outcry
sale or return
sales gimmick
sales manager
salesmanship
satisfaction
sell on credit
severance pay
share company
shareholding
short account
show business
slender means
sliding scale
sterling area
state lottery
steady market
stock company
stock dealing

stock in trade ten-cent store trial balance
stockholding the long green trustee stock
stockjobbery ticker market unemployment
street market trade balance variety store
strike action trade mission watered stock
strike it rich trading stamp Welfare State
superannuate travel agency without a bean
sustain a loss treasury bill working class
tax collector treasury note working order
tax exemption

HERALDRY

This general heading includes heraldic terminology
—blazons, colours and fabrics—flags, badges and
emblems—heralds—crosses—livery and armour—
orders of chivalry.

or	jamb	vert	giron	staff
bar	lion	wavy	gules	stake
orb	lure	York	gyron	tenné
rod	Lyon	aegis	label	tiara
ankh	orle	azure	luces	torse
arms	pale	badge	March	visor
bard	paly	barde	mitre	wyver
bend	pean	barry	molet	Albany
boss	pile	bendy	motto	argent
coat	ring	cadet	order	armour
coif	rose	chief	paled	banner
Cork	Ross	crest	pales	baston
coup	seal	crook	pheon	beaver
enty	sign	cross	plain	bezant
flag	sown	crown	plate	billet
foot	spur	dance	razed	blazon
fret	toga	dwale	rebus	border
gamb	umbo	fesse	rowel	braced
helm	undy	field	sable	burely
jack	vair	fusil	scion	burgeᴇ

camail	helmet	wreath	dolphin
cantel	herald	wyvern	dormant
canton	livery	annelet	*drapeau*
casque	lodged	armiger	engrail
charge	lorica	armoury	*estache*
checky	mantle	attired	estoile
collar	mascle	basinet	flanche
couped	morion	bearing	forcené
cuisse	mullet	bendlet	gardant
device	nebuly	bezants	garland
dexter	Norroy	bezanty	gironny
diadem	patent	bordure	grafted
dragon	pellet	buckler	greaves
Dublin	pennon	bunting	griffon
emblem	potent	Carrick	gyronny
ensign	raguly	chaplet	hauberk
ermine	rustre	charged	heralds
fillet	salade	checker	impaled
fitché	sallet	Chester	labarum
fitchy	scutum	chevron	leopard
flanch	shield	cockade	lozenge
fretty	signet	college	martlet
fylfot	sleeve	colours	maunche
garter	spread	coronet	nombril
gemels	symbol	corslet	oak leaf
gobony	tabard	cotices	pageant
gorget	Ulster	crozier	panoply
guidon	uraeus	crusily	parting
heaume	voided	cuirass	passant

pédieux	bearings	Lord Lyon
pendant	blazoner	mill-rind
pennant	blazonry	ordinary
pierced	brassard	powdered
potenté	cabasset	Richmond
quarter	caduceus	Rothesay
rampant	cantoned	sanguine
regalia	chamfron	scallops
roundel	cheveron	scocheon
salient	cinqfoil	segreant
saltant	corselet	siege cap
saltier	couchant	sinister
Saltire	crescent	Somerset
sceptre	crosslet	standard
sinople	dancetty	streamer
sixfoil	demi-lion	swastika
statant	erminees	synobill
surcoat	erminois	tau cross
trapper	fan-crest	tressure
trefoil	fountain	trippant
unguled	gauntlet	vambrace
unicorn	gonfalon	vexillum
uniform	half-mast	armorials
vermeil	heraldic	assigning
Windsor	heraldry	assurgent
accolade	herisson	backplate
ancestor	indented	banderole
armorial	insignia	blackjack
banneret	invected	blue peter

cadet line
casquetel
cross paty
cubitière
embattled
en surtout
epaulette
erminites
face guard
flaunches
gammadion
genealogy
gonfannon
Great Arms
great seal
habergeon
hatchment
head piece
jerserant
Lancaster
nose guard
nose piece
oriflamme
pageantry
phylogeny
powdering
prick-spur
privy seal
quarterly

red ensign
regardant
rerebrace
royal coat
royal seal
scutcheon
sollerets
spear side
spur rowel
trappings
tricolour
union down
Union Jack
assign arms
assignment
at half mast
barrel-helm
blue ensign
Blue Mantle
brigandine
brigantine
broad arrow
cap and gown
cheveronny
cinquefoil
Clarenceux
coat of arms
coat-armour
cockatrice

cross flory
cross formy
decrescent
dexter half
dexter side
difference
dovetailed
eagle crest
escutcheon
family tree
figurehead
fleur-de-lis
fleur-de-lys
gimmal ring
increscent
Jolly Roger
King of Arms
Lyon depute
ordinaries
parted arms
parted coat
plain cross
plain field
portcullis
purple pall
pursuivant
quartering
quatrefoil
roll of arms

Rouge Croix	gilded spurs	bend sinister
royal crown	grant of arms	bishop's apron
signal flag	*Leo fecialis*	border gobony
sloe charge	lion passant	cadet's shield
stall-plate	lion rampant	cardinal's hat
supporters	lion salient	charged field
wavy border	marshalling	couchant lion
achievement	mortarboard	cross botonny
ancient coat	*Pickelhaube*	differencing
assignments	privy signet	false colours
bar sinister	rampant lion	grand quarter
bishop's lawn	robe of state	granting arms
breastplate	rod of empire	grants of arms
counterseal	Rouge Dragon	heraldic seal
countervair	shield party	imperial seal
crested helm	spindle side	inescutcheon
demi-leopard	spread eagle	laurel wreath
differenced	subordinary	office of arms
dimidiation	triple crown	parted shield
display arms	triple plume	paternal arms
distaff side	true colours	purple ermine
dormant lion	vair-en-point	rowelled spur
engrailment	voided cross	sinister half
flag officer	white ensign	sinister side
fleurs-de-lys	armorial seal	tabard of arms

MYTHOLOGY

This general heading includes the gods and goddesses of Roman, Greek, Celtic, Scandinavian, Hindu, Egyptian and Babylonian mythology—spirits, fairies and evil demons—satanism, witches and witchcraft—fable and legend—charms and spells—fabulous creatures—enchantment, black and white magic.

Akh	Gog	Mut	Sol	Addu	Atar
Anu	Hea	nis	Sri	Aeon	Aten
Ara	Heh	nix	Tem	Afer	Atli
Ate	Hel	Nox	Tiu	Agni	Atmu
Aya	Hob	Nun	Tiw	Ajax	Aton
Bel	Ida	Nut	Tum	Akal	Atum
Bes	imp	Nyx	Tyr	Alea	Auge
Bor	Ino	Oba	Ull	Amen	Baal
Cos	Ira	obi	Uma	Amor	Bana
dea	Ker	Ops	Urd	Amun	Bast
Dia	Laz	Ore	Utu	Anax	Bora
Dis	Leo	Oya	Vac	Anna	Bori
elf	Ler	Pan	Van	Anta	Bran
ent	Lok	Ran	Zan	Apet	Bron
Eos	Lug	Seb	Zio	Apis	Buto
fay	Mab	Set	Ziu	Ares	Ceto
Geb	Min	Shu	Abuk	Argo	Ceyx
god	Mot	Sif	Adad	Askr	Civa

Clio	Frey	Iris	Maui	shee
Cora	Fria	Irra	Ment	Shri
deil	Frig	Isis	Mors	Siva
deus	Fury	jinn	Muse	Sobk
Deva	Gaea	jinx	Nabu	Soma
Devi	Gaia	joss	Naga	Spes
Dewa	Garm	Jove	Nana	Styx
Dian	Gerd	juju	Natt	tabu
Dice	Gere	Juno	Nebo	Tara
Dido	Geri	Kali	Neph	Tare
Dike	Goll	Kama	Nike	Thea
Duat	Hapi	kami	Nona	Thor
Echo	Hebe	Kapi	Norn	Tiki
Edda	hell	Ketu	Nott	Troy
Eden	Hera	Khem	Odin	Tyro
Edfu	Here	Kore	ogre	Tyrr
Egil	Hero	Leda	Otus	Ullr
Enki	Hler	Leto	peor	Upis
Enyo	Hödr	Loke	peri	Urth
Enzu	Hora	Loki	Ptah	Usas
Erda	Hoth	Luna	Puck	Usha
Eric	huma	Lyra	Rahu	Utug
Eris	icon	Maat	Rama	Vach
Eros	idas	magi	Rhea	Vale
Erua	idol	Maia	Rind	Vali
Fate	Idun	mana	Saga	Vans
Faun	Ilus	Mara	Sati	Vayu
Fons	Inar	Marx	seer	Vili
Frea	Iole	Math	Seth	Wate

Yama	avici	Dagon	fable	Horae
yeti	Baldr	Damia	Fagus	Horus
Ymir	Batea	Danae	fairy	houri
Zemi	Belus	deify	Fauna	huaca
Zeus	Bhaga	deity	Faust	Hyads
Zion	bogey	demon	fetch	Hydra
Aegir	Brage	Devil	fiend	Hylas
Aegle	Bragi	Diana	Flora	Hymen
Aello	Brute	Dione	Freya	Iasus
Aeson	Cabal	Diral	Frigg	ichor
afrit	Cacus	Dirce	Gauri	Idmon
Aiffe	Canis	Donar	genie	Iliad
Algol	Capta	Dorus	ghost	Indra
Ammon	Caria	Draco	ghoul	Irene
angel	Carpo	dryad	giant	Irmin
Aniel	Ceres	Durga	Gibil	Istar
Antea	Cerus	dwarf	gnome	Ister
Aralu	Cetus	Dyaus	Grace	Janus
Arcas	Chaos	Dylan	Gyges	Jason
Arges	charm	Dymas	Hadad	jinni
Argos	Circe	Egill	Hades	Kalki
Argus	Coeus	Ehlis	Harpy	Karna
Ariel	Comus	elves	Hatra	kelpy
Aries	coven	Enlil	haunt	Komos
Arion	Creon	Epona	Helen	Kotys
Artio	Creus	Erato	Helle	Laius
Athor	Crius	Erlik	Herse	lamia
Atlas	Cupid	Etara	Hoder	Lamos
Atman	Dagda	Eurus	Holda	Lares

larva	Ninos	Sheol	Venus
Lepus	Niobe	Shiva	Vesta
Lethe	nisse	Shree	Vidar
Liber	nixie	Sibyl	Virgo
Libra	Njord	Sinon	Vithi
limbo	Notus	siren	Wabun
Lupus	Nusku	Siris	wakan
Lycus	nymph	Solal	weird
Lydia	obeah	spell	Wodan
Maera	Orcus	spook	Woden
Magog	oread	Surya	Wotan
magus	Orion	sylph	Yasna
Marut	Othim	taboo	zombi
Mazda	ouphe	Terra	Abdiel
Medea	Paean	Theia	Adonai
Metis	pagan	theos	Adonis
Midas	Pales	Thoth	Aeacus
Mimir	Parca	Thrym	Aeëtes
Minos	Paris	Thule	Aegeus
Moira	Pitys	Titan	Aegina
Momos	pixie	totem	Aeneas
Momus	Pluto	Troad	Aeneid
Morna	Poeas	troll	Aeolus
Morta	Priam	Tyche	Aethra
Mysia	Remus	Uriel	afreet
naiad	Robur	Ushas	Agenor
Nanna	Satan	Vaman	Aglaia
Napal	satyr	Vanir	Alecto
Nerio	shade	Varah	Allatu

Alseid	Babbar	Cybele	*genius*
Amazon	Balder	Cygnus	Geryon
Amen-Ra	Baldur	daemon	goblin
Amenti	Baucis	Danaus	Gorgon
Amores	Belial	Daphne	Graces
amulet	Beulah	Decuma	Graeae
Amycus	Bootes	*diable*	Haemon
Anubis	Boreas	*diablo*	Hathor
Anytus	Brahma	dragon	heaven
Apollo	Buddha	durgan	Hebrus
Aquila	Cabiri	Egeria	Hecate
Ariske	Cadmus	Eirene	Hector
Arjuna	Cancer	Epirus	Hecuba
Arthur	Castor	Erebus	Hekate
Asgard	Caurus	Erinys	Helios
Assama	Cebren	Erotes	Hermes
astral	Chandi	Etolia	Hertha
Athena	Charis	Europa	Hestia
Athene	Charon	Euryte	Hobbit
Atreus	cherub	Faunus	Hoenir
Attica	Chiron	fetish	hoodoo
Auriga	Clotho	Freyia	Hyades
Aurora	Consus	Freyja	Hyllus
Auster	Corona	Frigga	Iasion
Avalon	Corvus	Ganesa	Iasius
avatar	Crater	Garuda	Icarus
avichi	Creusa	Gawain	Indara
Azazel	Cronus	Gefion	Iolcus
Azrael	Crotus	Gemini	Iseult

Ishtar	Mentor	Oileus	Scylla
Ismene	Merlin	Old Ned	sea god
Isolde	merman	Ondine	Sekume
Ithunn	Merope	oracle	Selena
jinnee	Minyas	Ormuzd	Selene
jumart	Mithra	Osiris	Semele
kelpie	Moerae	Ossian	Semnai
Khadau	Moirai	Pallas	seraph
kobold	Molech	panisc	Simios
korred	Moloch	panisk	Sinbad
kraken	Myrrha	Parcae	Sirius
Kronos	naguel	Peleus	sky-god
Laputa	Napaea	Pelias	Somnus
Libera	Naraka	Pelops	Sparta
Lilith	nectar	Phocis	Sphinx
Locris	Neleus	Phoebe	spirit
Lucina	Nereid	Pisces	sprite
Lugaid	Nereus	Placia	Stator
maenad	Nergal	pokunt	Stheno
Mammon	Nessus	Pollux	Strymo
manito	Nestor	Pontus	Sukune
Marduk	Nimrod	Pothos	sun god
Marmar	numina	Psyche	syrinx
mascot	Oberon	Pythia	Takaro
Matsya	obi-man	Python	Tammuz
Mavors	occult	Rhodus	Taurus
Medusa	Oeneus	Saturn	Tellus
Megara	ogress	Saxnot	Tethys
Memnon	Oicles	Sciron	Teucer

Teufel	war god	Arcadia	Camelot
Thalia	wizard	Argolis	cantrip
Thallo	wraith	Ariadne	Capella
Thebus	Xuthus	Artemis	Cecrops
Themis	Yahweh	Astarte	Celaeno
Thetis	Ydalir	Athamas	centaur
thrall	ye gods	Atropos	Cepheus
Thunor	Zephyr	Avadana	Cercyon
Titans	Zethus	Avallon	Chamuel
Tithon	zombie	Avernus	charmer
Tityus	Abaddon	Axierus	Chemosh
Tonans	Achalia	Azapane	chimera
Tophet	Achates	Bacchus	Chloris
Triton	Acheron	bad luck	Cisseus
Tydeus	Actaeon	bad peri	Clymene
Typhon	Ahriman	banshee	Cocytus
undine	Aladdin	Bellona	Curetes
Urania	Alcaeus	bewitch	cyclops
Uranus	alcmene	Bifrost	Cynthia
Utopia	Alcyone	Boeotia	Cythera
Vacuna	Ali Baba	boggart	Cyzicus
Varuna	Amphion	Bona Dea	Deasura
Vesper	Amymone	Brontes	Deipyle
Victor	Antaeus	brownie	Demeter
Vishnu	Antenor	bugaboo	demigod
vision	Anteros	bugbear	Derketo
voodoo	Antiope	Cabeiri	dervish
Vulcan	Aquilon	Calydon	dog star
Walwen	Arallis	Calypso	Echidna

Electra	gremlin	Laocöon	nymphet
Eleusis	griffin	Laodice	Oceanid
Elysian	griffon	Laputan	Oceanus
Epigoni	half-god	Leander	Oeagrus
Erginus	Hanuman	limniad	Oedipus
Erinyes	Harpies	Lorelei	Ogyrvan
erlking	Helenus	Lucifer	Old Nick
Eubulus	hellion	Lynceus	Olympus
Eunomia	heroine	Machaon	Omphale
Eupheme	Hesione	Mahuika	Orestes
Euryale	Himeros	Mamaldi	Orpheus
Eurytus	Horatii	Marsyas	Orthrus
Euterpe	Hyrieus	Megaera	Ouranos
evil eye	Iacchus	Mercury	Pandion
Evil one	Iakchos	mermaid	Pandora
Faustus	Iapetus	Michael	Panthus
fire-god	Icarius	Midgard	Parvati
Fortuna	Illyria	Miletus	Pegasus
Gabriel	Inarash	Minerva	Penates
Galahad	incubus	Mordred	Perseus
Galatea	inferno	Mycenae	Phaedra
Ganpati	Iuturna	Nariman	phantom
Gehenna	Jocasta	Nemesis	Philtre
giantry	Jophiel	Nephele	Phineus
Glaucus	Jupiter	Neptune	Phoebus
Glitnir	Kottyto	Nerthus	Phoenix
goat-god	Krishna	Niflhel	Phorcys
goddess	Laertes	Nirvana	Phrixus
godling	Lakshmi	Nisroch	Pleione

Pluvius	Thaumus	Antigone	Charites
Procris	the gods	Apollyon	cherubim
Procyon	Theseus	Aquarius	chimaera
Proteus	Tiphysh	Arcturus	Chrysaor
Pylades	Titania	Argestes	chthonic
Pyrrhus	Tristan	Argonaut	Cimmerii
rain-god	Troilus	Arimaspi	Clymenus
Raphael	Ulysses	Asmodeus	Cockayne
Rig-Veda	unicorn	Asterope	colossus
Romulus	vampire	Astraeus	Comaetho
Sagitta	Vingolf	Astyanax	Corythus
Sammael	Vitharr	Astyoche	Cretheus
sandman	warlock	Atalanta	Curiatii
Savitri	Wieland	Atlantis	Cyclopes
Scorpio	wind-god	Baalpeor	Cynosura
sea-maid	Zadkiel	bacchant	Daedalus
Serapis	Zagreus	bad fairy	Danaïdes
Serpens	Absyrtus	black art	Dardanus
serpent	Achelous	Briareus	Dea Syria
Shaitan	Achernar	Cabeirus	Deiphyle
Shamash	Achilles	Cadmilus	demiurge
Sigmund	Acrisius	caduceus	demonism
Silenus	Adrastus	Calliope	Despoina
sorcery	Aegyptus	Callisto	devaloka
spectre	Aganippe	Capareus	devil-god
Sthenno	Aidoneus	Casmilus	Diomedes
sylphid	ambrosia	Castalia	Dionysus
Taygete	Ameinias	Cephalus	Dioscuri
Telamon	Anchises	Cerberus	Doliones

dream-god	Heracles	Meleager
earth-god	Hercules	Menelaus
El Dorado	Hesperis	Mephisto
Electris	Hesperus	Merodach
elf-child	Hiawatha	Messenia
Epicaste	Himantes	Minotaur
Eridanus	Horatius	morganes
Erinnyes	Hyperion	Morpheus
Eriphyle	Iphicles	Myrtilus
Erytheia	jahannan	Nauplius
Eteocles	Juventas	Nephthys
Eurayale	Kalevala	Niflheim
Eurydice	Lachesis	Odysseus
exorcize	Laconica	Oenomaus
exorcism	Lancelot	Old Harry
fabulous	Laomedon	Old Horny
false god	Laputian	Olympian
Favonius	Leiriope	paganism
folklore	libation	Pan-pipes
Ganymede	Lilliput	Pantheon
giantess	limoniad	Paradise
Glasberg	Lycurgus	Pasiphaë
good luck	Lyonesse	Penelope
gramarye	magician	Pentheus
grimoire	Mahadeva	Percival
Harmonia	Marathon	Pergamus
Harpinna	Marnaran	Periboea
hell-fire	Maspiter	Persides
Hellotis	Melampus	Peter Pan

Phaethon	Thanatos	archangel
Philemon	the Deuce	archfiend
Philotis	the Muses	Aristaeus
Pierides	the Seven	Asclepiad
Pittheus	Thyestes	Asclepios
Pleiades	Tithonus	Asclepius
Podarces	Tristram	Ashtaroth
Polyxena	Tristran	Assaracus
Portunus	uturuncu	Astydamia
Poseidon	Valhalla	Atalantis
Quirinus	Valkyrie	Atargatis
revenant	were-folk	Atlantica
Teutates	were-wolf	Attic salt
Sabazius	Ygdrasil	Autolycus
Sarpedon	Zephyrus	Axiocersa
Satanism	zoolater	bacchante
sea nymph	zoolatry	Beelzebub
Sharrapu	Acarnania	bewitcher
Sisyphus	Aegisthus	Black mass
Sleipnir	Agamemnon	brimstone
smith-god	Agapemone	Britannia
sorcerer	Aigialeus	cacodemon
Steropes	Aldebaran	Caladbolg
succubus	Alexander	Carmentes
talisman	Alfardaws	Cassandra
tamanoas	Amphiarus	Centaurus
Tantalus	Andromeda	Cephissus
Tartarus	Anticleia	Charybdis
Teraphim	Aphrodite	chthonian

Cimmerian	glen nymph	magic wand
Cleopatra	golden age	magic word
cloudland	golden egg	Marspiter
Cockaigne	good fairy	Meilanion
Concordia	Great Bear	Melpomene
Corynetis	Guenevere	Mnemosyne
cupbearer	Guinevere	Myrmidons
Cupidines	hamadryad	Narcissus
Davy Jones	Heimdallr	occultism
Deianeira	Hippocoön	Palamedes
Delphinia	Houyhnynm	Palladium
Delphinus	Hippolyte	Pandareus
Dendrites	Hobgoblin	Parnassus
Deucalion	Holy Grail	Parshuram
devil lore	Hyppolita	Parthenon
diablerie	Ilmarinen	Phantasus
diabolism	Immortals	pied piper
Discordia	Jagannath	Philomelo
dreamland	Kumarpish	Polydorus
Electryon	labyrinth	purgatory
enchanter	Launcelot	pyrolater
Eumenides	love charm	pyrolatry
Euphorbus	lucky bean	Robin Hood
Excalibur	Lugalgirn	Ruritania
fairy ring	Lycomedes	Sangarius
fairyfolk	Lyonnesse	Sarasvati
fairyland	Mt. Helicon	Schamander
Friar Tuck	Mt. Olympus	Shangri-la
Gilgamesh	maelstrom	sorceress

Sthenelus	Axiocersus	fairy queen
Strategis	Beulah land	Gargantuan
Teiresias	bewitchery	ghost dance
Telegonus	black magic	Glathsheim
the Furies	broomstick	Greek Fates
Tisiphone	Callirrhoe	hagiolatry
totem pole	Canis major	Happy Isles
tree nymph	Cassiopeia	heathen god
Trojan War	cast a spell	heliolater
Tyndareus	changeling	heliolatry
Ursa major	Chrysippus	Hellespont
Ursa minor	cloven foot	Heosphoros
Valkyries	cluricaune	Hephaestus
Valkyriur	Cockatrice	Hesperides
winged cap	Coriolanus	Hippocrene
wood nymph	cornucopia	hippogriff
Yggdrasil	Cretan Bull	hippogryph
Zernebock	Demogorgon	Hippolytus
Zeus Pater	demonology	hippomanes
Alexandros	Eileithyia	Hippomenes
Amphiaraus	Electryone	Hitopadesa
Amphitrite	Epimetheus	hocus-pocus
Amphitryon	Erechtheus	Hyacinthus
Andromache	Estotiland	idolatrous
apotheosis	Euphrosyne	idolomancy
apparition	Euroclydon	invocation
Argus-eyed	Eurystheus	ivory tower
Arion's lyre	evil genius	Juggernaut
Armageddon	evil spirit	Juno Lucina

King Arthur	Phosphoros	Vardhamana
korriganes	phylactery	water nymph
leprechaun	pipes of Pan	water witch
Little Bear	Polydectes	white magic
Little John	Polydeuces	wishing cap
lucky charm	Polyhymnia	witchcraft
lucky piece	Polymestor	Wonderland
magic spell	Polyneices	Yggdrasill
Maid Marion	Polyphemus	abracadabra
Melicertes	Procrustes	Aesculapius
Memnonides	Prometheus	amphisbaena
Menestheus	Proserpina	Aonian fount
minor deity	rabbit-foot	Aonian mount
mumbo-jumbo	River of woe	Aristomenes
myrmidones	round table	bedevilment
Nebelkappe	salamander	Bellerophon
necromancy	Samothrace	Britomartis
Nemean lion	Santa Claus	Brobdingnag
ocean nymph	Saturnalia	Capricornus
Oedipus Rex	sixth sense	charmed life
open sesame	soothsayer	demigoddess
Orion's belt	St. Nicholas	demonolatry
Pallantides	sun worship	enchantment
Pantagruel	Telemachus	fetch-candle
Peirithous	the Dickens	fire worship
Peripheles	the Tempter	flower nymph
Persephone	Thruthvang	Gog and Magog
Pheidippes	Triangulum	Golden Bough
Phlegethon	underworld	golden goose

Gorgon's head	Pandemonium	water sprite
Happy Valley	Pandora's box	were-animals
Helen of Troy	pastoral god	wishing well
hippocampus	patron saint	witch-doctor
Hippodamcia	Persephassa	wooden horse
Hypermestra	Philippides	Achilles' heel
Juno Curitis	Philoctetes	Aesop's fables
Kabibonokka	poltergeist	Aetolian boar
kingdom come	Polymnestor	Aladdin's lamp
Lilliputian	Prester John	Amphion's lyre
Locrian Ajax	Reimthursen	Arcadian hind
lotus-eaters	Rosicrucian	Athena Pallas
lycanthrope	Sagittarius	Augean stable
magic carpet	Scamandrius	avenging fury
magic circle	second sight	Bower of Bliss
meadow nymph	Shawandasee	Bull Poseidon
medicine man	spellbinder	Chrysomallus
Megapenthes	Stygian oath	Clytemnestra
Midas touch	sylvan deity	Dyanean rocks
moon goddess	Symplegades	*Doppelgänger*
Morgan le Fay	Terpsichore	Erichthonius
mother earth	the black art	exsufflation
Mudjekeavis	three Graces	Garden of Eden
necromancer	thunderbolt	golden apples
Neoptolemus	Triptolemos	golden fleece
nether world	Trojan horse	Golden Legend
Nymphagetes	tutelary god	heavenly host
Orion's hound	under a spell	Hesperethusa
Orion's sword	water spirit	hippocentaur

horn of plenty
household god
Hyperboreans
Isle of Apples
Juno Quiritis
Kriss Kringle
Laestrygones
Lake Tritonis
Land o' the Leal
lap of the gods
Lernean Hydra
little people

Marathon bull
Mount Helicon
MountOlympus
ordeal by fire
Pallas Athene
Panchatantra
Parthian shot
Periclymenus
Phoebus Apollo
Promised Land
Rhadamanthus
Serpentarius

Stygian creek
Stygian gloom
supernatural
thaumaturgus
Thesmophorus
ultima Thule
vestal virgin
Wandering Jew
Weird Sisters
Will Scarlett
wishing stone
witches' coven

FIRST NAMES

This section lists male and female first names and some of their diminutives.

Abe	Guy	Net	Tim	Bart
Ada	Ian	Nye	Tom	Bert
Alf	Isa	Pam	Una	Bess
Amy	Jan	Pat	Val	Beth
Ann	Jim	Peg	Vic	Bill
Bab	Joe	Pen	Viv	Cara
Bea	Joy	Pip	Wal	Carl
Bel	Kay	Pru	Zoe	Chad
Ben	Ken	Rab	Abel	Ciss
Bob	Kim	Rae	Abie	Clem
Dan	Kit	Ray	Adam	Cleo
Don	Len	Reg	Alan	Dave
Dot	Leo	Rex	Aldo	Dawn
Ena	Liz	Roy	Ally	Dick
Eva	Lyn	Sal	Alma	Dirk
Eve	Max	Sam	Amos	Dora
Fay	May	Sid	Andy	Drew
Flo	Meg	Sis	Anna	Duke
Gay	Nan	Sue	Anne	Earl
Ger	Nat	Tam	Avis	Edna
Gus	Ned	Ted	Babs	Ella

Elma	Jock	Olaf	Yves	Caleb
Elsa	John	Olga	Aaron	Carol
Emma	Josh	Oona	Abbie	Cathy
Enid	Judy	Owen	Adele	Cecil
Eric	June	Paul	Aggie	Celia
Evan	Karl	Pete	Agnes	Chloe
Ewan	Kate	Phil	Aidan	Chris
Fred	Lena	René	Ailie	Clara
Gail	Lily	Rhys	Alfie	Clare
Gene	Lisa	Rick	Algie	Cliff
Gill	Lois	Rita	Alice	Clive
Gwen	Lola	Rolf	Aline	Colin
Gwyn	Lucy	Rory	Alvin	Coral
Hope	Luke	Rosa	Angus	Cyril
Hugh	Lynn	Rose	Anita	Cyrus
Hugo	Mark	Ross	April	Daisy
Iain	Mary	Ruby	Avril	Danny
Iona	Matt	Ruth	Barry	Darby
Iris	Maud	Sara	Basil	D'Arcy
Ivan	Mick	Saul	Becca	David
Ivor	Mike	Sean	Bella	Davie
Jack	Muir	Stan	Benny	Delia
Jake	Myra	Tess	Beryl	Denis
Jane	Neal	Theo	Betsy	Derek
Jean	Neil	Toby	Betty	Diana
Jeff	Nell	Tony	Biddy	Diane
Jess	Nick	Vera	Brian	Dilys
Jill	Nita	Walt	Bruce	Dinah
Joan	Noel	Will	Bruno	Dodie

Dolly	Frank	Jenny	Marge	Norma
Donna	Freda	Jerry	Margo	Orson
Doris	Garry	Jesse	Maria	Oscar
Dylan	Garth	Jimmy	Marie	Paddy
Eamon	Gavin	Josie	Mario	Patty
Eddie	Geoff	Joyce	Marty	Paula
Edgar	Gerda	Julie	Maude	Pearl
Edith	Giles	Karen	Mavis	Peggy
Edwin	Ginny	Keith	Merle	Penny
Effie	Grace	Kevin	Miles	Perce
Egbert	Greta	Kitty	Milly	Percy
Elias	Harry	Lance	Mitzi	Perry
Eliot	Hazel	Laura	Moira	Peter
Eliza	Helen	Leila	Molly	Polly
Ellen	Helga	Lenny	Morag	Ralph
Ellis	Henry	Lewis	Moray	Rhoda
Elmer	Hilda	Libby	Morna	Rhona
Elsie	Hiram	Linda	Moses	Robin
Emily	Honor	Lindy	Myles	Rodge
Enoch	Inigo	Lloyd	Myrna	Roger
Ernie	Irene	Lorna	Nancy	Rufus
Errol	Isaac	Louis	Nanny	Sadie
Ethel	Jacky	Lucia	Naomi	Sally
Faith	Jacob	Lydia	Nelly	Sandy
Fanny	James	Mabel	Netty	Simon
Felix	Jamie	Madge	Niall	Sonia
Fiona	Janet	Magda	Nicky	Steve
Fleur	Janey	Mamie	Nicol	Susan
Flora	Jason	Manny	Nigel	Susie

Sybil	Arnold	Darsey	Evadne
Tanya	Arthur	Davina	Evelyn
Terry	Astrid	Debbie	Fergus
Tilly	Athene	Denise	Gaston
Tracy	Aubrey	Dermot	George
Vicky	Audrey	Donald	Gerald
Vince	Aurora	Doreen	Gertie
Viola	Austin	Dougal	Gideon
Wanda	Aylwin	Dudley	Gladys
Wendy	Barney	Dugald	Gloria
Adrian	Bertha	Dulcie	Gordon
Agatha	Billie	Duncan	Graham
Aileen	Blaise	Dwight	Gregor
Albert	Bobbie	Easter	Gretel
Aldous	Brenda	Edmund	Gwenda
Alexis	Bryony	Edward	Hamish
Alfred	Calvin	Edwina	Hannah
Alicia	Carmen	Eileen	Harold
Alison	Carrie	Eilidh	Harvey
Althea	Caspar	Elaine	Hattie
Amanda	Cedric	Elinor	Hector
Amelia	Cherry	Elisha	Hester
Andrea	Claire	Elvira	Hilary
Andrew	Claude	Emilia	Horace
Angela	Connor	Ernest	Howard
Antony	Conrad	Esmond	Hunter
Arabel	Damian	Esther	Imogen
Archie	Daniel	Eugene	Ingram
Arline	Daphne	Eunice	Ingrid

Irving	Lionel	Morrie	Robina
Isabel	Lolita	Morris	Rodney
Isaiah	Lottie	Morven	Roland
Isobel	Louisa	Muriel	Ronald
Isolde	Louise	Murray	Rowena
Israel	Lucius	Myrtle	Roxana
Janice	Luther	Nadine	Rupert
Jasper	Maggie	Nathan	Sabina
Jemima	Magnus	Nessie	Salome
Jeremy	Maisie	Nettie	Samuel
Jerome	Manuel	Nicole	Sandra
Jessie	Marcia	Noelle	Selwyn
Joanna	Marcus	Norman	Serena
Joseph	Margie	Norris	Sheena
Joshua	Marian	Odette	Sheila
Josiah	Marina	Oliver	Sidney
Judith	Marion	Oonagh	Sophia
Julian	Marius	Oriana	Sophie
Juliet	Martha	Osbert	Stella
Julius	Martin	Oswald	Steven
Justin	Maxine	Pamela	Stuart
Kenelm	Melvin	Petrus	Sydney
Kirsty	Melvyn	Petula	Sylvia
Larrie	Merlin	Philip	Thelma
Laurie	Mervyn	Phoebe	Thomas
Lesley	Minnie	Rachel	Trevor
Leslie	Miriam	Regina	Tricia
Lester	Monica	Reuben	Trixie
Lilian	Morgan	Robert	Trudie

Ursula	Belinda	Dorothy	Jeffrey
Verity	Bernard	Douglas	Jessica
Victor	Bertram	Drusilla	Jocelyn
Violet	Blanche	Eleanor	Juliana
Vivian	Brendan	Elspeth	Justine
Vivien	Bridget	Emanuel	Kenneth
Wallis	Bronwen	Erasmus	Lachlan
Walter	Cameron	Estella	Lavinia
Warner	Camilla	Eugenia	Leonard
Warren	Candida	Ezekiel	Leonora
Wilbur	Carolyn	Fenella	Leopold
Willie	Cecilia	Florrie	Lindsey
Winnie	Celeste	Flossie	Linette
Yvonne	Charity	Frances	Lucille
Abigail	Charles	Francis	Lucinda
Abraham	Charlie	Gabriel	Malcolm
Adriana	Chrissy	Geordie	Margery
Alfreda	Christy	Geraint	Marilyn
Alister	Clarice	Gilbert	Matilda
Ambrose	Claudia	Gillian	Matthew
Annabel	Clement	Giselle	Maureen
Annette	Clemmie	Godfrey	Maurice
Anthony	Corinna	Gregory	Maxwell
Antonia	Cynthia	Gwyneth	Melanie
Ariadne	Deborah	Harriet	Melissa
Aurelia	Deirdre	Heather	Michael
Baldwin	Desmond	Herbert	Mildred
Barbara	Dolores	Horatio	Mirabel
Barnaby	Dominic	Hubert	Miranda

Modesty	Stanley	Bertrand	Georgina
Montagu	Stephen	Beverley	Gertrude
Murdoch	Stewart	Carlotta	Hercules
Myfanwy	Susanna	Carolina	Hermione
Natalie	Terence	Caroline	Humphrey
Natasha	Theresa	Cathleen	Iseabail
Neville	Timothy	Catriona	Jeanette
Nicolas	Valerie	Charmian	Jennifer
Obadiah	Vanessa	Clarence	Jonathan
Ophelia	Vaughan	Claribel	Kathleen
Ottilie	Vincent	Clarissa	Lancelot
Patrick	Wallace	Claudius	Laurence
Pauline	Wilfred	Clemence	Lawrence
Phyllis	William	Clifford	Llewelyn
Queenie	Winston	Collette	Lorraine
Quentin	Wyndham	Cordelia	Madeline
Raphael	Yehudi	Cressida	Magdalen
Raymond	Yolande	Cuthbert	Margaret
Rebecca	Adrienne	Danielle	Marianne
Richard	Alasdair	Diarmaid	Marigold
Roberta	Alastair	Dominica	Marjorie
Rosalie	Aloysius	Dorothea	Matthias
Rudolph	Angeline	Drusilla	Meredith
Rudyard	Arabella	Ebenezer	Montague
Russell	Augustus	Euphemia	Morrison
Sabrina	Barnabas	Farquhar	Mortimer
Shirley	Beatrice	Felicity	Nicholas
Solomon	Benedict	Florence	Octavius
Spencer	Benjamin	Geoffrey	Odysseus

8–11

Patience	Anastasia	Marmaduke
Patricia	Annabella	Millicent
Penelope	Archibald	Mirabelle
Percival	Augustine	Nathaniel
Perpetua	Cassandra	Nicolette
Philippa	Catherine	Peregrine
Primrose	Charlotte	Priscilla
Prudence	Christian	Rosabella
Prunella	Christina	Sebastian
Reginald	Christine	Sephronia
Roderick	Constance	Seraphina
Rosalind	Cornelius	Siegfried
Rosamund	Ebenezer	Stephanie
Rosemary	Elizabeth	Sylvester
Samantha	Esmeralda	Véronique
Scarlett	Ethelbert	Antoinette
Sherlock	Ferdinand	Bernadette
Silvanus	Francesca	Christabel
Sinclair	Frederica	Christiana
Somerset	Frederick	Clementine
Theodora	Genevieve	Jacqueline
Theodore	Geraldine	Maximilian
Veronica	Gwendolyn	Montgomery
Victoria	Henrietta	Petronella
Violette	Jacquetta	Wilhelmina
Virginia	Josephine	Bartholomew
Winifred	Katharine	Christopher
Alexandra	Madeleine	Constantine
Alphonsus	Magdalene	